Extending Educational Reform

In an effort to improve student achievement, thousands of US schools have adopted school reform models devised externally by universities and other organizations. Such models have been successful in improving individual schools or groups of schools, but what happens when educational reform attempts to extend from one school to many?

Through qualitative data from several studies, this book explores what happens when school reform "goes to scale". Topics covered include:

- Why and how schools are adopting reforms
- The influence of the local context and wider constraints on the implementation of reform
- Teachers and principals as change agents in schools
- The evolution of reform design teams
- The implementation, sustainability and expiration of reform, and its impact on educational change

Each chapter concludes with guidelines for policy and practice.

This book will be of interest to educational leaders and staff developers, educational researchers and policy makers, in the US and internationally.

Amanda Datnow is Assistant Professor in the Department of Theory and Policy Studies at the Ontario Institute for Studies in Education, University of Toronto.

Lea Hubbard is an Assistant Research Scientist in the Sociology Department at the University of California, San Diego.

Hugh Mehan is Professor of Sociology and Director of The Center for Research on Educational Equity, Access and Teaching Excellence at the University of California, San Diego.

Educational Change and Development Series

Series Editors: Andy Hargreaves, Ontario Institute for Studies in Education, Canada and
Ivor F Goodson, Centre for Applied Research in Education, University of East Anglia, Norwich, UK and
Warner Graduate School, University of Rochester, USA

Re-schooling Society
David Hartley

The Gender Politics of Educational Change
Amanda Datnow

The Rules of School Reform
Max Angus

Whose School is it Anyway? Power and Politics
Kathryn Riley

Developing Teachers: The Challenges of Lifelong Learning
Chris Day

Change Forces: The Sequel
Michael Fullan

The Color of Teaching
June A. Gordon

The Sharp Edge of Educational Change: Teaching, Leading and the Realities of Reform
Edited by Nina Bascia and Andy Hargreaves

Reforming Education: From Origins to Outcomes
Benjamin Levin

Authentic School Improvement
David Hopkins

Extending Educational Reform: From One School to Many
Amanda Datnow, Lea Hubbard and Hugh Mehan

Extending Educational Reform

From One School to Many

Amanda Datnow, Lea Hubbard and
Hugh Mehan

London and New York

KH

First published 2002 by RoutledgeFalmer
11 New Fetter Lane, London EC4P 4EE

Simultaneously published in the USA and Canada
by RoutledgeFalmer
29 West 35th Street, New York, NY 10001

RoutledgeFalmer is an imprint of the Taylor & Francis Group

© 2002 Amanda Datnow, Lea Hubbard and Hugh Mehan

Typeset in Garamond by M Rules, London
Printed and bound in Great Britain by TJ International Ltd,
Padstow, Cornwall

British Library Cataloguing in Publication Data
A catalogue record for this book is available
from the British Library

Library of Congress Cataloging in Publication Data
Datnow, Amanda.
    Scaling-up school reform / Amanda Datnow, Lea Hubbard, and
    Hugh Mehan.
        p. cm. – (Educational change and development series)
    Includes bibliographical references (p.) and index.
    1. School improvement programs – United States.
2. School management and organization – United States.
3. Educational innovations – United States. I. Hubbard, Lea, 1946–
II. Mehan, Hugh, 1941– III. Title. IV Series.

LB2822.82 .D38 2002
371.2′0097 dc21   2001048816

ISBN 0-415-24069-7 (hbk)
ISBN 0-415-24070-0 (pbk)

11/22/04

Contents

Foreword by Michael Fullan   vii
Acknowledgments   ix
Frequently Used Abbreviations   xi

1   Introduction   1
2   How Does Reform Adoption Happen? The Role of Power,
    Politics, and Perspective   18
3   Is All Change Local? How Context Shapes Implementation   39
4   Change Agents in the School Reform Process   62
5   Building the Plane While It's Flying: The Evolving Design
    Team   90
6   The Life of External Reform Models: Sustainability and
    Expiration   117
7   Prospects for Educational Change   138

Appendix   Description of Reform Designs   146

Notes   158
References   159
Index   175

Foreword

Michael Fullan

The twin concepts of the last and present decade are large scale reform and sustainability. Since about 1990 reformers have been concerned about how to go to scale involving the vast majority of schools in a given system not just a few, and latterly how to sustain reforms as they occur on a large scale.

Little comprehensive research has been conducted on these twin topics. Datnow and colleagues provide a superb, insightful and highly readable account, tracing the vicissitudes of large scale reform efforts. They reveal the complexities of adoption decisions on which power and politics dominate decisions even when it appears no decisions are being made on a democratic basis.

Extending Educational Reform uses a model of structure, culture and agency to examine all levels of the change process. The interplay of local context, change agents, and design teams forms the basis of the book. Especially helpful are the strategic recommendations at the end of each chapter. Together they constitute a goldmine of insights for tackling large scale reform. What makes these ideas so powerful is that they are derived from careful and insightful analysis of what is happening on the ground.

Datnow and colleagues have taken an enormously complex topic, one that is at the heart of educational reform in the 21st century, and have rendered it understandable. We see the various key pieces and how they interrelate. Above all, we see a way forward. The strategic recommendations, as a set, form a comprehensive plan for pursuing large scale, sustainable reform.

Using the ideas and strategies in *Extending Educational Reform* is the best place to start for anyone who is seriously concerned about the prospects for achieving and sustaining large scale reform.

Acknowledgments

The work reported herein was supported by a grant from the Office of Educational Research and Improvement, U.S. Department of Education, to the Center for Research on Education, Diversity, and Excellence under the Educational Research and Development Centers Program, PR/Award Number R306A60001, and a grant to the Center for Research on the Education of Students Placed At Risk (Grant No. R-117D-40005). However, any opinions expressed are the authors' own and do not represent the policies or positions of the U.S. Department of Education. Support was also provided by a University of Toronto Connaught grant. We are greatly indebted to the participants of our research studies who welcomed us into their schools, districts, and offices and gave so freely of their time. We also wish to thank our colleagues who worked with us on some of these studies, most notably Sam Stringfield and Marisa Castellano. Our thanks to Mandira Raksit for her help in formatting and editing the final draft. We also wish to thank Michael Fullan for being supportive of this book project and for writing the Foreword. Finally, we wish to sincerely thank our series editor Andy Hargreaves and our colleague Peter Hall for their very helpful comments on an earlier draft.

Frequently Used Abbreviations

AC – Audrey Cohen College Purpose-Centered System of Education
AVID – Achievement Via Individual Determination
CSRD – Comprehensive School Reform Demonstration Program
CES – Coalition of Essential Schools
Comer SDP – Comer School Development Program
CK – Core Knowledge
MRSH – Modern Red Schoolhouse
NAS – New American Schools
SFA – Success for All

1   Introduction

This is a book about a movement to change schools on a grand scale. Over the past five years, we have had unique opportunities to examine the "scaling up" phenomenon, which involves the transfer of school reform models that have been successful in one or a few schools to many schools. The scaling up of externally developed school reform designs is occurring at an unprecedented rate, affecting thousands of schools in the United States and elsewhere. There are currently more than 1300 Accelerated Schools, more than 1000 schools in the Coalition of Essential Schools, more than 500 schools implementing the Comer School Development Program, more than 800 Core Knowledge schools, over 1600 Success for All schools, over 700 schools implementing the Achievement Via Individual Determination (AVID) program, and more than 2000 schools implementing New American Schools reform designs. All of these reform designs were originally implemented in one location and, as they became successful, were exported by design teams and adopted by educators in other locations.

By the time this book is published, the statistics on the number of schools implementing these models are sure to be outdated. Each of these reform designs has increased the number of participating schools substantially over the past few years. There are dozens of other school reform designs, most with national and/or international support networks, most rapidly growing. The passage of the Comprehensive School Reform Demonstration Program (CSRD) in the U.S. Congress in 1997, which allocated $145 million dollars (and additional funds in subsequent years) to schools willing to adopt "research-based" school reform designs, is spurring further expansion of these models in the United States. Some of these models are also being implemented in other countries as well, including the United Kingdom, Canada, Australia, South Africa, Mexico, and Israel, among others.

While the growth in the use of these models is perhaps an indicator of their success, effectively transferring an innovation across school contexts is said to be difficult at best, and perhaps impossible (Elmore 1996; Fullan 1999; Hargreaves and Fink 2000; Stringfield and Datnow 1998). Meanwhile, some argue that the current generation of externally developed reform models provides the best hope for school improvement on a grand scale that has existed in the past several decades (Slavin and Madden 1998).

In this book, we present data from several nationwide (U.S.) studies to explore what happens when school reform designs go to scale. We will begin with an assessment of why and how schools are adopting reforms with such incredible fervor at the current time. We discuss the transportation of models to new contexts, and how local politics around race, class, and gender affect this process. Next, we investigate teachers' and administrators' activities and relationships that change when schools implement externally designed reforms. We also examine the possibilities and boundaries of the school-design team relationship to ascertain how design teams change over time to adapt to local needs and policy demands. We discuss the life cycle of external reform models in schools, from adoption to implementation, and later, sustainability or expiration, as well as what counts as successful reform.

In addressing these key topical areas related to scaling up educational reforms, we illuminate the actions of federal, state, district, design team, and school community members that facilitate or hinder the viability of external reforms. Our hope is that this book pushes the discussion beyond the typical list of countervailing conditions necessary for successful reform implementation and toward a deeper understanding of how the scale up of reforms, and school improvement more generally, is constructed through the interaction of multiple institutions and individuals. In sum, this book provides a comprehensive understanding of the dynamics of school change in the era of externally developed reform designs. This book also speaks to the large-scale reform movement more generally, which involves not just the reform designs we discuss here, but also the global movements to implement educational reform across an entire district, state, or nation (Fullan 2000). Such large scale reform efforts are currently occurring in such diverse places as England, the Canadian province of Ontario, Chicago, Boston and San Diego, among others.

The New Language of the Scaling Up Movement

The scaling up movement has introduced some new language into the discourse of educational reform. In case it is not yet clear, we use the term *scaling up* to refer to the deliberate expansion of an externally developed reform model. Scaling up is similar to what was once referred to as planned replication. However, for some, replication implies that the program will and should look the same everywhere, which, by design, is not true for some of the reforms we have studied. Thus, we operationalize the term scaling up to mean the transfer of an external reform model to multiple settings.

The term *externally developed reform design* refers to a model for school improvement that is developed by an organization external to the school or district. With the exception of one, almost all of the reforms we discuss are whole-school reform designs, which are also now known as "comprehensive school reform designs". It bears noting that the term reform "design" was brought into use by the New American Schools (NAS) corporation (Kearns and Anderson 1996), which has borrowed some corporate and organizational development terms and applied them to the education reform world. Other terms currently in vogue in education – and the practices that accompany them – also derive from business and include "accountability" – including financial incentives for student test improvement, and financial punishments for student test decline. When students (and teachers) are referred to as "clients", when reform assistance is purchased from private vendors, not provided as part of state-support to schools, and vouchers are advocated as a way to improve schools, we are witnessing an increased degree of connection between private and public spheres. Expressions and practices derived from business have come into wide use among policymakers, educators, and researchers since the early 1990s. Therefore we use them here as well, while acknowledging the limitations of corporate concepts as applied to schools.

The reliance on external partners to provide educational services and staff development represents a shift from the traditional arrangement where services were provided by district offices or state departments of education (Sunderman and Nardini 1998). In this era of increased accountability, decentralization, and bureaucratic downsizing, schools are increasingly looking toward external reform groups for assistance with school improvement efforts. In an attempt to help meet state and local accountability demands, schools now purchase school reform assistance or reform models from vendors, or what are called reform *design teams*. The design team is the group that conceives of the reform design, engineers the principles, implementation strategy, and/or materials that accompany the reform; and often provides support to local schools and districts in the form of training, consulting, follow-up checks, or other types of professional development. The term *design team* is also borrowed from the business world.

Design teams come in a variety of different forms and serve different functions. Some design teams, such as the Coalition of Essential Schools at Brown, Success for All at Johns Hopkins, and the Comer School Development Program at Yale, originated in or still exist within universities. There are also many other university-based school reform groups that work with smaller numbers of schools in communities across the U.S.A., some of these functioning as process facilitators in school change efforts. Private, non-profit, organizations – such as the NAS corporation, AVID Center, the Modern Red Schoolhouse Institute, and the Core Knowledge Foundation – have also developed and disseminated school reform models. For-profit organizations, such as the Edison Project, are also part of the design team ecology (Rowan 2001), as are federally funded regional educational development labs.

By *implementation* we mean the use of a specific, externally developed school reform design within a school not previously using the reform. The term "implementation" tends to be associated with a technical-rational perspective (Snyder, Bolin and Zumwalt 1992) and, as a result, connotes a particular way of studying school reform. We do not intend to invoke this

3

definition. Indeed, the reforms we studied embody different notions of what is meant by implementation, with some viewing it as the appropriate term to apply to the program carried out by teachers, and others eschewing the term and its connotations. In sum, we do not mean to imply that a school's implementation should be or is an exact copy of a reform design. Quite the contrary, as we explain in forthcoming chapters. As defined here, implementation is simply the act of "doing" the reform or a component of the reform, which may mean teaching a prescribed curriculum, providing college counseling, or engaging in a vision-setting meeting, depending on the reform design.

Description of the Reform Designs

The reforms that we study in this book array along a continuum of those that are highly specified and provide curriculum, lesson plans, school organizational models, implementation plans, and professional development, to those that are much less specified, asking schools to commit to a guiding set of principles and engage in an inquiry-guided, locally-driven process of self-renewal. In this regard, some reform designs are more nearly "prepackaged," whereas others are much looser and presume local development of the change effort. Reform designs also have different foci, with some focusing more directly on pedagogical practices, and others attempting to change the school culture or structure. Accordingly, the design teams have different theories of school change and theories of action.

At the less specified end of the continuum, the Coalition of Essential Schools (Sizer 1984) and the Comer School Development Program (Comer *et al.* 1996) provide frameworks for reform and leave particulars to each school. These designs point to the primacy of local development efforts, so long as the process is guided by a set of overarching principles (and school management structures, in the case of the Comer program). Such reform designs operate according to a "concept dissemination" approach, rather than a program dissemination approach.

A bit further along the continuum, the Core Knowledge Sequence (Core Knowledge Foundation 1998) provides detailed curricula for one half of each day for each elementary grade while leaving issues of how to teach and how to organize the school to the judgment of the principal and faculty. Similarly, with the Audrey Cohen College System of Education and Modern Red Schoolhouse designs, some materials and technical assistance are provided with these reforms, but typically teachers in local schools develop lesson plans. The Achievement Via Individual Determination (AVID) untracking program also reflects this middle ground approach, providing some materials and implementation guidelines, but not daily lesson plans. Also, AVID differs from the other reforms in that it starts as a partial-school program and has fairly modest ambitions of reaching the entire school, whereas the other models discussed here are all deliberately "whole-school" reform models.

At the most "highly specified" end of the continuum is Success for All, a design that provides detailed descriptions of how to organize both schools and classrooms with respect to reading (Slavin *et al.* 1996). Success for All is known as a prescriptive school reform design. However, importantly, it only is prescriptive in the area of reading, not in all school subjects. While differing in their fundamentals, the Success for All, AVID, Audrey Cohen College, and Modern Red Schoolhouse design teams all operate somewhat according to a "franchise approach." The design team grants a school the right to the reform design and assumes that the school will use the entire package of standardized components, including manuals, materials, and training. Table 1.1 provides a brief description of each of the reform designs discussed in this book.

Table 1.1 Description of Externally Developed Reform Designs Discussed*

Design	Major Characteristics
New American Schools	
The Audrey Cohen College System of Education	*Developer:* Audrey Cohen College, New York *Primary goal:* Development of scholarship and leadership abilities using knowledge and skills to benefit students' community and larger world *Main features:* 1 Student learning focused on complex and meaningful purposes 2 Students use what they learn to reach specific goals 3 Curriculum focused on Constructive Actions (individual or group projects that serve the community) 4 Classes structured around five dimensions (e.g., Self and Others, Values, etc.) that incorporate core subjects For grades K–12. Materials and training provided
The Modern Red Schoolhouse	*Developer:* The Modern Red Schoolhouse Institute, Nashville *Primary goal:* To combine the rigor and values of little red schoolhouse with latest classroom innovations *Main features:* 1 Challenging curriculum (Core Knowledge recommended in K–6) 2 High standards for all students 3 Emphasis on character 4 Integral role of technology 5 Individual education compact for each student For grades K–12. Some materials and training provided

Table 1.1 cont.

Design	Major Characteristics
Success for All/Roots and Wings	*Developer:* Robert Slavin, Nancy Madden, and a team of developers from Johns Hopkins University. Now based at the Success for All Foundation in Baltimore *Primary goal:* To guarantee that every child will learn to read *Main features:* 1 Research-based, prescribed curriculum in the areas of reading, writing, and language arts 2 One-to-one tutoring; family support team; cooperative learning; on-site facilitator; and building advisory team For grades K–6. Mostly all materials provided. Training required

Independent Reform Designs

AVID (Achievement Via Individual Determination)	*Developer:* Mary Catherine Swanson, San Diego County Office of Education Primary goal: To ensure that all students, but especially disadvantaged students in the middle with academic potential will succeed in rigorous curriculum and will increase their enrollment in four-year colleges Main features: 1 Elective program of academic and social supports to facilitate student success in a rigorous curriculum 2 AVID methodologies are WIC (writing, inquiry and collaboration) 3 Strong emphasis on study skills and college awareness 4 AVID Site Team (school-wide support team for AVID students) composed of teachers, administrators and counselors 5 AVID Essentials detail compliance to the AVID philosophy and ensure permission to use the AVID Trade name For grades 7–12. Curriculum guidelines and materials provided. Training required
Core Knowledge	*Developer:* E.D. Hirsch, Jr. (University of Virginia) and the Core Knowledge Foundation, Charlottesville, VA *Primary goal:* To help students establish a strong foundation of core knowledge for higher levels of learning

Table 1.1 cont.

Design	Major Characteristics
	Main features: 1 Sequential program of specific grade-by-grade topics for core subjects; the rest of curriculum (approximately half) is left for schools to design 2 Instructional methods (to teach core topics) are designed by individual teachers/schools For grades K–8. Curriculum guidelines provided. Training available but not required
Coalition of Essential Schools	*Developer:* Ted Sizer, Brown University, Providence, RI. Now based in Oakland, CA *Primary goal:* To help create schools where students learn to use their minds well *Main features:* 1 Set of Ten Common Principles upon which schools base their practice 2 Personalized learning 3 Mastery of a few essential subjects and skills 4 Graduation by exhibition. 5 Sense of community 6 Instruction and organization depend on how each school interprets the Common Principles (may involve interdisciplinary instruction, authentic projects, etc.) For grades K–12. No materials. Range of training options mostly provided by regional centers
Comer School Development Program	*Developer:* James Comer, Yale University, New Haven, CT *Primary goal:* To mobilize entire community of adult caretakers to support students' holistic development to bring about academic success *Main features:* 1 Three teams (school planning and management team, student and staff support team, parent team) 2 Three operations (comprehensive school plan, staff development plan, monitoring and assessment) 3 Three guiding principles (no-fault, consensus, collaboration) For grades K–12. Training and manual with materials

Note: * With the exception of the description of AVID, this table draws information from *The Catalog of School Reform Models*, Portland, OR: Northwest Regional Educational Laboratory. http://www.nwrel.org/scpd/natspec/catalog/

In the Appendix we provide more detailed descriptions of each of the reform designs. We discuss: (1) the reform design's history, including primary players and the extent to which the reform has been implemented in schools; (2) the guiding philosophy and goals of the reform; (3) the reform's components and implementation strategy; and (4) the broader support framework for the reform, including training, materials, and support provided by the design team.

We do not review the research studies that have been conducted on these various reform designs, as the "effects" of reform are not the focus of this book. Moreover, such reviews (e.g., Herman *et al.* 1999) have inspired controversy among some reform design teams who have argued that they do not adequately reflect the progress that has been made in schools implementing their reforms. We do not wish to become part of this debate. The research upon which we draw was qualitative in nature, and thus while it allows us to generalize to theory, we cannot and do not wish to make judgments about particular reform models. Moreover, the reform designs themselves were at various stages of development during the period of our study and all have evolved since then. Hence, the experiences of the schools we describe may not apply to schools adopting these reforms now. Our primary intent in this book is to bridge theory and data to better understand the process of bringing reforms to scale.

The Scaling Up Studies: Methodology

We were fortunate to study the aforementioned reform designs in various research projects that we conducted separately, together, and with other colleagues during the period 1996–2000. We draw primarily upon data from two comprehensive, longitudinal studies of scaling up school reform and, to a more limited extent, upon data from several other related studies.

First, this book draws upon data from the *Scaling Up School Restructuring in Multicultural, Multilingual Contexts Study* in which Amanda Datnow, Sam Stringfield, and Steve Ross and a research team at Johns Hopkins University and the University of Memphis studied 13 elementary schools in a large, culturally and linguistically diverse urban district (Sunland County[1]) in a southeastern U.S. state over a four-year period (see Datnow, Stringfield, Borman, Rachuba, and Castellano, 2001; Datnow and Stringfield 2000; Stringfield, Datnow, Ross and Snively 1998; Yonezawa and Datnow 1999). Each of the schools was implementing an externally developed school reform design. The reform designs include three of the New American Schools (NAS) models (e.g., Success for All/Roots and Wings, Modern Red Schoolhouse, and the Audrey Cohen College System of Education) and three independently developed reform designs (not part of NAS) including the Core Knowledge Sequence, the Coalition of Essential Schools, and the Comer School Development Program.

Over a period of four years, the team conducted annual two-day, two-to-three person site visits to each of the 13 schools in our study. We conducted focus groups with teachers at every grade level, as well as interviews with school and district administrators and design team representatives to capture their perspectives on the implementation process. Each year, we systematically observed classrooms using a four-pronged observation system, which used ethnographic, semi-structured, and low-inference strategies, to ascertain how the reforms were being implemented and how teachers accommodated student diversity with the reforms (see Datnow and Yonezawa in press). The study also involved more limited data collection at 30 replication sites in schools throughout the U.S. We also gathered student achievement data over the four-year period; those findings are reported elsewhere (Datnow *et al.* 2001).

The second major data source for this book is the *Tracking Untracking* study, led by Hugh Mehan and Lea Hubbard at University of California, San Diego. In the *Tracking Untracking* study, Hubbard and Mehan and their research team studied the scale up of the Advancement Via Individual Determination (AVID) untracking program in 12 high schools in four U.S. states (Virginia, California, Kentucky, and North Carolina) over a three-year period (Hubbard and Mehan 1999a, 1999b). Datnow assisted with data collection in two sites in this study. This book will also draw on a prior longitudinal study of AVID that took place during the program's development in San Diego (Mehan *et al.* 1996).

In the *Tracking Untracking* study, with the exception of one site in North Carolina, which was added during the third year of our study, we visited each of the school sites twice each year, once in the fall and again in the spring for approximately one week. We observed in AVID classrooms and some academic classes. We interviewed school principals, counselors, teachers, students and parents. At some schools we were able to attend AVID student recruitment sessions. These observations were instructive because we were able to ascertain which students applied to the program and how decisions were made by the AVID teachers regarding selection of students for admittance to the program.

We also interviewed school board members, district superintendents as well as AVID regional directors. In Kentucky and Virginia we interviewed state education officers. To gain a more thorough historical understanding of implementation, we also interviewed superintendents who were responsible for the initial implementation of AVID in their states. Several times over the course of the study we interviewed members of the AVID Design Team. All of our interviews lasted approximately one hour, although many of the interviews with Design Team members and district and state officials were two hours or longer.

In addition to our observations and interviews, we attended the AVID Center's Board of Directors' Meetings. We also attended many special district and state educational events that pertained to AVID in each state. We attended AVID's Eastern Division Summer Institute, California's Summer Institute, various Regional Directors' conferences in all of the states in our study, San Diego sponsored "Awareness Sessions" and an Executive Leadership conference held in Louisville, Kentucky. The purpose of many of these conferences was to educate local educators and those from around the country about AVID. Interviews and informal chats with participants offered us an opportunity to understand the way in which AVID familiarizes its own people with the program and the types of requirements it places on those implementing the reform. At many of these occasions we were asked to present research data from our previous study on the implementation of AVID in San Diego.

Finally, this book also includes data from an in-depth qualitative study of implementation and teaching in three Success for All schools in California (see Datnow and Castellano 2000a, 2000b, 2001). Amanda Datnow and Marisa Castellano conducted this study during the period from January 1998 to August 1999. Our two-person research team conducted a total of four two-day site visits to each school. At all three schools, we conducted individual interviews with principals, SFA facilitators, and teachers. We interviewed the principal and, in most cases, the facilitator, during every site visit. At two schools, we were able to interview almost every teacher in each school individually. At one newly implementing site, we conducted individual interviews with about one-third of staff, as well as a group of several additional teachers. We also interviewed district level administrators in each site. In total, we conducted over sixty interviews and sixty systematic classroom observations. We also observed and took detailed notes on the training that teachers received prior to the implementation of Success for All at one school.

In sum, we will rely on multiple sources of rich data gathered in hundreds of interviews with teachers, principals, design team representatives, and district administrators, and in observations of classrooms, schools, staff development sessions, and meetings in elementary and secondary schools across the U.S. All of the interviews were transcribed verbatim and transcripts and field notes from observations were coded for the purposes of analysis. We also drew upon case reports that our research teams had written on each school under study. The observations we report in this book rely upon our integration of within- and cross-site analyses of reform efforts with the theoretical framework described below.

Educational Reform as a Co-constructed Process

This book develops a novel theoretical framework for making sense of reforms going to scale. We believe that one of the reasons why "scaling up" has proven to be a vexing and seldom successful endeavor is that educators and researchers have underestimated the co-constructed nature of the implementation process. First, studies which treat the implementation process as unidirectional, technical, and rational (Smith and Keith 1971; Pressman and Wildavsky 1973) do not fully capture how educational innovations play out as social, negotiated features of school life. As school change theorists suggest, organizational models of school improvement that grew up in reaction to these technical-rational models also do not suffice for understanding school reform implementation (Fullan 1991; Louis 1994). Because their focus is on school level strategies for self-renewal and improvement, they downplay the actions that initiated reform and the governmental, community, and district actions that occurred away from and before the school attempted rejuvenation and renewal. Neither technical-rational nor organizational development models help us fully understand educational implementation, which we believe involves a dynamic relationship among structural constraints, the culture of the school, and peoples' actions in many interlocking sites or settings.

We believe that formulating reform implementation as a co-constructed process coupled with qualitative research is helpful in making sense of the complex, and often messy, process of school reform. Our research builds upon work in the sociocultural tradition, especially Rogoff (1995) and Tharp (1997: 12) who identify personal, interpersonal and community "levels" or "planes" of interaction and McLaughlin and Talbert (1993a) who depict organizations as successively contextualized layers. We extend this work by explicitly calling attention to the political and economic conditions that enable possibilities and impose constraints on education in general, and school reform in particular. We also try to avoid privileging any one context in our discussion of educational implementation by showing the reciprocal relations among the social contexts in the policy chain.

In some ways, the theoretical framework guiding our work is similar to Fullan's (1999) use of chaos and complexity theory as a vehicle for understanding school change, as well as Helsby's (1999) use of structure, culture, and agency as concepts for addressing how reforms change teachers' work. Both Fullan and Helsby argue that change unfolds in unpredictable and non-linear ways through the interaction of individuals in different settings under conditions of uncertainty, diversity, and instability. We agree, and in this book we will use empirical data to provide additional evidence for the non-linear, non-deterministic characteristics of the school change process. However, as we explain shortly, we attempt to lend increased understanding of the dynamics of change by giving more primacy to the role of power and perspective.

Reform Implementation as a Set of Interrelated Conditions and Consequences

Pressman and Wildavsky (1973: xii) observed: "If one is always looking for unusual circumstances and dramatic events, he cannot appreciate how difficult it is to make the ordinary happen." That is, school reform is to be found in the mundane details of the every day life of the school – getting meetings set up, assigning tasks, carrying them out; settling petty feuds.

While we agree with Wildavsky that reform occurs in mundane social situations, school reform, like any human activity, does not take place automatically, in isolation, in separate, autonomous situations. At the same time, social actions are not generated entirely and spontaneously in locally organized contexts. To capture the *interrelations* among social contexts, we analyze the reform process as a co-constructed, conditional process, "as a web of interrelated conditions and consequences, where the consequences of actions in one context may become the conditions for the next" (Hall and McGinty 1997: 461). That is, interactions in one policy context generate "outcomes," such as policy statements, new rules or procedures, which in turn potentially condition the interactions of other actors in other contexts in the policy chain.

Formulating the scaling up of reforms as a co-constructed process is heuristic because it instructs us that reform implementation is generated in face-to-face interactions among real people, confronting real problems in concrete social contexts, such as classrooms, school board meetings, courts of law, and state legislatures. Because contexts are inevitably connected to other contexts (Sarason 1997), contexts *throughout* the social system must be considered. At a given point in time in research on implementation, the interaction among social actors in one context is foregrounded, and of necessity, the other contexts are backgrounded. But in order to render a complete analysis, the interconnections among contexts throughout the social system must be described (cf. Sarason 1982; 1997; McLaughlin and Talbert 1993a; Engestrom 1993; Cole 1996; Tharp 1997; Hall and McGinty 1997; Rogoff 1998).

A Relational Sense of Context

Reform implementation formulated as a co-constructed process relies on a *relational* sense of context in which part and whole shape each other. By a relational sense of context we mean parts are "inextricably intertwined into one thick chain or braid" (Star and Bowker 1997: 17; McDermott 1980: 14–15). That is, people's actions can not be understood without understanding the sense of the setting in which the actions are situated, and reciprocally, the setting can not be understood without understanding the actions of the people within it. Here, the meaning of people's actions is dependent upon the circumstances of their occurrence, including the biography and purposes of the actor, the previous course of interaction, the social setting, and the relationships among the people present. All of these contextual particulars need to be in play in order for participants and observers to make sense of a given action or a package of them. The intertwining of the individual parts yields a sense of the whole, which in turn transforms the indeterminacy of actions into meaningful patterns.

Lave (1993), McDermott (1993), and Cole (1996) point out that social scientists have not routinely employed a relational sense of context. Instead, they focus on the task or activity of people in one setting and describe how it is constrained by broader levels, often represented as concentric circles. Cole (1996) cites Brofenbrenner's (1979) formulation of human development as a prime example of this *embedded* conception of context. Brofenbrenner conceives of social life as starting with the microsystem at the core, and proceeding outward through mesosystems and exosystems to the macrosystem. In educational research, the embedded sense of context appears in Fullan's (1991: 49) description of the classroom, school, district, state, and nation "levels" of the implementation system, Wilcox's (1982) description of classroom socialization shaped by organizational and community constraints, and McLaughlin and Talbert's (1993a) analysis which places the classroom in the center of school, community, higher education institutions, professional and environmental contexts.

The embedded sense of context is important because it calls our attention to the fact that face-to-face interaction occurs within wider dimensions of social life. It is limited, however, because it often puts one site, and only one site, in the center. Furthermore, the embedded sense of context is susceptible to the conceptual traps of structural determinism and unidirectionality.

When reform implementation is portrayed as a linear sequence or mechanical process of program testing, adoption and institutionalization, or educators in schools are depicted as passively responding to directives mandated from higher levels of bureaucracies (Carlson 1965; Havelock 1969; Smith and Keith 1971; Pressman and Wildavsky 1973), then models of educational implementation are susceptible to structural determinism. These models minimize the fact that educators are active agents, not just responding to but making policy. In concrete educational encounters, educators may act in a variety of ways in response to reforms – initiating alternatives, advancing or sustaining reform efforts, resisting or actively subverting reform efforts. Most importantly, the agency of educators is part of a complex dynamic, *shaping* and *shaped by* the structural and cultural features of school and society.

The embedded sense of context can also leave the impression that social life is unidirectional; forces emanating from higher levels of context cause or determine action at lower levels. While actions initiated at some distance away from local events may indeed constrain or shape actions, they do not totally determine them. And actions initiated in local events generate or construct conditions or structures that have consequences in settings far removed from local events.

The relational sense of context helps avoid the conceptual traps of structural determinism and unidirectionality that potentially plague the embedded sense of context. Whereas the embedded sense of context can be interpreted to mean that events at higher levels of the context occur first and are more important analytically, the relational sense of context does not automatically assign an *a priori* sense of importance to any one context. Events certainly occur in the chronological past, present and future, near to or far away from us. And we can use these divisions to clarify our statements about events. But we must also recognize the mutual influence of one context upon the other when accounting for social action in general, the implementation of educational reforms in particular.

Perspective and Power

Our theoretical framework gives primacy to the role of power and perspective as important features of the school reform process. We believe that the meaning that people derive from the social world varies according to their perspective (Thomas and Thomas 1928; Wittgenstein 1952; Austin 1961; Garfinkel 1967). A person's location in social institutions and cultural arrangements can influence their interpretation of events (Bakhtin 1981). People are "ineluctably situated in a sociohistorical matrix, whose cultural, political, economic, social and personal realities shape the discourse" (Gee *et al.* 1992: 228). Gender, ethnicity, and social class are particularly powerful realities that shape differences in meaning. These power relations are constituted on the terrain of everyday discourse in societal institutions, including schools, and influence the perceptions that men and women have on social events and objects, such as educational reform efforts (Datnow 1998).

All perspectives are not equal, however. W. I. and D. S. Thomas (1928: 572) were certainly correct when they said that people define situations as real and these definitions are real in their consequences. Because of institutional arrangements however, some positions accrue material and symbolic resources that enable incumbents of those positions to impose meanings upon others. Psychiatrists, for example, have the power to confine patients in hospital against their will even if they think they are healthy, judges can confine people in prisons even if they think they are innocent, and educators have the power to alter the course of students' educational careers (Erickson and Shultz 1982; Mehan *et al.* 1986; Sjöström 1997). Power is certainly a central feature of the educational policy process, both in development and in implementation (Berliner and Biddle 1995; Hargreaves and Fullan 1998).

As a result of the institutional distribution and application of power, the meaning of the reform effort or its aspects is not necessarily shared; there can be disagreement, or conflict over the meaning of actions, events, even the reform itself. If there is consensus, it is not the automatic result of a shared culture. Consensus is achieved, not given. It is achieved through negotiation and often strife, which means it is fragile, subject to revision and change.

We recognize that the knowable world is incomplete if seen from any one point of view and incoherent if we try and see it from all points of view at once. Given the choice between incoherence and incompleteness, we align with Shweder (1996) who opts for incompleteness. His "view from manywheres" (Shweder 1996: 4) is preferable to the view from "only here" because the latter falls into the trap of ethnocentrism. Attempting to obtain multiple perspectives is preferable to the view from "nowhere in particular" because the ideal of perfect objectivity is, after all, a myth. The view from manywheres is preferable to "no view at all" because the perspective of postmodern skeptics can lead us into the trap of nihilism. Our ethnographically informed research tries to overcome these conundrums by exposing our subjectivities and displaying as many perspectives on the implementation process as possible.

The Interplay of Structure, Culture and Agency

Ethnomethodologists say social action is "mutually constitutive" or "reflexive" (Garfinkel 1967; Cicourel 1973; Wieder 1973; Mehan and Wood 1975) by which they mean social actions simultaneously constitute social structures and cultural artifacts and are constrained or enabled by them. Giddens' (1979, 1984, 1993) idea of "structuration" in which agents (i.e., people), social action and social interaction are constrained by, yet generative of, the structural dimensions of social reality makes a similar point: "By the duality of structure, I mean the essential recursiveness of social life, as constituted in social practices: structure is both medium and outcome of the reproduction of practices and 'exists' in the generating moments of this constitution" (Giddens 1979: 5).

These ideas provide a different, reflexive, perspective on what have been called "macro phenomena" (social structures) and "micro phenomena" (social actions). Durkheim's (1938) depiction of social structures as objective and external to social action but constraining upon it is a classic formulation of the position that treats structure as independent of action. Suggesting that social structures are the contingent outcomes of practical activities that are produced in micropolitical encounters departs from conceptions of macro structures conceived to be independent of the observable actions of everyday life.

These concepts (which we collapse into the idea of "co-construction") are particularly helpful for the study of educational reform because they provide a heuristic way to look at the relationship between social interactions in schools and the impact of the major structural forces that characterize, indeed contribute to the reproduction of society. To be more than heuristic for our understanding of the policy implementation process however, structural forces must be located in the social actions that take place in encounters situated in classrooms, schools, districts, communities, design team meetings, courts of law, and governmental offices. We examine these sites in our study and find that *policy is made* in them. A policy enacted in the initial stages of implementation is added to, changed, subtracted from, and otherwise modified in later stages in the process. These transformations suggest that the policy process is an active and creative, not a passive flow-through device (Hall and McGinty 1997).

A lingering problem in ethnomethodology and Giddens' theory of structuration is that they tend to subsume culture in the structure–agency dynamic. Inasmuch as culture involves power and is the site of social differences and struggles, we believe that culture is of equal importance and profoundly impacts both structure and agency. In order to depict the equal albeit reflexive relations among structure, culture and agency, following Cole (1996), we represent them in Figure 1.1 as a "mediational system." Figure 1.1 attempts to show that structure, culture, and agency construct each other. Structure and agency work reflexively. So do agency and culture, structure and culture. In the agency of individuals we see structure and culture operating; in culture, we see structure and agency; and in structure, we see agency and culture.

We believe that this perhaps seemingly abstract discussion will come to life as we describe the reform efforts we observed. However, to provide a brief summary, the complex and often messy reform implementation process is marked by several important considerations:

- Analyzing scaling up and reform implementation as co-constructed processes affords us a better opportunity to understand the complexities confronting the implementation of a successful prototype than is provided by unidirectional (especially "top down") interpretations. Reform efforts in schools do not succeed on simple technical considerations alone, nor do they proceed in a linear fashion, fixed in time and space.
- Any one context is inevitably interconnected with other contexts. And, the consequences of actions taken in one context become the conditions for actions taken in other contexts.
- Reform efforts are viewed differently from different perspectives or points of view. We expect that teachers, principals, design team trainers, and district administrators will all view the reform differently, as will the individuals occupying each of those positions. No doubt, not all teachers in a school view reform in the same way.
- The culture of the school mediates educators' actions and structural constraints. Some educators may initiate reform efforts, others may push or sustain them, and still others may resist or actively subvert

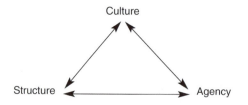

Figure 1.1 Culture, Structure and Agency as a Meditational System.

reform efforts. This range of actions shows that the agency of educators is part of a complex dynamic, *shaping* and *shaped by* the structural and cultural features of school and society.

- The incumbents of some positions have the power to impose meaning on others. Educators in schools must sometimes respond to realities that are created in discourse among powerful people – some who may have accrued power due to their race, class, or gender position. Actions, while sometimes seemingly mundane, are rarely neutral. We must explicitly attend to the possibilities and constraints of the political and economic conditions (including, but not limited to the changing nature of work, capitalism, and race, class, and gender inequalities, etc.) of society at large when we attempt to understand, much less implement, school reform.

Organization of This Book

The format of the book will be as follows: we will begin each chapter with a review of the extant literature on the topic and then present data from our studies, informed by our theory, to illustrate key points about scaling up school reform. Each chapter will end with "bullet point" implications for policy and practice.

In Chapter 2, we will assess why and how schools are adopting reforms with such incredible fervor at the current time. We will place the scaling up movement in historical and political context by discussing its relationship to prior school reform movements in the U.S. In Chapter 3, we will discuss how external reform designs interacted with local contextual conditions, and how their implementation was affected by the social dynamics of race, class, and gender. We discuss these findings in relation to studies regarding local variation in implementation and its root causes. Chapter 4 focuses on the agency of teachers and administrators in the school reform process.

Chapter 5 focuses on the design team as a changing, dynamic entity, and the consequences of design team actions for educators in schools. In Chapter 6, we explore the life of external reform designs in schools, discussing sustainability and expiration. We also discuss the politics of how reform effectiveness is defined and how varying measures of reform success impact the scaling up movement and the day-to-day activities of people in schools, design teams, and boardrooms. Finally, in Chapter 7 we summarize the findings presented in this book and their implications for school change. In doing so, we will discuss how our findings add conceptually and practically to extant research. We also pose new questions for research and practice.

2 How Does Reform Adoption Happen? The Role of Power, Politics, and Perspective

Why are schools adopting externally developed reforms with such fervor at the current time? How exactly does reform adoption come about? In this chapter, we argue that economic, social and political conditions – including growing public dissatisfaction with public schools, the push for strong systems of accountability and systemic reform, and beliefs about the effectiveness of "research-based" decision-making – have all set the stage for the adoption of external reform designs. These events combine to cause schools and districts to look to the possibilities of reform. As a result of these conditions, we have discovered – perhaps not surprisingly – that the impetus for the adoption of an external reform seldom arises from teachers. Rather, as we will explain, these reforms are introduced by state legislators, district administrators, and principals.

Why Are Schools Adopting Reforms *Now?*

Current economic, social, and political forces have combined to create a climate in which schools feel great pressure to change. First, there is a persistent and growing sentiment that public schools are failing to meet societal expectations, especially concerning students' academic achievement. Public schools are believed to be deficient in certain respects for all students (Elmore 1996), and most importantly, there are wide disparities between income and ethnic groups in educational outcomes. African-American and Latino students consistently obtain lower scores on standardized tests at all educational levels. They have lower attendance rates, lower passing rates, lower graduation rates, lower college matriculation rates, and higher drop-out rates than their white counterparts (Haycock 1999). These inequities increase even as the proportion of racial and ethnic minorities is growing in American public schools. The explanations given for the low achievement of poor and minority students are varied, but increasingly research has shown that these students are not offered equal or even adequate opportunity to learn in American public schools.

While the inequities are certainly real, the news media and policy-makers have also successfully manufactured a discourse of chaos that has destabilized public confidence about education and provided the pretext for the imposition of reform (Berliner and Biddle 1995; Hargreaves and

Fullan 1998). Provoked by the damning indictment of public schooling initiated by *A Nation At Risk* (National Council on Education and the Economy 1983) which condemned public schools for perpetuating a "rising tide of mediocrity," citizens, educators and researchers have produced a dizzying array of educational reforms in the U.S. over the last 20 years. During this period, we have witnessed a pendulum swing from reform policies aimed at increasing the centralization of authority over schools to those emphasizing a more decentralized governance structure (Tyack 1990). *A Nation at Risk* sparked a major wave of proposals that focused on a need for greater governmental regulation of schools by raising standards for graduation and increasing testing requirements. Mandates and inducements were the favored policy instruments to promote excellence and efficiency, thus reducing local control at the school site. These reforms allowed teachers little freedom to decide the curriculum as a whole or what was taught in their classrooms (McNeil 1988).

A countervailing set of proposals came to an opposite conclusion: top-down implementation of standardized policies did not meet the diverse needs of students in the classroom. The lack of professional control at the local level was perceived to de-skill or de-professionalize teaching, and the compelling argument was made that teachers are best positioned to make decisions about what their students need (Darling-Hammond 1988). While some were arguing that teacher autonomy undermines efforts to professionalize, in 1986, the Carnegie Foundation and the Education Commission of the States called for a shift in the locus of control from the states to local school districts, presumably giving more discretion to teachers. The political push toward district control ushered in a second wave of reform emphasizing upgrading standards for teachers, providing incentives linked to student achievement, and restructuring schools in order to give teachers a greater role in decision-making. It should be noted that many teachers still considered this move to be a "top down" arrangement. Although the second wave of reform focused on teachers, a basic formula was beginning to emerge: tightly connect the educational establishment to outcomes, while loosely connecting them to means (Sergiovanni *et al.* 1992).

The tenor of the second wave of reform continued into the 1990s, with the emergence of the "systemic reform" movement. Systemic reform is predicated on the belief that simultaneous centralization of accountability and decentralization of administration will free schools from bureaucratic constraints, allowing them to innovate, while assuring that all students meet the same high standards (Smith and O'Day 1991). Advocates argue that neither purely top-down nor bottom-up strategies of reform have proven to work; rather, a combination of the two might be more effective (O'Day and Smith 1993). The era of systemic reform was bolstered by the enactment of the federal Goals 2000: Educate America Act in 1994.

While there is strong political support for systemic reform, research suggests that there are substantial practical and political barriers to broad deregulation in general, and systemic reform in particular, as well as some possible negative consequences for equity (Borman and Cookson 1996; Cohen 1995; Fuhrman and Elmore 1995; Hannaway and Carnoy 1993; Gamoran 1996). Despite some skepticism about systemic reform among researchers, states are moving full speed ahead to establish high stakes accountability systems. Examples include the Tennessee Comprehensive Assessment Program, the Maryland School Performance Accountability Program, and the Kentucky Education Reform Act. Principals and teachers are held accountable for improving outcomes for all students on standardized tests. Some state accountability systems, such as those in Florida and Texas, also include mandates for closing achievement gaps between white and minority students. If student outcomes improve, educators are praised and often schools receive monetary rewards. If student outcomes decline or fail to show improvement over a period of time, schools may be subject to punishment, the final form of which can be the reconstitution of the school.

One of the intentions of the systemic reform movement is to inspire change at the local level. While some schools begin their own reforms in response to increased accountability, other schools have looked to the adoption of externally developed reform designs. By contracting with an external design team for assistance with school reform and, in some cases, a pre-packaged curricular and instructional model, educators hope to find a more expeditious route to improved student outcomes. This impulse is reinforced by several high profile research studies and reports that have shown implementation of reform models can lead to student achievement gains. For example, the *Special Strategies* study (Stringfield *et al.* 1997: 30) found that within the sample of schools observed longitudinally, "students in schools using externally developed designs tended to achieve greater academic gains than did students in locally developed programs." In separate reviews of research, Slavin and Fashola (1998), Herman and Stringfield (1997), and Herman *et al.* (1999) found that several externally developed reforms had the potential to improve students' academic achievement.

Adopting an externally developed reform design allows schools and districts to act locally in response to public pressures and external accountability measures, without having to create reform anew, a process that takes considerable time and effort. Studies have found that externally developed reforms, particularly those that are more prescriptive, can be implemented more easily and more quickly than change efforts that involve local development (Bodilly 1998; Nunnery 1998; Stringfield *et al.* 1997). Externally developed reforms also have name recognition, which can help educators garner resources for their change efforts, even if much of the work actually takes place locally (as may be the case with more principle-driven reforms such the Coalition of Essential Schools).

Actions at the federal level have also set the stage for the adoption of externally developed reform models, and in particular whole-school reforms. Perhaps the most significant of these actions has been through Title I, the U.S. government's approximately $8 billion a year program for improving the education of disadvantaged children. Title I has been in existence since 1965, initiated by President Johnson as part of his Great Society program. Changes in federal Title I regulations in 1988 and 1994 through the Improving America's Schools Act (IASA) have meant that schools serving large numbers of students in poverty can use Title I funds for schoolwide programs, rather than only targeted assistance programs as in the past (Desimone 2000) and recent studies have supported the educational benefits of this change (D'Agostino *et al.* 1998). In the past decade, many schools have used Title I funds for the costs associated with implementing externally developed reform models, including a number of the schools we studied. Additionally, as we mentioned in Chapter 1, the new federal funding available for research-based reforms through the Comprehensive School Reform Demonstration Program has also spurred reform adoption since 1998. However, none of the schools we studied received funding through this source, as it came along several years after our research was underway.

With the press for school improvement from national and state agencies and local constituencies and the growing number of reform options available, it is important that schools adopt a reform design that is a good fit and for which there is substantial local buy-in (Bodilly 1998; Consortium for Policy Research in Education 1998; Datnow *et al.* 1998; Desimone 2000; Education Commission of the States 1999; U.S. Department of Education 1999). A free and uncoerced choice for reform is essential to ensuring a successful change effort (Slavin 1998). Yet, research suggests that educators in schools adopting reforms feel uninformed and lack sufficient time to make educated choices (Berends and Bodilly 1998; Consortium for Policy Research in Education 1998; Stringfield and Ross 1997). How does this set of circumstances arise, or how exactly are reforms adopted?

In this chapter, we will open up the "black box" of the reform adoption process to examine how and why schools adopt reforms and the consequences of those processes for implementation efforts. We find that political dimensions of schooling, as well as seemingly mundane practical circumstances and everyday interactions, influence how and why reforms are chosen. Social actors – often those who do not work at the classroom level, such as school or district administrators or state legislators – are most often the force behind the adoption of the reform. Thus, those who are most responsible for implementing a reform (i.e., teachers and, in the case of district initiation, principals) are strongly encouraged to go along with the plans. School change is an inherently political process (Malen 1995; Noblit *et al.* 1991). Indeed, some argue that reforms enter schools already politically organized (Noblit *et al.* 1991). Because a hierarchical approach is evident in most reform adoption scenarios, we analyze our data in light of a framework that addresses the issues of power and perspective discussed in Chapter 1.

Our intent is not to favor either a macro or a micro version of politics, but instead attempt to "understand politics as a force, for good or ill, and to work to develop a keener understanding of the complexities and the consequences of power relations and political processes" (Malen 1995: 160). Therefore, we attempt to display political processes as not negative, but rather as a taken-for-granted feature of how reform arises within a school, district, or state. This framework is useful for understanding how schools adopt reforms, as it acknowledges that differing, often conflicting perspectives, representing how power differentials are features of the process, and these dynamics have consequences for teacher buy-in and for the future implementation and sustainability of reform efforts. It also highlights the multiple and dynamic interrelationships among the reform initiators and reform implementers.

In the sections that follow, we begin to concretize the theoretical framework described in Chapter 1 with respect to reform adoption processes. We discuss how the vector of reform varies. We find that sometimes it flows from state to district, as in the case of the adoption of AVID in Kentucky. More frequently for the reform adoptions in our study, the impetus to adopt a reform came from the district either in the form of mandates to principals, or in the use of more subtle tactics designed to persuade teachers. Without exception, differential power relations shaped reform adoption. Next, we examine how practical constraints influenced the best-laid plans for reform choice and how these constraints are also connected to issues of power. We illustrate how the politics of representation influenced decisions around reform, showing how the meaning of events around reform adoption varied, as did educators' responses to the initiation of reform. We draw upon case study data to specifically illustrate each of these points in their own right; however, we believe that all of themes are evident within every discussion. We conclude the chapter with implications for policy and practice.

Differential Power Relations Are Central Features of the Reform Adoption Process

The Role of the State

When we examine the encounters that occur among individuals in states, districts and schools, we find that policy is made in these encounters. Indeed, the educational policy process is influenced by the educators who have power. Often these people are at the state level.

The adoption of AVID in Kentucky was the result of a hierarchical approach to reform adoption. It was the particular actions of a powerful leader at the state level that placed this reform on the agenda. In 1989, the Kentucky Supreme Court declared that "state revenues were unequally allotted to local school districts" (Richardson *et al.* 1991) and directed the state legislature to remedy the problem. In response to the court's decision, the state legislature passed the Kentucky Education Reform Act (KERA), which mandated a total overhaul of the K–12 public educational system and increased state funding for education. As part of KERA, systemic reform was initiated through a centralized accountability system coupled with decentralized decision-making. Site-based decision-making was mandated. Each school was directed to improve test scores by 5 percent each year. There were financial and oversight consequences for schools that did or did not achieve rigid accountability standards.

The selection of a new educational leader helped AVID move to the center of KERA. In 1990, Dr. Thomas Boysen was recruited from his position as San Diego County Superintendent of Schools and appointed Commissioner of the State Department of Education in Kentucky. Boysen had promoted AVID in his previous position because of the program's success in raising the academic achievement of minority students in San Diego schools. Responding to the imperatives of KERA, Boysen lobbied for AVID to be introduced in Kentucky schools. He viewed AVID as a program that could help many of the students who had been previously poorly served and were underrepresented on college campuses.

Boysen appealed to the legislators for financial support of AVID and convinced the state legislature to devote $500,000 to AVID in fiscal year 1993. Because the state was willing to support the implementation of AVID as a significant vehicle in the KERA reform program, districts were eager to get their share of reform funds. In 1993, the state approved applications from 19 schools to implement AVID. When the state is poised to accept educational change, the results are significant. Actions of those at this level of the system can dictate decisions regarding the adoption of educational reform.

The Role of the District

When actors interact together in situations, their positionality is neither neutral nor is their power evenly distributed. Rather, powerful people can impose meaning on others, and this happens through decisions that often advantage some groups over others. In this case, district superintendents, with their ability to interact in fortuitous ways with state legislators and exert power over principals, and principals who are able to exert power over teachers, decided the fate of reform adoption and implementation.

The story of the adoption of the AVID program in Virginia illustrates the impact that a powerful district administrator played in policy creation and reform adoption. In 1991, Samuel Evans, then superintendent of the White Wake School District in Virginia, attended a conference in Florida and by chance learned of AVID, a topic that was not even on the agenda. Evans explained:

> I got to the opening session late, sat in the back, and wound up next to a teacher from California who said she taught AVID. She ended up being a lot more interesting than the keynote speaker. We talked right through lunch, and her enthusiasm and description of AVID was intriguing. When I returned, I told my staff to track down this AVID program.

This serendipitous encounter set into motion a series of actions by Evans that motivated principals to adopt the program. When the powerful district superintendent returned from the conference he convinced educators that AVID could help the students in their community who had been ignored by the educational system. Evans brought achievement gaps between white and black students to center stage and charged the atmosphere with calls for educational change and improvement. A district official who worked closely with Evans remembers that he was a "mover and a shaker" and that AVID fit his goals.

The policy process and the adoption of reform unfolded from there – in a more deliberative fashion. Evans skillfully created a particular discourse around AVID that would help him achieve his goals of reform adoption. Evans was careful not to present AVID as a program designed for a special segment of the community. With the assertion, "what is good for AVID kids will be good for other kids," he persuaded the community and teachers that the whole school would benefit from implementing the program and using AVID methodologies. Middle school parents were especially supportive and turned out in large numbers at parent meetings. Evans also secured "buy in" by convincing teachers and principals that AVID was not an add-on program. Because AVID is built into the school day, teachers would not have extra work, he asserted.

Evans astutely worked at the state level to secure funding for AVID. Evans' position as superintendent gave him access to the state legislature. He convinced a state legislator from White Wake to enable him to present a funding proposal to a subcommittee that had been created by the state to examine minority enrollment in higher education. The timing was fortuitous, as the subcommittee had just prepared a report that reflected some very dismal statistics about minority high school students in Virginia. Legislators were impressed with Evans' presentation of AVID and made the program a separate line item in the state budget commencing in 1994–95.

Program implementation in White Wake moved quickly. Starting up this new program on such short notice was described by an AVID educator as a "whirlwind kind of adoption to get it going" and very "challenging." According to an administrator, who was put in charge of the district-wide program at the time, "we made a lot of mistakes but our superintendent wanted to get it in place to get some focus for state funding." Schools scrambled to respond to the superintendent who employed his power to insist that this reform take hold. Over the course of several years, strong district commitment was secured, and all five high schools and all seven middle schools in the White Wake school district adopted AVID.

In the White Wake example we find dynamic interactions that occur across time and space in the policy process and the importance of representing the reform in a particular way. Most importantly, this example points to the role of powerful district leaders in shaping the adoption of a reform across an entire school district and ultimately across the state. The state legislature's decision to jump quickly onto the reform bandwagon and fund AVID is not unusual, as it occurred during a period of increased state involvement in educational reform beginning in the late 1980s and continuing through the 1990s. As Mazzoni (1995: 60) states, "reform proposals by the many hundreds were picked up, packaged, and promoted by elected officials across the country." The actions of district superintendents, in both planned and unplanned encounters, are pivotal in reform adoption.

The power issues surrounding reform adoption were more highly charged in an urban district in California, where a district administrator promoted the adoption of Success for All. After extensively researching SFA, visiting SFA schools in other districts, and winning the support of the school board, the assistant superintendent strongly encouraged ten low-performing schools to adopt SFA. She explained, "I've done my homework. SFA is the only model that does anything." SFA fit well with the district's goal of having all students reading at grade level. The carrots for schools were generous: the district offered to pay fully for the first three years of SFA implementation. In addition, the sticks were sharp: the district informed the schools that if they chose not to adopt SFA they would need to develop their own literacy programs and achieve comparable gains, without support from the district.

After attending an SFA Awareness Presentation, the staff at Bayside Elementary School discussed the pros and cons of SFA. The principal was in favor of adoption, as were some newer teachers, but some veteran teachers were vehemently against SFA. The teachers who were hesitant about SFA felt that the district was coercing them and their principal to adopt yet another program. As one of these teachers remarked in an interview, "The people at the top threatened the principals." What finally led them to vote unanimously in favor was the staff's unwillingness to develop a program in lieu of SFA. According to the principal, "The clincher was when one teacher said, 'Look guys, this is reality. If we don't do this, then which one of you is going to work over the summer to develop and design a program?'" After deliberation, the staff voted unanimously to adopt SFA. Not surprisingly, given the district's strong encouragement, seven of the ten other low-achieving schools in the district also voted to adopt the reform.

Often times, this imposition of meaning from the district does not take the form of simple mandates as we might expect, but rather it occurs in a series of interconnected and nuanced events, in which compromise, resistance, and negotiation all figure strongly. These competing interests, ideologies, and the informal negotiations of turf in schools and districts are the essence of school micropolitics (Iannacone 1991; Marshall and Scribner 1991). We found that informal negotiations were often part and parcel of the reform adoption processes. For example, in Sunland County, the administrators employed at the district's Office of Instruction helped some schools to decide to adopt reforms by visiting the schools and making presentations to the faculty. As part of an effort to revitalize the school, a district liaison approached the principal of Sawgrass Elementary about implementing the Audrey Cohen College System of Education, one of the

New American Schools designs. As the district liaison described, "I knew their population was changing . . . so I said 'Let me come to your school and do a presentation.'" Sawgrass Elementary had experienced a considerable demographic shift in the past few years from a school which was white and middle-class, to one which served 1000 students, grades K–5, of whom the majority were Black and Latino recent immigrants. The principal, however, believed that they were chosen for the presentation because they were known to be a progressive school. Clearly, the reasons for reform looked different from the points of view of the district and the school site educators. Rather than impose a reform adoption on this school, however, the district with the help of the principal, skillfully manipulated an event that was designed to persuade teachers of the merit of the Audrey Cohen model.

The principal agreed to let the district administrator give a presentation of the design to the faculty. Subsequently, a vote was held to determine faculty interest in implementing the design. The requisite 80 percent of the teachers voted in favor; however some staff voted "yes" grudgingly. The principal explained that the teachers "know that I like new things, and that if it wasn't Audrey Cohen, it would be something else." A teacher corroborated this point. She stated, "We kind of knew that it was that or this scripted reading thing" that a number of other schools in the district had been mandated to adopt. The Sawgrass principal clearly developed a strategy to deal with the tension, appeasing her staff on the one hand and the district on the other. Principals are commonly caught in political dilemmas of this kind (Malen 1995).

To be sure, hierarchical relations of power strongly impact school reform efforts. Power dynamics are present in all relationships in schools: students vs. teachers, teachers vs. principals, principals vs. district administrators, districts vs. state departments of education (Sarason 1996: 338), and teachers vs. teachers (Datnow 1998). As others have noted, research on school change often ignores these micro-political interactions (Ball, 1987; Hargreaves *et al.* 1996). Whereas organizational theory tends to emphasize shared goals, consensus, and similarity, we agree it is necessary to emphasize power, ideological diversity, and political action (Ball 1987). By studying how politics work in interaction, we gain an understanding of how and why certain individuals and groups shape what happens in schools through their power and dominance over others.

Practical Circumstances And Power Constrain Reform "Choice"

Practical circumstances have been demonstrated to act as constraints to actors, sometimes in distinctly political ways. Structural constraints come into play with respect to the amount and kind of information given and the use of this information by individuals. Even when people in an organization intend to use all information in making decisions, they often behave in "boundedly rational" ways because they have too much information, unreliable information, or not enough (Simon 1957). "In practice, individuals and organizations consider only a relatively small number of alternatives, and frequently stop searching once they find a tolerable course of action, rather than seeking the best possible" (Black 1997: 37). As we will explain, power relations often also influence what information is presented, as well as how much.

The "reform design fairs" by which reform adoption occurred in numerous schools in our studies reveal instances in which structural constraints, particularly with respect to time, resources, and information, combined with power dynamics in the local arena, disrupted even the most carefully thought out plans. Reform design fairs are one of the most prevalent routes through which schools currently adopt externally developed reforms. Design fairs began in 1995 when the New American Schools (NAS) Corporation attempted to effect large-scale reform by bringing a "menu" of school restructuring models to numerous partner districts (Kearns and Anderson 1996; New American Schools 1997).

The Sunland school district was one of the original NAS scale up jurisdictions. The district chose to offer five of the NAS designs to its schools, as well as several others including the Comer School Development Program and the SRA reading program. The district negotiated with NAS to offer an exhibition of reform designs (Ross *et al.* 1997). In the spring of 1995, the first exposition was held in Sunland, where design teams exhibited their school restructuring designs to teams of educators from all schools that were invited to send groups to the exposition. After attending the exhibition, schools were given some time to gather additional information through meetings with design team representatives and through videos and printed information about the designs.

Schools that were interested in adopting particular designs were required to conduct a vote among staff to ensure an adequate level of teacher buy-in. In schools where the proper number of teachers voted to implement a NAS design, the district agreed to pay for teacher training, materials, and a full-time program facilitator for each school. In Sunland, 80 percent of the teachers needed to vote in favor of a design for the district to support its implementation. However, a close look at how reform choice unfolded in schools suggests that the process was not so neat and clean, despite the best intentions of district leaders.

Educators in schools were clear about the fact that the district was promoting reform. In 1995–96, Sunland's then-superintendent was very much in favor of promoting the use of externally developed reforms. While principals did not describe themselves as forced to adopt a reform after attending the design fair, they were keenly aware that money and resources flowed to schools that did choose a reform. Therefore, they set out to select one. In most cases, principals pushed their staff to vote in favor of reform quickly and often apparently without much information. Uniformly, the principals we interviewed expressed more knowledge and interest in the reform at the outset than the teachers did.

It appears that structural constraints and relations of power had as much to do with reform adoption as the information about the reforms themselves. In most cases, principals realized that they would be able to garner additional resources and curry favor from the district if they adopted a reform. As a result, they encouraged their teachers to vote in favor and vote quickly. While they were successful in doing so, the lack of genuine teacher buy-in at the outset often negatively impacted the success of the implementation of the reform in the long run, as we will see in subsequent chapters.

The Politics of Representation Influence Decisions About Reform

The politics of representation is the competition that takes place among individuals or factions over the meaning of ambiguous events, people, and objects in the world. The way in which events, objects, or people are represented in discourse gives them a particular meaning (Mehan 1993). Representations do not mimic reality, but rather are the practices by which things take on meaning and value (Shapiro 1987). The key to the politics of representation is the inextricable connection between language and power: "the more powerful the people, the larger their verbal possibilities in discourse" (Wodak 1995: 33). The strategic use of discourse is among the most influential micropolitical processes (Corson 1995; Marshall and Scribner 1991; Berger and Luckmann 1967).

Contests over the meaning of reforms were a significant element in adoption processes, and they played themselves out in a number of different ways. First, the adoption of school reform models was influenced by a discourse of "research-based" educational reform, an expression that has come into widespread use among educators and policymakers in recent years. Research-based reforms are presumed to be "proven" as well as "replicable" and thus the term brings with it considerable cache and power. The adoption of Success for All at Peterson Elementary School in California exemplifies how a "research-based" reform prevailed over other choices. Success for All was initially suggested to the school's principal by a grant writer, who had been employed to help write a federal grant to improve the school's bilingual and early literacy programs. The principal, already somewhat familiar with SFA, invited SFA trainers to describe the program to the faculty. After the presentation, the teachers unanimously voted against the reform, explaining that they were concerned about its structured nature and the prescriptive curricular materials.

When the school finally did receive the federal grant, the staff were told by the principal that they needed a "research-based" bilingual literacy program in order to use the funding. The principal searched for other programs, but found that none were as well substantiated by research as

SFA. The teachers agreed to have the SFA trainers visit the school one more time to answer questions and address concerns about the program. After their visit, the principal impressed upon the teachers the need to adopt a program. The staff took another vote, resulting in 18 in favor of SFA and only one against. Several teachers noted that they were not given many options, since SFA was the only bilingual reading program that had "statistics behind it," which was the grant requirement. Some teachers were still not sold on the program, even though they actively voted for it. As this illustration reveals, the politics of representation influences reform adoption. Reforms that carry the label "research-based" have more power than those that do not. Even when several programs are supported by research, those in positions of power often decide how information about the various choices is presented.

How models were presented to faculty and, most importantly, by whom was a second way in which the politics of representation influenced reform adoption. Those in positions of greater power, such as principals, were able to use their leadership roles and their ability to control information flow to affect school-site decision-making in potent ways (Malen 1995: 150). For example, at Tupelo Elementary, school administrators attended the Sunland reform design fair and considered adopting one of three reforms. Subsequently, the principal made presentations about each reform to the faculty. The principal believed that while the teachers had the opportunity to give input into the reform they wanted, she openly admitted that her presentation of the reforms was weighted in favor of Modern Red: "Obviously, I presented Modern Red to them with a lot more positives than I did some of the ones I didn't want." The requisite 80 percent of teachers then voted in favor of adopting the Modern Red Schoolhouse design. How the Modern Red reform was represented and the fact that it was presented by the principal strongly influenced the teachers' decision for adoption.

The Meaning of Events Around Reform Adoption Varies with Perspective

One's perspective is usually influenced by the standpoint from which one sees and experiences the world. As a result of differential power and positionality, the definition or meaning of events by various actors can become contested terrain. Different opinions can surface over the course of actions that lead to reform. The Sawgrass Elementary School example described above suggests that there were differences in perspective between the principal and the district administrator who had brought the reform to her attention. Most often, we found differences in perspective among teachers in a school or between teachers and administrators. These perspectival differences were not surprising, given the varied positions and ideologies of the individuals within each group.

An interesting case in point is Forest Elementary, a school in Sunland

County that adopted the Comer School Development Program in 1992, preceding the district's push for externally developed reform designs in 1994. The principal learned about Comer SDP from the principal of another school that was implementing the model. Believing that the program fit with her leadership style and philosophy, she took a group of teachers to visit the Comer school. The team subsequently presented information about their visit to the faculty. Revealing differences in perspective on the reform adoption process, a member of the administrative team stated that "the teachers were really part of this from the outset," whereas some teachers said they had little involvement in the decision to adopt the Comer model. A vote was not held, and the administration explained that sufficient support for the program had been achieved through consensus. The assistant principal admitted that some teachers were "disinterested" in Comer and that "we had to accept that it's not going to be one hundred percent." None of the teachers we interviewed appeared upset about the way the reform was adopted at the school.

The issue of some teachers feeling coerced to vote in favor of a reform because their principal desired it was also apparent at Jetty Elementary, a Core Knowledge school in Sunland County. In 1991, after receiving a copy of the Core Knowledge Sequence from another principal, the principal at Jetty gave teachers copies and invited them to teach lessons on the topics in the sequence, if they chose to. The following year, the majority of the faculty voted to have Core Knowledge included in the school improvement plan. Some teachers were very supportive of Core Knowledge and believed that the program had been introduced gradually, after they had had time to develop and pilot lessons. Others had a different perspective, arguing that the principal effectively mandated it because she liked the program. "We were given the books and we were told that we were going to do something 'wonderful'," remarked one teacher. Another teacher explained that, "it's been voted on more than once. The desired response was not secured the first time so the vote was taken again." Despite resentment from some teachers at Jetty, the majority of teachers accepted that Core Knowledge was a part of their school, and many were actually enthusiastic supporters, feeling ownership for the program and the lessons that they had developed as a consequence.

In summary, while principals reported that teachers often had a strong voice in decision-making, teachers often stated they had little choice but to comply with the principal's initiative. Teachers are, after all, in a vulnerable position and realize that there may be consequences for expressing divergent opinions (Malen 1995). Teachers' perceptions of their involvement in reform adoption decision-making often correlated with their perceptions of the reform itself. Those who felt ownership reacted favorably to the reform adoption; others, reacting to the fast pace of adoption, feeling no part in the decision-making process and who had little time to try out the program, reacted negatively. In the end, teachers' perspectives were less significant in the adoption process, as administrators held the power to shape events. Most principals realized that they would never bring all staff along in the reform process, but they were mostly successful in creating the feeling that the reform was simply a given at the school.

The Reactions of Educators Vary in Response to the Advent of Reform

Our framework for making sense of reform is premised upon the fact that educators in schools do not passively respond to directives mandated from higher levels of organizations. Rather, educators may respond in a variety of ways to such directives – through advancing reform efforts, symbolically displaying reforms, or resisting them overtly or covertly. Conflicting ideologies are often the source of educators' divergent responses to change. That is, educators who find that their ideologies are consistent with the proposed reform often support it, whereas those who find their ideologies are inconsistent with it may actively or passively resist the change (Bailey 2000; Muncey and McQuillan 1996; Sikes 1992). Ideology and response to reform also can correlate with teachers' personal characteristics, such as age or career stage (Huberman 1989; Riseborough 1981), gender (Datnow 1998; Hubbard and Datnow 2000), or race and culture (Bascia 1996; Casey 1993; Foster 1993).

Educators' perspectives and responses to reform can be deeply embedded within a larger societal context. For this reason, it is important to focus both on schools as units of change and on the external communities of which the schools are a part (Little 1990; Louis 1990; McLaughlin, Talbert and Bascia 1990; Siskin 1994). Events outside schools profoundly affect what happens inside them. Budget changes, new tests or curriculum guidelines, and the election of local officials can disrupt even the best-laid plans for reform (Siskin 1994). Additionally, the social, historical, and economic context in which a school is located can affect how educators respond to reforms (Louis 1990; Sarason 1990).

The efforts of one district superintendent to bring AVID to North Carolina illustrates the way in which perspective, informed by social context, impacts reform. As we explained earlier, Virginia superintendent Evans was successful in promoting the adoption of AVID in his district. Thereafter, Evans moved to North Carolina and assumed the superintendency of an urban district in that state. He attempted to bring AVID to their schools. Evans was friendly with a North Carolina State Senator and was very quick to gain support and a modest sum of money from the legislature for AVID.

Evans benefited from support of the local school board but he met resistance from many educators and community members who were not convinced that AVID should be in their schools. Evans explained:

> Race is an issue. This is a program that is designed for a specific classification of students. The "I want my kid to get the good stuff too" type of mentality comes up. See, so you get the backlash from folks who would normally be [supportive]. Those are some major issues.

The teachers and principals were also suspicious of the program because they had seen many pet programs come and go. One high school principal explained his reservations and why he ultimately adopted AVID at his school:

> We were *told* to have it by the superintendent. It became one of his initiatives here when he came to [this district]. The AVID piece is one that I raised questions about and did not eagerly decide to do it. As a matter of fact I delayed and delayed and delayed . . . and then finally made that decision. My reservations? Is this going to be something that is going to positively do something and have some long-term impact or is this another of these morning dew [programs] that will come out with this present superintendent and be gone again when the sun comes out? Is it something that we're playing smoke and mirrors with?

Evans once again convinced his constituents that AVID was more than smoke and mirrors. As we will discuss later, his efforts to achieve district-wide implementation of AVID succeeded. However, the adoption of AVID in schools in North Carolina demonstrates resistance that had both racial overtones as well as the typical "is this just another program that will come and go?" concern that educators often voice about reform.

A second case in point was when AVID began to spread to districts throughout Virginia. Some principals and teachers resisted the adoption of the program. In some instances they were already operating other programs and either saw AVID as redundant or as competition. In other instances, they resented the legislature that directed them to adopt AVID. Decision-makers in the district offices of Jonesville and Walnut Grove had a different perspective than teachers and principals. They were loath to turn their backs on state money. Adopting AVID, after all, meant that Jonesville and Walnut Grove would receive $100,000 a year from the state. Since each of these districts had only two high schools, implementing the AVID program gave each school a considerable amount of money, especially helpful in troubled economic times.

It appears that educational decision-makers in the Freeport district in Virginia were particularly ambivalent about the relevance of AVID. Because they had already lent their support to another program, they felt no sense of urgency in applying for funds to support AVID. Eventually delegates from Freeport concluded that they could no longer ignore this funding opportunity and received state funds to implement AVID. Economic considerations in the end drove their decision to adopt AVID. Their ambivalence toward the program, however, has had consequences. AVID is limited to ninth and tenth graders only. It operated in three of 23 Freeport high schools and two of 22 middle schools at the time of this study. There were no plans to expand it further.

In contrast, educators at Callaway, an elementary school in Sunland, chose to embrace and advance a reform that was also brought in from the outside. District administrators encouraged Callaway Elementary to adopt Core Knowledge, not because the school was stagnating, but because they believed reform would be likely to succeed there. As a result, the school would then become a model for Core Knowledge in the district. The principal recounted that in 1993, two years before the superintendent offered a menu of reform designs, she received phone calls from two district administrators who wanted to see Core Knowledge implemented in Sunland County Public Schools. One administrator specifically thought that it would be good to implement it in Spanish. Given that Callaway was the district's flagship two-way bilingual school that had long been successful, they were the obvious choice. As the principal explained, "So it was something that came from the district. They did support us financially. They gave us money at least for the first year we did it to purchase books and materials to help us implement the program. Of course then once we had made the commitment we set out to find out how we're going to do it."

There was initial hesitation on the part of the teachers, who felt they had little option but to say "yes" to the adoption of Core Knowledge. In the end, the teachers decided that they would expend the effort to try to make Core Knowledge work at their school. They spent considerable amounts of time planning for implementation (e.g., deciding the language of instruction, coordinating Core with the district's curriculum, and writing lesson plans). In the process, this already professional and motivated staff developed substantial ownership of the program. Core Knowledge continues to be successfully implemented at this school eight years later. One district administrator commented about Callaway being an example of reform institutionalization, stating "Callaway has completely changed populations but they have maintained a high level of commitment" both to Core Knowledge and its two-way bilingual program that had been in existence for over 20 years. This was an exemplary school that had sustained effectiveness on traditional measures for long periods of time.

As these illustrations reveal, externally developed reforms meet with varying types of agency among educators, depending on their ideologies, prior experiences with change, and local interests, constraints, and circumstances. Educators' responses to reform are almost never uniform within a school, much less within a district or state. In order to understand support for and resistance to the adoption of educational reform, it is essential that we pay attention to the social, historical and economic context in which these decisions are made. Individuals formulate perspectives that are driven by societal context and their interaction with externally developed reform models account for the tensions and ambiguities that we find in the process.

The Vector of Reform Is Multidirectional

As we explained in Chapter 1, deterministic models that portray reform flowing only from the top down do not explain school reform efforts. In fact, the examples above show evidence of the push–pull that often arises in reform adoption. Reform adoption also flows from the bottom up, rather than from the top down. Although unusual among the schools we studied, teachers occasionally brought a reform to their schools and districts. We found the greatest evidence of this in California with the AVID program. As AVID teachers changed locations, they told their new administrators about the reform and the reform spread throughout the state. As a result, knowledge about AVID was quite widespread in California. Many teachers heard about AVID from other educators and felt it would meet the needs of their population of students. One district official from California recalls:

> A group of innovative school administrators and teachers on the [high school] campus who had heard about the AVID program visited Mary Catherine Swanson, the founder of AVID. [They] learned about the program and decided that this would be something that could really help them turn their school around, particularly in terms of the expectations that teachers had for their students.

Teachers brought their passion for the program to the attention of their districts. The California district in our study viewed themselves as "pro-active about issues of diversity and integration" and thus were very receptive to the AVID program. The superintendent claimed that, "It was kind of a perfect match at the perfect time between a model that seemed to hold a lot of promise and our own need to respond to the increasing diversity in the district." The school board also endorsed AVID and one member even felt compelled to give testimony about AVID at a National School Board Association meeting claiming it was the "best decision" their district had ever made.

While the vector of reform adoption can flow in an upward rather than a downward direction, people in positions of power are still needed for teachers to achieve school level goals. Teachers' success in having AVID adopted was due in large part to the strong district support, both philosophically and financially that they were able to secure. The district provided "more than mere lip-service" to the support of AVID. While teachers did inspire the adoption of AVID, as this example makes abundantly clear, they needed the powerful backing of school and district officials to make it a reality.

Conclusions and Implications

As our case studies illustrate, power and politics played into decisions in every arena. This was true whether teachers initiated a particular reform, the district pushed a myriad of reform choices, the state provided funding for a single reform, or the principal initiated reform at his/her school. Whichever individuals saw a reason for a reform, the onus of responsibility was on them to convince those with power about the merit of adopting it. State legislation and funding for the AVID reform provided strong inducements for districts to adopt the reform, and districts proceeded regardless of whether individual schools felt they needed the program or whether they had funding to fully support it. So too, the strong push for restructuring from the district level led few educators to question whether or why they needed to reform their particular school. Even when they did challenge efforts to adopt reform, as educators in a number of schools saw no need to restructure or change, they found that their voices were over-shadowed by the more powerful voices at the top.

Offering a menu of reform models is a process used by districts to encourage reforms, while not appearing to mandate them. Yet, this some-what hyperrational approach (Wise 1977) does not account for the fact that schools are social institutions characterized by hierarchical relations of power and competing interests and ideologies. What programs are pre-sented and how they are presented are politically strategic events. Moreover, if local educators feel forced to choose a reform model in order to avoid having one foisted upon them, reform adoption will be motivated by an interest in retaining autonomy, following administrative mandates, or securing additional resources. A school then might choose a reform simply for the purposes of legitimacy (Scott 1998), which can be achieved simply by showing external (often superficial) compliance.

In many cases, teachers stated that the reform adoption voting process was not genuine. Either teachers voted several times until the desired out-come was achieved, or they were strongly encouraged to vote for the reform the first time. In such cases, teachers occupy a relatively powerless role in the reform adoption process. The vote gives the presumption of buy-in, and allows administrators to later point to the fact that staff chose to adopt the reform. Yet, this pseudo-democracy ignores the system of power relations in which the reform process is embedded. Teachers know that they may fall out of favor with administrators, or with colleagues, if they subvert reform.

As we analyze the origins and consequences of reform attempts, we must be careful to recognize that some retrospective sense-making (Weick 1995) may be occurring among educators. On the one hand, teachers who are happy with how the reform is now working at their school, or whose ideologies match those of the reform, may be more likely to describe having participated in the reform adoption process. On the other hand, teachers who are not in favor of the reform may be more likely to pick apart the adoption process, minimizing their role in it. Indeed, we heard varied perspectives on the role of teachers in reform, depending upon which teachers were interviewed in a particular school. The tensions that often existed between teachers who were for and against the reform may have contributed to teachers' sense-making about reform adoption.

Perhaps it is not the particular reform choice that makes the most dif-ference to the reform's sustainability; it is the context into which those reforms were introduced. Our research shows that the perspectives of teachers, principals and district administrators are strongly influenced by their social, historical and economic experiences.

Where does this leave us? In many respects our studies suggest the difficulties of achieving commitment to the adoption of an external reform, regardless of the origin of its impetus. This would point to a renewal of faith in local change efforts. However, some might argue that the need for school improvement is so great that we cannot solely rely on grass-roots efforts, which are much slower to evolve. The press to improve schools continues unabated and states continue to develop high stakes accountability systems designed to push schools to change. Externally developed reforms are here to stay, at least for the time being. How can the adoption of these models be more genuine? How can schools, districts, and states better construct environments that encourage genuine staff buy-in to a particular change process? We have several suggestions, albeit with accompanying caveats.

- *Policymakers, educators, and design teams need to think about external reforms as part of overall, long-term plans for school change, not as simple technical fixes for isolated school "deficiencies"*

The promotion of reforms by powerful actors in schools and districts often proceeds as if schools had only a few more years to live. Moreover, externally developed reforms are seen as cures for school "illnesses" such as low reading scores, traditional instructional methods, or incoherent curricula. Externally developed reforms need to be understood as part of an overall change process that is intended to orient the school towards continual improvement, not simply things that schools can insert and then abandon when test scores do or do not improve. In Chapter 6, we will further address the issue of how measures of reform success constrain school change.

- *Districts and states need to understand the difference between supporting reform and mandating or strongly inducing it*

Even when districts and states did not specifically mandate reform, the inducements and/or strong encouragement that they provided led the reforms to be viewed essentially as top-down directives. When hierarchical power relations surround reform adoption, it is likely that a reform becomes highly politicized within a school or district. There is also a very strong chance that educators will react to inducements for reform adoption opportunistically, particularly given the recurring need for extra school funding or outside resources. District and state support for reform initiation is no doubt essential. However, initial buy-in and long-term commitment to reform among teachers – the people who must initiate reforms day-in and day-out – will make or break a reform effort.

- *Expand the time in which schools make decisions about reforms*

Expanding the time allowed for reform adoption is essential. Keep in mind that two systematic reforms that improved the academic performance of underrepresented students – The Kamahameha Early Education Program [KEEP] in Hawaii (Tharp and Gallimore 1995) and the high performance learning community in New York's District 2 (Elmore and Burney 1997a, 1997b) took almost a decade each to institutionalize. We recognize that it will be difficult to implement the recommendation to expand the time for schools to make decisions in the current climate of high-stakes account-ability. Schools are under extreme pressure to improve outcomes on standardized tests and are eager to adopt reforms that might lead to those improvements quickly. Parents and community members look to school districts to show the results of their investments in time and effort quickly, sometimes causing educators to abandon reforms before they have had the opportunity for success. Moreover, resource bases, such as the Comprehensive Reform Demonstration Program, often have timelines of their own. While acknowledging these constraints, building additional time for reform adoption into the professional lives of educators will contribute to reform success.

- *Genuinely increase the level of teacher involvement in reform adoption*
Genuine teacher involvement in reform adoption certainly needs to be increased. If teachers are going to be convinced that they can contribute to the solutions for school problems they must also be convinced that they have the power to effect change. They must be respected for the knowl-edge they have. Even in this era when we believe that the teacher is a change agent, we found so few schools in our studies in which the impe-tus for adopting a reform came from the teachers. Teachers need to be encouraged and empowered to identify school level problems and consider how the various reforms may help solve these problems (Hargreaves 1994). According to Sirotnik and Oakes (1986: 39), this inquiry process should ideally be characterized by "free exploration, honest exchange, and non-manipulative discussion of existing and deliberately generated knowledge in light of critical questions like: 'What goes on in this school? Who bene-fits from the way things are?'" The critical inquiry process can play an important role in adopting the right reform (or developing a local change strategy instead) and in promoting long-term teacher development and empowerment for change. But obviously, the teacher inquiry process is not sufficient in and of itself. Districts must demonstrate to teachers that their ideas are actually becoming part of the decision-making process. The redis-tribution of power is an important struggle if all stakeholders are to be given a voice in the process of school reform.

- *Increase the amount of information schools have about reforms prior to adoption, but also acknowledge its limits*
Many people seem to think that simply by improving the amount and level of information that is given to schools about reforms, educators will be able to make better choices among reforms. Of course more information can be helpful to decision-making, but it does not necessarily make for a

more "rational" process. A more powerful actor (e.g., a principal, a school leadership team, or a district administrator) is often in a position to decide what information to present, and thus structures the process so that one particular reform receives support.

Second, as studies of problem solving in ambiguous situations show (Wason and Johnson-Laird 1972 or D'Andrade 1997), too much information can shut down decision-making. Third, as Weiss (1995: 588) found in her study of shared decision-making, for teachers the "lack of extensive information coalesced with self-interest in the status quo and was reinforced by selective attention to those elements in their value system that stressed continuation of present practice." That is, teachers may choose to ignore information that does not fit with their ideology or their interest in avoiding change. In this regard, no amount of information will change whether teachers feel informed about a reform prior to adoption but efforts can be made to expand the discourse and present alternative views that otherwise may not have been available to them. The process of critical inquiry has to flatten hierarchies of control in order to achieve genuine participation and to enable educators to make better choices among reforms.

- *Policymakers need to recognize that educational reform will not be met with unanimous agreement among all stakeholders. They must be prepared to build a context for discussion and a capacity to implement the reform*

Whether the reform is teacher driven, district mandated or state mandated, undoubtedly everyone will not be in agreement with adoption nor welcome the pressure to change. The success of the reform will weigh heavily on a school system's ability to communicate and negotiate concerns among all those involved. Communication between district administrators and teachers must be actively promoted. Part of that communication process must include the assurance that the necessary support to carry out the reform will be available. Teachers, district administrators, state officials must be given the opportunity to understand the benefit of the reform but also must be given the tools, strategies and support to carry out the work.

3   Is All Change Local? How Context Shapes Implementation

Tip O'Neill, the legendary congressional leader from Massachusetts, is famous for having coined the maxim "all politics is local." In this chapter, we consider a corollary in the domain of educational reform "all change is local."

A key issue when reforms go to scale is the extent to which models developed in one school can be successfully transported to other schools with entirely different teacher and student compositions and district and state policies. Some reform design teams market their models on the basis that they can be implemented in any school, anywhere, at any time. However, in reality, context is extremely important in school reform. In fact, one of the most consistent findings in studies of educational reform since the 1960s concerns variability due to local circumstances. Whether initiated by the government, higher levels of the school system, university faculty, local practitioners, or business leaders, educational reforms have changed to adapt to schools more often than schools have adapted to accommodate educational reforms. Given the robustness of this finding, we were not surprised to find that the reform designs, particularly those that were highly specified, were modified at school sites in response to the constraints, circumstances, and ideologies of local educators.

This chapter is about how local educators molded externally designed reforms to fit their local contexts. We begin this chapter with a discussion of the technical-rational and co-construction perspectives on local variations in implementation. We describe how context, defined in broad terms, shaped the implementation of reform in the schools we studied. We examine how local structural conditions, including school organizational characteristics, district and state policies, and the composition of the student population, shaped reform. Next, we discuss how cultural considerations, especially educators' ideologies about teaching and learning, race, ethnicity, and intelligence influenced how reforms were implemented. We conclude with guidelines for actions that reform designers and local educators might take together to begin to improve practice based on our findings.

Technical-Rational and Co-Construction Models of Reform

Numerous research studies have found that the level of reform implementation is predictive of student achievement gains on standardized tests (Crandall *et al.* 1982; Datnow, Borman and Stringfield 2000; Stallings and Kaskowitz 1974; Stringfield *et al.* 1997). Despite this finding, the level of fidelity with which schools must implement reforms to achieve desired outcomes – whether they are student achievement gains or other school improvements – is not well understood (Elmore 1996; Stringfield *et al.* 1997). Meanwhile, numerous comprehensive and important studies in the field (Hall and Loucks 1976; Berman and McLaughlin 1978; Stringfield *et al.* 1997; Muncey and McQuillan 1996) have found that variation in implementation – often due to local contextual demands – is a hallmark of educational change processes (Datnow and Stringfield 2000). School change is rarely a linear process whereby teachers implement "the innovation as developed in the classroom" (Snyder, Bolin and Zumwalt 1992: 404). Even when policies are seemingly straightforward, they are implemented very differently across localities, schools, and classrooms (Elmore and Sykes 1992).

How do researchers and policymakers explain the variation in implementation that is observed? Explanations for the roots of variation in implementation, what could or should be done about it (if anything), and how to study it tend to be influenced by two dominant approaches: the technical-rational perspective and the mutual adaptation, or what we extend and call a "co-construction" perspective (Snyder, Bolin and Zumwalt 1992[2]). A summary of the two approaches is provided in Table 3.1, and in the subsequent section we discuss them in more detail.

Table 3.1 Comparison of Technical-Rational and Co-Construction Approaches

Technical-Rational	Co-construction
Psychometric methods	Multiple methods, including ethnographic
Rational, classical management theory	Socio-cultural theory
Emphasis on measuring fidelity of implementation	Emphasis on contingent processes of implementation
Reform designers as primary driver of change; local educators as receptors	Local educators and reform developers as jointly constructing change
Reform failure located in the actions of local educators	Reform failure located in insensitivity of reform to local context
Implementation as unidirectional process	Implementation as a multidirectional process
Local variation as dilemma	Local variation as inevitable

The Technical-Rational Perspective: Reform as a Rational and Technical Process

The technical-rational perspective is the most extensively used approach for studying reform. It operates on classical management theory, which places a premium on planning, organization, command, coordination, and control. Many educational reforms originated by the U.S. government circa 1965 until 1980 (e.g., Follow Through, Education for All Handicapped Students, Vocational Education) exemplify this perspective. The presumption was that ". . . authority and responsibility should flow in a clear unbroken line from the highest executive to the lowest operative . . ." (Masie 1965, quoted in Smith and Keith 1971: 241). The Disseminating Efforts Supporting School Improvement (DESSI) project, while developed more recently, also incorporates the assumptions of the technical-rational reform model. The research, development, and dissemination concept of innovation used in DESSI assumed an ordered sequence of activities which involved planning, a division of labor, and a passive consumer (the teacher) (Havelock as cited in Snyder, Bolin and Zumwalt 1992).

The assumption that organizations operate according to what Weber called "technical rationality" infuses this perspective's definition of implementation, as we can see in one of the very first studies of the process: "Implementation is the ability to forge subsequent links in the causal chain so as to obtain the desired results" (Pressman and Wildavsky 1973: xv). Pressman and Wildavsky's conception of implementation identifies actors, actions, and the objects of action. Two classes of actors are implicated: the program designers (what we call "the design team"), and the "implementers" – the people who operate and work at the local or street level of bureaucracies. Likewise, two classes of actions are identified: "planning" and "implementing." Significantly, the actions are segregated and the actors are stratified. The design team, at the top of the hierarchy, "makes plans" while the educators – the people down the causal chain – are relegated to "carrying out the plans," that is, completing the pre-determined goals and objectives of the design team. In this "grammar of implementation," the causal arrow of change travels in one direction – from active, thoughtful designers to passive, pragmatic implementers.

Other studies of reform implementation that exemplify the technical-rational perspective are Hall and Loucks (1976) and Gross, Giaquinta and Bernstein (1971). More recent investigations of school reform (e.g., Nunnery *et al.* 1997) also adopt the technical-rational perspective. In these studies, implementation is measured according to an objectified standard. The desired outcome is fidelity to the established reform model. Factors are identified which hinder or facilitate planned implementation (Snyder, Bolin and Zumwalt 1992). Quasi-experimental methods are used to connect carefully measured levels of implementation to student outcomes.

When reform fails, the technical-rational perspective tends to place the blame on local educators who did not implement models properly. Educators in schools are said to circumvent well-intended reforms, either because they are irrational, or they are protecting their own interests, or they don't understand the intentions of the planners. Certainly, not all those who treat reform as a technical and rational process believe that recalcitrant educators undermine reform. However, we wish to raise the point that the technical-rational perspective is more likely to see local variation in implementation as problematic, or as a dilemma rather than as inevitable – that is, a natural, normal routine feature of everyday life in schools (Snyder, Bolin and Zumwalt 1992). Furthermore, reforms built on rational grounds often assume that reforms can be sustained on technical considerations alone, and downplay or do not account for the social, cultural, and political factors that lead to local variation.

Mutual Adaptation and Co-Construction Perspectives: Reform as Multidirectional

New ways of talking about school change emerged when researchers attempted to understand the implementation "problems" at the local level that resulted from the limitations of the technical-rational approach to reform. Some researchers argued that government-mandated, technically-driven reforms were not as successful as planners envisioned because reformers in distant locations were not sensitive to the culture of the school or the perplexities of the daily life of educators (Berman and McLaughlin 1978; Sarason 1982; Sizer 1984), not because educators in schools subverted innovations out of hostility, indifference, or slough. These realizations have lead researchers to see school change as an ongoing process, rather than as an event (Fullan 1991) and to focus more attention on the context of schooling.

In the emerging critiques of the technical-rational model, context was not treated as just one factor in an equation attempting to explain the variability of implementation; it began to be seen as part and parcel of the school change process. The phrase "mutual adaptation" was first coined by Berman and McLaughlin (1978) in the Rand Change Agent Study to characterize this dynamic conception of context that we employ here. Berman and McLaughlin argued that implementation should be seen as "a mutually adaptive process between the user and the institutional setting – that specific project goals and methods be made concrete over time by the participants themselves" (McLaughlin 1976 cited in Snyder, Bolin and Zumwalt 1992). As Berman and McLaughlin imply, not only was mutual adaptation inevitable, it was desirable. Negotiation, flexibility, and adjustment on the part of educators and reform designers were key to successful reform (Snyder, Bolin and Zumwalt 1992).

While the Rand Change Agent study is certainly the classic example of mutual adaptation, numerous other studies have adopted this perspective on reform. Most of these studies were conducted in the late 1970s and early-mid 1980s (e.g., Hannah 1979; Lotan and Navarette 1986; Matthews 1978; Bird 1986; Firestone and Donner 1981). A host of other studies focused on what might be termed mutual adaptation even though they do not label it as such. Examples include: Smith and Keith's (1971) study of innovation at Kensington School; Popkewitz, Tabachnick and Wehlage's (1981) study of Individually Guided Education in six schools; and Mehan *et al.*'s (1986) study of the implementation of federal special education mandates. Most of these studies employed qualitative methodologies, in the form of case studies, ethnographies, or some mixture of quantitative and qualitative methods. These studies all suggest that reform implementation involves an active and dynamic interaction between local educators, the reform directives, and the social, organizational, and political life of the school. Reform is seen as a two-way street between developers and local educators (Firestone and Donner 1981).

The aforementioned studies illustrate a dynamic implementation process in various ways, emphasizing different types of contextual features. For example, the Rand Change Agent Study and Mehan *et al.*'s (1986) ethnographic study demonstrate how educators' actions in implementing federal special education mandates are constrained by "practical circumstances" (e.g., standard operating procedures in local schools and multiple competing goals). Some other studies of reform have emphasized how reforms, new curricula, or policies are adapted to fit teachers' professional and personal ideologies (Helsby 1999; McLaughlin and Talbert 1993b; Popkewitz, Tabachnick and Wehlage 1981; Tyack and Cuban 1995).

To a lesser degree, the aforementioned studies connect actions and contexts inside the school to the larger social, political, and organizational sphere in which the schools are located. Several studies of reform have made these connections more explicit (Bascia and Hargreaves 2000; Blackmore 1999; Helsby 1999; Oakes and Wells 1996; Muncey and McQuillan 1996). Bascia and Hargreaves' (2000) recent volume on school change explicitly addresses the social and political dynamics, as well as the emotional consequences of reform. In their study of secondary school reform, Oakes *et al.* (1997) found that deep-seated cultural beliefs about intelligence held by educators and parents blocked detracking efforts. Muncey and McQuillan (1996) found similar cultural impediments to change in their ethnography of schools attempting to implement the principles of the Coalition for Essential Schools (CES). Belief systems that exist among educators and community members are robust examples of social norms and politics that shape reform in local schools. These narratives in which reforms run into "obstacles" in school sites seems, at first blush, to simply recapitulate the Pressman and Wildavsky (1973) narrative in which erstwhile reform efforts are sabotaged at the local level. The positions of Oakes and Muncey (with which we agree) are different, however. They do not characterize local educators as irrational or uninformed; they introduce the vocabulary of "interests" and "resistance" to the conversation. This new vocabulary shifts the emphasis away from irrational, recalcitrant or uninformed local educators and toward the presumably technical and rational characteristics of the reform itself.

We build upon the concept of mutual adaptation by showing interrelations between actions in schools and the wider social and political sphere. Moreover, the notion of multidirectionality is important to this extension which we call "co-construction." Political and cultural elements of context do not simply constrain reform. Rather, in the "grammar of co-construction" the causal arrow of change travels in multiple directions among active participants in all domains of the system and over time. This grammar makes the reform process "flexible," with people who have "different intentions/interests and interpretations [and who] enter into the process at different points along the [reform] course. Thus many actors negotiate with and adjust to one another within and across contexts" (Hall and McGinty 1997: 4). This interaction over time and space constructs consequences for future actions. While actions initiated at some distance away from local events may indeed constrain or shape actions, they do not totally determine them. And actions initiated in local events generate or construct conditions or structures that have consequences in settings far removed from local events. This emphasis upon multidimensionality marks the co-construction perspective and departs from the technically driven, unidirectional focus of the technical-rational perspective.

In sum, the central thesis behind this general perspective, whether it be termed mutual adaptation or extended to co-construction as we define it, is that "context matters when studying school level reforms" (Wells *et al.* 1995: 21). While that proposition is clear, just what constitutes local context varies from study to study. Here, we define local context broadly as being comprised of conditions including the school's history of dealing with change, the population served by the community, school and community norms, school, district, and state policies, and ideologies about teaching, learning, race, class, and gender. Our broad view of context derives from our belief that the agency of educators is interconnected with events taking place elsewhere. Understanding the local politics and social norms that permeate the walls of schools can lead to a better understanding of why educators act the way they do in the face of reform (Wells *et al.* 1995).

Structural Considerations Enable and Constrain Reform

Local context, broadly defined, played a very important role in the implementation of reform models in our studies, and it functioned in several important ways. Conditions in local contexts caused educators to modify reform models to better suit their needs. Some adaptations were enhancements to the designs, whereas others threatened the intensity and potential success of the reform. Other adaptations were rather benign. Design teams had varied responses to these adaptations, depending upon their stance towards fidelity and their receptivity to local variation. As you will recall, Chapter 1 provided a description of how each reform design team approaches and attempts to ensure fidelity, if important to their model. (The Appendix enlarges on these themes.) In the section that follows, we discuss the structural conditions that shaped the implementation of reform in local contexts, and in the subsequent section we discuss cultural conditions shaping implementation.

Molding Reform Designs to Accommodate Organizational Constraints

Many of the schools made adaptations to reforms to accommodate organizational constraints in their school settings. These organizational constraints were typically related to school size, level of resources, school organizational features, time, and staffing arrangements. In some cases, the constraints led teachers to simply implement program features less frequently, or not at all. For example, one school working with the Coalition of Essential Schools found it difficult to schedule time in the school day for teachers to meet with "critical friends," an important design feature of this reform model. Another school implementing the Modern Red Schoolhouse found the technology features of the model, which called for fully wired computers in every classroom, to be a "pipe dream" and not practicable when teachers worked without overhead projectors or other more simple technology.

Most schools were able to find the tension point between organizational constraints and reform design demands, and found rather creative solutions. For example, in the 12 schools implementing AVID, educators described tutoring as "probably the most critical component of the whole program . . ." and yet, "one of the most difficult 'AVID essentials' to implement." The lack of qualified college tutors, the difficulty in coordinating university and high school schedules, the difficulty in obtaining funds to reimburse tutors in a timely manner are just some of the practical problems that plagued the schools that attempted to meet the expectation of this AVID essential and, in turn, the needs of their students. As one state education official explained, "We have very isolated schools. Some are six hours away from a college. Getting tutors to come to them is impossible."

Some schools responded in very innovative ways to these sorts of problems. In North Carolina, the tutoring component of an AVID program has been embellished by the use of graduate students and teachers. This program has also introduced content-based tutoring to supplement AVID's Socratic approach. Tutors with deep knowledge of subjects such as chemistry, math, and English bring a high level of expertise to the tutoring situation. According to educators in North Carolina, these modifications have enhanced the AVID prototype. However, in some cases, local modifications became constraints to program success. One California school responded to the difficulty of attracting and retaining tutors by holding tutoring sessions after school with a teacher who volunteered her time. This arrangement excluded many AVID students who were not able to stay after school due to transportation problems. Other schools chose to subsist without tutors, or with sparse coverage. This meant that some AVID students did not have the benefit of interacting with tutors who could both assist them with their schoolwork and could share their college experiences.

Similarly, large school size impacted the implementation of Success for All in three elementary schools in Sunland County, leading to significant adaptations that hindered the success of the reform. Success for All calls for reading classes of no more than 20 students. This design feature is facilitated through the use of classroom as well as non-classroom teachers who act as reading group leaders for 90 minutes per day. The program also requires that the reading period be offered at the same time for all students, to facilitate movement among the groups. These critical program features could not be implemented as designed in the Sunland schools, each of which served over 1000 students and were severely overcrowded, operating at up to 75 percent over their designated space utilization rates.

At Mangrove Elementary, the dearth of space was so severe that some teachers had to share a cramped classroom during the reading period, making for a noisy, distracting environment. One teacher led a reading group on the stage in the school auditorium. Due to the restrictions of space and the number of teachers available, some reading groups had as many as 32 students, instead of the 20 suggested by SFA. At all three schools in Sunland, two reading periods were offered at different times, in order to maximize the use of space and resources. This constrained students' ability to move among groups (e.g., a first grader reading at the third grade level could not be grouped with third grade students). The sheer number of teachers and students to monitor in these large schools meant that the job of the SFA facilitator, already a taxing one, was even more difficult. As one facilitator described, "When I was at the SFA convention, there were schools that had 400 students and one facilitator," whereas her school, Orchid Elementary, served 1400 students. She explained: "That's three times the materials I have to organize, three times the teachers I have to work with . . . because of that I'm limited in what I can do with the teachers." The large number of students that needed to be tested every eight weeks, according to the SFA design, also was too much for the facilitator and the tutors to accomplish by themselves, outside of the 90-minute reading period. "We'd never get done. And it would be impossible . . . it would take us eight weeks to do it the way they wanted to us to do it. So we cheat." The school has made a significant adaptation by having reading teachers conduct testing during the reading period. This took time away from reading instruction.

As these vignettes illustrate, educators modified reforms to fit within their organizational constraints. Furthermore, educators in local school settings were not passively implementing programs designed elsewhere. They were actively making policy through their adaptations. In the case of AVID's tutoring component, some schools responded in creative ways to their practical circumstances and enhanced the reform, but others did not. The educators in Sunland County also responded in practical ways when the SFA reform demands bumped up against the constraints of their large school size and overcrowding – both features that were unchangeable. However, their solutions tended to compromise the success of the program in providing all students with small class sizes for reading and created significant headaches for school leaders. Reforms, as a result, were co-constructed in the negotiations that were required to meet the practical demands of their everyday teaching lives.

Laminating a New Reform Over Existing Reforms

Often, multiple reforms existed in a school at a given time, leading educators to make modifications in order to accommodate the various program goals and demands. In some schools, this meant forgoing components of particular reforms, or not enacting reforms fully. In each case, it appeared that existing practices were strong enough to suppress the new reforms, and thus adjustments to the new reform needed to be made, rather than the other way around. These modifications were necessitated by the press of circumstances in local contexts; they were not sloppy or irrational actions.

Reform designs – such as Comer's SDP model – that involve the creation of new governance structure, such as school-based management teams, were often adapted in local schools as educators fit existing structures into the new model. Sometimes these teams simply changed names when the new reform was adopted. In other cases, educators struggled to meet the team goals as established by the reform design team as well as those that the team formerly organized around. Forest Elementary, a Comer SDP elementary school in Sunland, provides an interesting case in point. The Comer SDP model requires schools to institute three teams: a School Planning and Management Team, a Student and Staff Support Team, and a Parent Team. The teams are designed to "work in tandem and synergistically to design and implement the social and academic program of the school" (Haynes 1998: 5). When it came time for Forest to institute their teams, the faculty decided that they wanted to change the name of the Student and Staff Support Team to the Home School Services Team (HSST). Some of the components of the team were already in place because of the school's prior and ongoing involvement as an integrated services school. For instance, the school had three or four psychological or counseling agencies that already sent full-time counselors to the school. They had legal aid representatives on site and were connected to agencies addressing domestic violence. The HSST was formed by bringing together representatives of these groups, rather than by forming new connections. This was an easy, benign, and successful integration of the SDP reform model and the school's existing reform integrated services.

Although some schools were able to make effective adaptations in response to the layering of reforms, in other cases, pre-existing reforms threatened the integrity and success of the new reform. For example, one Coalition of Essential Schools site did not implement the "teacher as generalist" principle as recommended by the design team because the teachers were implementing a local university-developed program which was explicitly aimed towards organizing teachers by subject specialization and rotating students among them. The teachers felt that the local initiative was working well for them, and did not see it conflicting with the goals of the Coalition reform. However, clearly it did. The "teacher as generalist" principle of the Coalition calls for teachers to see themselves as general educators and scholars, rather than just experts in a particular subject. The move towards this principle is often much more difficult in secondary schools but usually requires no changes in elementary schools, as teachers usually teach multiple subjects in self-contained classrooms. Due to the local program, the teachers in this school were deliberately doing the opposite.

In Freeport, Virginia, the success of the AVID program was seriously undermined when the district implemented AVID solely as a 9th and 10th grade program, rather than offer it for four years because of conflicts with another reform designed to help minority and low-income students that was well-entrenched in the district. The "College Partnerships" program was perceived as "the GATE program for African-American kids." Apparently the two programs could only coexist at different grade levels because of the competition for students and prior agreements that protected the College Partnership "territory." Their turf battle resulted in minimizing the support available to AVID students.

A problem arose, therefore, when students completed two years of AVID but were not accepted into College Partnerships. They were left to struggle with the more difficult classes offered in their junior and senior years without support structures. The AVID teacher complained that many students were trying to take rigorous academic classes, including International Baccalaureate classes, but were dropping out because they lacked the help they needed to do well. Ironically, early participation in AVID actually disadvantaged students who were unable to take advantage of College Partnerships later.

In sum, existing practices and procedures operated as both opportunities and constraints to new reform models that were introduced. A local program prevented one Coalition school from moving towards the "teacher as generalist" principle, something that is usually taken for granted in elementary schools. Similarly, the long-standing College Partnership program in Freeport competed with AVID, and the students lost opportunities for academic and social support as a result. The Comer team structure fit in fairly well at Forest Elementary, where the team structure and the school's existing full services model were very complementary.

Adapting Reforms to Address Linguistic Diversity

In Sunland County, the most significant local "conditions" that caused educators to adapt reform designs were those related to the linguistic diversity of the student population. With the exception of Success for All, which includes a Spanish version, most externally developed reform designs were not created to serve students who speak English as a second language. As a result, educators had to make adaptations to all reforms at the local level, more successfully in some cases than in others. Not only did the extant needs of language minority students come into play, but also district and state policies with respect to Limited English Proficient (LEP) students.

The most significant – and successful – adaptation to accommodate language differences occurred at Callaway, a school implementing the Core Knowledge Sequence. The Core Knowledge Sequence is a list of topics and is not accompanied by materials or a teacher's manual. Rather, lesson plans are locally developed by teachers, thus allowing for substantial flexibility in methods of presentation. At this school, bilingual instruction of Core Knowledge topics in Spanish and English enabled students to benefit from this curriculum reform, regardless of English language proficiency.

While the teachers at this school believed that this bilingual adaptation of Core Knowledge has been successful, they had some difficulty finding age-appropriate materials on Core Knowledge topics in Spanish. Because of the demands required by teaching Core in both languages, the teachers have elected not to teach all of the topics. Rather, they teach a selection of them. Meanwhile, the Core Knowledge Foundation suggests teaching all topics in the Sequence. It is notable that this school received a waiver, long before implementing Core Knowledge, to conduct two-way bilingual instruction. Teachers in another Core school that conducted instruction in English attempted to make the content accessible to students by utilizing visual aids and peers as interpreters for LEP students.

Other schools struggled to make programmatic adaptations to serve LEP students effectively. Teachers at an Audrey Cohen school felt that the design would be far more adaptable in a context where students were all native speakers of English. A teacher at one school explained that since her first grade students could not read in English, she read the books to them, explaining the concepts in Spanish at times, and then writing the main points on the board for students to copy. Audrey Cohen College was willing to make some adaptations to accommodate speakers of other languages. For example, they allowed students to write in their "purpose record books" in their native language. However, they did not provide any materials in languages other than English.

The schools in Sunland that had the most difficulty adapting the reform to meet the needs of LEP students were Success for All schools. While SFA has a Spanish version of the curriculum (hence, a significant LEP student accommodation), this was not helpful in the Sunland schools that served students who spoke languages other than Spanish or English. Even so, the district's policies prohibited reading instruction in students' native languages. The SFA design team began working on an ESL adaptation, but it was completed only after some schools had attempted implementation of SFA for three years. The principal at Newton Elementary was frustrated by the design team's lack of immediate response to the needs of his school's population.

Moreover, because the district required that LEP students be taught by ESL-certified teachers, the LEP students could not be placed in reading groups according to level, as SFA specifies. Instead, the LEP students in the primary grades remained in self-contained classes that were heterogeneous by reading level. The principal permitted significant adaptations to SFA by ESL teachers, acknowledging that the curriculum as written did not work well with LEP students. The teachers at Newton did a number of things in their classrooms in order to adapt the SFA materials for use with their LEP students, including rewriting some materials and replacing some of the SFA vocabulary with words the students may have been more familiar with. Teachers also occasionally dropped the SFA lesson plans in favor of using ESL strategies for oral language development. The curriculum was often significantly diluted for LEP students in terms of time and pacing.

The molding of reform models to fit the linguistic diversity of school populations is a significant issue, as the demand for change and the number of LEP students continues to grow, particularly in urban areas. What makes these matters all the more tricky are the differences of opinion that surround bilingual education and how best to teach second language learners. Reform models, which bring their own theories about language, can conflict with teachers' beliefs. These issues become even more heated when they reach political levels outside the school.

Reform Adaptations in Response to State and District Policies

As the previous illustrations suggest, it was quite common in Sunland County for educators to make adaptations to reform designs in order to comply with state and district policies, not just with regard to bilingual education, but in other areas as well. As school educators explained to us time and time again, they were most accountable to these administrations, not the design team. We will now discuss how state and district policies occupy an influential place in the context, causing schools to attempt and balance multiple demands.

Teachers in Sunland County felt bound to teach the district curriculum first and foremost. Where the reform design's curriculum conflicted, these components were left aside or implemented only sparsely in some schools. For example, about the county curriculum, one teacher remarked, "That's who we have to answer to first . . . If Audrey Cohen is thrown in there, it's thrown in. It is just on the little back burner for me." Conflicts with district curricula were often not an issue in Comer and Coalition schools, as these reform designs did not specify curricula. However, planning for district curricula sometimes competed with the reforms for teachers' time.

Opinions sometimes varied as to whether a reform model's curriculum fit or did not fit with the district curriculum, and how conflicts might be dealt with. Teachers in one of the Core Knowledge schools felt that the state curriculum dovetailed with Core topics: "It kind of all fits together." However, the topics were not necessarily covered at the same grade levels in each curriculum. The teachers chose to cover topics twice in these instances, but in less depth. On the other hand, teachers in another school made the accommodation of simply leaving out Core in favor of the district curriculum. As one teacher stated, "You know we're being held accountable for teaching objectives for the county, and there aren't enough hours in the day to get everything in. You have to pick and choose and, consequently, this year we chose not to cover some things in Core that we have in the past."

In many cases, school educators saw district policies as hindrances and at times expressed that little could be done at the local level to accommodate both district and reform demands. For example, teachers in one school that implemented the Modern Red Schoolhouse design were annoyed by the district's strict policies regarding curriculum, staff development, and ESL instruction. One teacher stated, "I feel like the concepts of Modern Red sound like paradise, but when you get to reality, we have to go by Sunland County guidelines." Another teacher at this school lamented that a district administrator spent an entire inservice related to Modern Red telling them what elements of the school they were not allowed to change to do district mandates, "He was there to say, 'no, you can do this, you can't do that. . . .'" The teachers and the principal wondered why they should even bother developing a new scope and sequence when the district would still hold them accountable for the county curriculum. The district's tying of hands frustrated teachers, particularly since the district had encouraged them to adopt the reform to begin with.

Fortunately, as the principal explained, the Modern Red design team reacted by trying to accommodate the reform design to fit the district's requirements:

> Modern Red worked with us to try and work it out. . . . They understood the role of the school district and the relationship we had to have with that district and respected it all the time. They never tried to get us in a conflicting situation with our district at all.

Nevertheless, the school never got reform implementation fully off the ground, due to a combination of factors, not the least of which were the change in district administrators and the lack of teacher buy-in at the outset. These issues will be addressed in more detail in Chapter 6.

Not only did district standards and curricula impact reform, but state standards as well. Reflecting the federalist approach to education that currently permeates education in the U.S., several states (and many more districts) have established performance standards for their students. The standards movement has eclipsed federal mandates, decentralization, and multiculturalism and seems to be holding its own against moves to privatize education, such as vouchers and some forms of charter schools, and takes many forms.

Of the states where we have been studying the implementation of AVID, Virginia and Kentucky are notable because they adopted strong and comprehensive standards: KERA in Kentucky and "Standards of Learning" (SOLs) in Virginia. One reason for AVID's initial success in Kentucky was the perception that AVID's program aligned with that state's standards. Conversely, AVID's curriculum has been faulted by some Virginians because it does not adequately address their SOLs.

Soon after his election in 1998, Governor George Allen convinced the Virginia legislature to establish the "Virginia Standards of Learning" (SOLs). Students in selected grades were tested in the areas of English, math, science and history. Results from the first year of testing were disappointingly low. Local newspapers reported that almost half of the students across the state failed at least one test, with the worst failing rates in the areas of history and math.

Because of these poor results, tests administered to students in May 1999 took on additional significance. Teachers strived to meet the increased demands of accountability made by their district and their state. Teachers feverishly reviewed tests and tutored students after school without complaint. During our visits to Virginia we found that these tests were the main topic of conversation and concern. Virginian educators needed the tools to help them succeed on these tests. While AVID is poised to respond to the demands of the SOLs, the AVID curriculum's alignment with the standards was not clearly articulated by the AVID design team. This resulted in local AVID educators scurrying to rewrite curriculum. This additional work was perceived by Virginia educators as a burden on their already demanding schedules.

As these examples point out, local educators dealt with the competing demands of the state, the district, and the design team. These structural constraints led many educators to lament that the litany of district and state requirements were almost too much to bear, regardless of the reform. As one reform facilitator pointed out, "We have so many things going on. I know all systems do, but we feel as though we are just overwhelmed. At least I do, and so do the classroom teachers, due to all of the programs that we have."

Cultural Considerations Enable and Constrain Reform Efforts

We proposed in Chapter 1 that cultural considerations mediate structural constraints and the actions that people take (their agency). Educators' beliefs are a fundamentally important cultural consideration, because they often constitute people's actions. Educators' and policymakers' ideologies about ability, race, language, social class, and most fundamentally, education strongly influenced how they implemented reforms. Some educators socially constructed students' identities in a way that allowed them to see the reform as a way to challenge stereotypes and as an opportunity to celebrate and build upon the linguistic and cultural resources that students brought to the classroom. In these cases, belief systems became enablers to reform. In numerous instances, however, educators' constructions of students on the basis of race, language, and ability served as a constraint to the reform. We also found that reforms cohered or conflicted with educators' ideologies about teaching and learning – and were accordingly implemented in varied ways in local schools and classrooms.

Educators' Social Constructions of Student Ability Shape Reform

Teachers' ideologies are produced in the course of their interactions within the school context and the larger society in which they exist (Apple 1985). Teachers naturally vary along many objective dimensions, including the grade levels they teach, their subject areas, length of experience, gender, racial and ethnic background, and the type of teacher training they received. These variations greatly impact their ideologies and in turn their classroom practice and propensity towards reform (Sarason 1996). Not surprisingly, ideology is often contested in schools as different subcultures of teachers and individual teachers hold different ideologies (Hargreaves 1994; McLaughlin 1994).

AVID teachers overwhelmingly held positive views of their students' ability to succeed in school and go onto college. The AVID coordinator at Palm Valley High School explained that AVID students have the potential to do well in school but many of them could fall through the cracks unless they received the kind of academic support that AVID could provide. She said:

> AVID works, whether it's the label and making the kids feel like they can do it or that they [feel that they are] special. Because at this school there are *not* a lot of positive programs and so all of a sudden, here's one that says, hey, we believe in you, we know you can do it, and we're going to help you.

AVID teachers repeatedly articulated these beliefs to their students. As a result, students came to believe in their own efficacy (Mehan *et al.* 1996). Similarly, an AVID teacher in North Carolina explained his philosophy of education "for students whom success may not have been predicted," including AVID students. He stated:

> I have always believed that we had many students who were not being served [in this community] and particularly, African-American students, that is the

underrepresented and the underserved population. I have been involved with a lot of kids whose potential was so clear and whose performance didn't always match it. I have worked with kids who were having difficulty in our public school who, when given some other opportunities and support, were producing the same kinds of results that . . . [successful] AVID students were producing.

For these AVID teachers, student ability was socially constructed (Berger and Luckmann 1967), not naturally allocated. Like the teachers in Oakes *et al.*'s (1997) study, these teachers believed that disadvantaged students might need different opportunities to achieve or might require special efforts or compassion by the teacher, but they had the capacity to achieve at high levels of success.

In their comprehensive study of schools attempting to dismantle high school tracking programs, Oakes and colleagues (1997) found that intelligence was viewed by many parents and educators as innate, fixed and race-based. These beliefs became translated into rationalizations for maintaining tracking that were tied to power and privilege. As Oakes and her colleagues point out, the culturally based standard against which students are measured was never questioned and thus, unjust practices remained intact.

We also found several examples of how the social construction of minority, immigrant students as low ability and lacking in basic skills served as a constraint in both educators' initial receptiveness to reform designs as well as their subsequent implementation of them. For example, the positive attitudes and support of AVID teachers were often in conflict with the stereotypes of the academic ability of minority students held by other faculty members at their schools. These ideologies threatened AVID students' opportunities for success. An AVID teacher at a high school in California explained the struggle she faced when she tried to place her students in advanced placement classes: "We pride ourselves in diminishing the number of honors students until we get to this 20 kids out of 500. And we've excluded as many kids as possible and that makes us good in this society in that they are the cream of the crop."

AVID students at this school could not easily break into the honors elite, given teachers' long standing beliefs that these spots were reserved for a select, highly able few. Apparently some faculty members suggested that admitting AVID students would "water down" their classes. AVID teachers and site team members had to fight to prove to their colleagues that their AVID students were qualified to be in the advanced classes. As one teacher explained, they "try to open doors for them" so that they can "open doors for other kids" as well.

Similarly, when AVID was implemented in the Oakwood School District in North Carolina, the reform confronted educators' entrenched beliefs about African-American students' inability to achieve. In some cases, teachers resisted the placement of African-American AVID students in their Advanced Placement classes, arguing they were not qualified. For example, an English department chairperson supported existing placement practices by saying that she is afraid that placing "under-qualified" black students in advanced courses will "cripple them." She stated, "I'm afraid I'm just one of those old-fashioned people who believes self-esteem follows a job well done; it doesn't always precede it" (Oakwood Times, December 15, 1996). An African-American parent and member of the Oakwood high school governance team explained her perception of the problem, "I think there are a lot of people who truly believe that all of it lies within the kids . . . [that] there are no forces that are external to the kid that contribute to their success or failure."

Even when the AVID coordinator was able to succeed at getting AVID students into higher level classes, race-based attitudes and practices continued to impede the success of African-American students. A teacher related the story of one of her African-American AVID students who she believes was the victim of racism. He was the only African American in his Spanish class and he was earning an A. But, he did not receive that grade on his report card. The teacher told him he didn't give him an A because "you were talking, you know you talk too much." The AVID coordinator confronted the Spanish teacher, and she changed his grade. Yet, injustices like this one often were not rectified, because parents and teachers in Oakwood were often reticent to challenge the system.

In Sunland County, local educators' ideologies about ability, race, and culture also impacted reforms, but in a different way. The constraints that operated as a result of educators' constructions of student ability connected to language background, race, and culture were not unique to a particular school, or a particular reform. For example, a teacher at Keys Elementary, a school that worked with the Audrey Cohen College System of Education, found that the design was difficult to implement because, "the students are not high. They don't have high abilities. They come from second languages and they need a lot of basic drilling. They lack a lot of skills they need in order to do Audrey Cohen well."

According to some teachers at this school, not only did students lack the innate abilities to do well with the reform's Purpose Centered System of Education, but they also came from a culture that did not ready them for taking responsibility for their own learning. Speaking from her own experience as a Hispanic, one teacher explained, "They [the Hispanic students] need to take charge. . . . They're not used to it. So we had a doubly hard time. . . . I saw it in those kids that were American. They did do better. Right away they came up with something" for a lesson on inventions. Her view was applied to all Hispanic children, whether they were born in the U.S. or not, "because it comes with their culture."

Reinforcing this finding from another angle, the reform facilitator argued that the program worked particularly well with gifted students, "who see beyond where they are now. . . . They're the ones that read something in the paper and they worry about it. . . . And I don't find that to be typical with the other students." The comments by these educators reveal beliefs in intelligence or ability as a fixed entity and as innate, not as skills that were malleable through engagement in new types of learning activities. These beliefs in the importance of ability rather than effort led them to have little faith in the reform design.

We were fortunate to find some counter examples in Sunland as well. In some schools serving populations that were similarly comprised of low-income immigrant students of color, educators celebrated students' backgrounds and saw them as the building blocks of the reform. For example, the principal at Holly Elementary, a Comer SDP school that had formed very strong partnerships with parents described the families stating, "Even though they don't have formal education, they really want a good life for their children. So they're very involved with the school." Educators at another Comer SDP school explained that the Comer philosophy "helps us see the child as an individual. And we look for their strengths instead of weaknesses." The teachers also stated that Comer's unstructured nature allowed them to be more sensitive to various cultures in their curriculum. "The program allows us a lot of flexibility in the classroom," said one teacher, "so it allows us to bring more of a cultural awareness to the other children."

In sum, we found educators with two types of basic beliefs. One group believed in innate intelligence. Educators in this group felt that the reform did not fit their schools well because it did not "fix" the primary problems of the low-income, immigrant, language minority students they served. A second group believed student success could be nurtured. Educators in this category saw their chosen reform designs as in fact helping them better understand or celebrate the cultures of children in their communities. These attitudes caused them to embrace, rather than resist, the reform. Both sets of attitudes point to the influence of social constructions of student achievement as applied differentially to students of diverse backgrounds. As all of these illustrations reveal, educational reform requires cultural change as well as organizational rearrangements. Unfortunately, prevailing attitudes about race, intelligence, and ability were seldom confronted when schools implemented reforms.

Reforms Cohere or Conflict With Educators' Ideologies About Teaching and Learning

We often think of beliefs as privately held opinions. But beliefs are social, influencing the actions that people take together. Inevitably, reform designs cohered or conflicted with teachers' collective beliefs about education. When reform elements conflicted or were unclear, educators sometimes resisted these elements outright or they made adaptations. Most often, educators simply molded the reforms in ways that made sense with their professional knowledge. These findings are consistent with prior studies that show that teachers resist reforms when the rhetoric of the changes does not match the realities of their experiences (Bailey 2000). As a result, reform efforts need to be grounded in an understanding of teachers' professional lives and development (Fullan and Hargreaves 1996; Helsby 1999; Hopkins and Wideen 1984).

For example, some of the teachers we interviewed in Success for All schools cited instances where the structure of the curriculum did not fit with their own ideologies of teaching and learning. The Success for All reading curriculum includes an active pacing of specified activities for a daily 90-minute period. Most commonly, teachers were concerned that students were pushed on from one level to the next too quickly and that the pace of the program was too fast. As one teacher said, "Using my teacher judgment, I know they were rushed." This teacher, in fact, refused to start her group on the next level when she was told to do so. Teachers complained that SFA's pacing did not allow them the opportunity to individualize instruction and to do what they felt was best to meet students' needs. As one teacher explained: "Every class has it's own personality. And there are different kinds of learners everywhere . . . How can you tell me that your strategies are going to meet the needs of my students?"

The majority of teachers we interviewed made adaptations regarding the amount of time spent on particular activities, typically spending more time than allotted in the manuals. While time expansion is acceptable in some circumstances (e.g., for a group of English Language Learners for one very low reading group in the school), slow pacing across an entire school is seen as a major problem by SFA trainers. The SFA training manual states that "it is better to err by going too rapidly, than to hold students back by going too slowly. It is not necessary for every student to master every aspect of each lesson" (Madden, Livingston and Cummings 1998, p. Monitoring-11). This recommendation ran contrary to some teachers' judgment, however.

The majority of teachers made adaptations for what they saw as pedagogical reasons, although some also admitted to adapting the program to make teaching easier or more enjoyable for them. Ironically, teachers' comments about their lack of autonomy and creativity in implementing SFA were often accompanied by strong statements that the program was working well for students. For example, one teacher stated:

> I think it really takes away from the teacher being able to do what the teacher feels . . . not necessarily is best, but what they're good at, and I think that's probably the hardest part for a lot of teachers. It is ninety minutes where maybe they're not really good at this type of teaching. But we do it, and the kids are fine, and they're learning, and that's what is important.

Teachers in Success for All schools commonly complained about the lack of opportunities to be creative and the difficulty of staying on pace, particularly when they felt students' needs might have demanded otherwise. Yet, while teachers may have had trouble letting go of the freedom to create their own lessons that they had long enjoyed, most were willing to make these adjustments (Datnow and Castellano 2000b).

Educators' ideologies about school organization conflicted with the AVID program's commitment to rigorous curriculum. The hallmark feature of AVID's untracking effort is the placement of students who had been in non-academic tracks into college-prep classes for all four high school years. Previously underachieving students are expected to benefit academically by learning side-by-side with high-achieving students. Almost all high schools in the districts we studied implemented this feature as designed by AVID Center, but educators at Palm Valley High School in California implemented this design feature quite differently. They placed AVID students in college-prep classes to be sure, but these classes were segregated both academically and physically. AVID students took all their classes as a "team" in a separate wing of the school. In this organizational arrangement, AVID students were not mixing with high-achieving students, thereby significantly modifying a program design element. The educators at the high school explained they arrange AVID students' education in this manner to "sequester" them from negative influences, such as the less-achievement oriented or troublesome students attending classes elsewhere in the school.

This adaptation had the unintended consequence of disabling AVID students from enrolling in honors courses because those classes are reserved for students in another "team" which meets in another part of the campus. At this school, then, a school culture was created that disempowered AVID students. If students who do not take honors classes do not obtain the same opportunity for college admissions as those who do, then AVID students do not achieve their goals, or the goals established by the AVID program.

As these examples illustrate, educators molded reforms in ways that are consistent with their own ideologies about how teaching should be conducted and schools organized. Teachers embraced reforms that allowed them to extend their professional expertise and openly resisted elements of the reform that did not fit with their professional judgment. Sometimes, modifications were to the detriment of the "fidelity" of a reform model. In some cases, modifications were also detrimental to the students.

Yet, as Cuban (1998: 459) states, "What becomes especially important for teachers is how they can put their personal signature on the mandated reform and make it work for their students and themselves." The opposite is especially important for some reformers. For these reformers, alterations in their design, and variations in practice become evidence of decay and failure. To teachers the very same modifications are viewed as healthy signs of inventiveness, active problem solving: "To one, the end product is everything; to the other, getting to the end product is as important as the outcome" (Cuban 1998: 459). Here, then, are concrete examples of what we called "perspectival differences" in Chapter 1. Educators with different locations in educational space have different values about "what counts as success" and therefore, what criteria they apply to judge how reforms work in their local contexts.

Conclusions and Implications

The departures from the reform designs we have described in this chapter exemplify Sarason's (1997: 176) point that, "without exception, each new school became other than its planners had envisioned." Contextual features, from practical circumstances such as resource limitations to state and district policies, influenced educators at school sites to modify program features to meet local needs. Because reform is a co-constructed process, as most well-researched reforms are adopted, and as "they are implemented, [they] undergo changes that transform them in ways that few of the designers of the original reform could predict or even claim ownership" (Cuban 1998: 455). The ubiquity of local variation demonstrates once again the most pervasive finding in the study of school reform, "schools change reforms as much as reforms change schools" (Cuban 1998: 455).

In some cases, reforms are enhanced. In other cases, reforms are constricted. Such modifications sometimes caused friction between school sites and the design teams, because some of the design teams wanted schools to implement the reform features as planned, not produce free variations. This was most often the case with highly specified models. We do not mean to imply, however, that all design teams are insensitive to local contextual demands. Quite the contrary, some explicitly attempt to address local considerations or use them as the building blocks of reform and all design teams attempt to work within them. Even so, local educators who existed in differing cultures, policy systems, and organizational constraints molded reforms in unique ways. No design team, no matter how sensitive or well organized, could possibly anticipate all of the conditions in local settings that might shape reform implementation.

These examples also show that local educators make educational reform, not just respond to actions imposed upon them. Actions that educators take during later stages in the implementation process modify the reform that was originally designed. As Fullan and Hargreaves (1992: 13) state, "However noble, sophisticated or enlightened proposals for change and improvement might be, they come to nothing if teachers don't adopt them in their own classrooms and if they don't translate them into effective classroom practice."

These locally generated modifications urge us to see the policy process as a co-construction, not an imposition of policy from the top down, or as an organic bottom-up process. Consistent with Hall and McGinty's (1997) proposal, we found that the stage model of the public policy process did not apply to this educational reform effort. The reform agenda was not set and formulated by the design team, and then simply and faithfully implemented by educators in their local school sites. Educators made reform in their local contexts; they did not simply respond to directives issued elsewhere. Local adaptations to specified models occurred even in the face of fairly vigilant monitoring on the part of in-school facilitators and design teams (Datnow and Castellano 2000b).

Socio-political factors interact with cultural beliefs and practices to shape reform initiatives "on the ground." Reforms are shaped and reshaped by actors with competing interests. Recall the case of AVID teachers who fought against the beliefs and practices of other teachers at their school sites in order to effectively implement the reform. The success of the reform thus relied heavily on the agency and daily negotiations of those at the site level.

Educators' local adaptations to reforms sometimes impacted who benefited and who didn't. Sometimes these decisions were unconscious, reflecting past practices more so than poor intent. In other cases, actions reflected deep-seated beliefs. Long-standing cultural beliefs about the distribution of intelligence and ability along racial lines constituted constraints for reform. These findings imply that educational reform requires cultural change as well as organizational rearrangements. We agree with Oakes *et al.* (1999: 19) who argue that reform is not simply a process of setting policy, providing resources, and proceeding with implementation and monitoring. "Reform is much less logical and technically rational. It is much more idiosyncratic – dependent upon the context of local relationships, histories, and opportunities." Yet, as Desimone (2000) found in a review of studies on comprehensive school reform, only a few studies have actually examined the contextual variables that influence the implementation of comprehensive school reform. Perhaps this omission recurs because at the present time, school reform policies are driven largely by technical-rational approaches that treat local context as a nuisance and not as a constitutive feature of reform.

In addition to describing the enactment of reform in local context, we have developed the following guidelines for action from our findings:

- *Reform designers would be well advised to . . .*
  - (a) view local context and the diversity of the language, race, class and gender of those involved as a strength to build upon;
  - (b) approach schools with flexibility and develop a set of strategies for attending to local conditions;
  - (c) see teachers as an asset and as collaborators, not uninformed obstacles or passive implementers of reform;
  - (d) address the cultural, and political dimensions of change not just the technical dimension (Oakes and Wells 1996); and
  - (e) include equity as an explicit goal in their reforms.

- *Successful implementation requires sensitivity and adaptability (without academic compromise) on the part of the local policymakers*

Design teams, states and districts must be willing to change along with schools. Such active, shared growth is at the heart of the co-construction of a successful change effort. Policies need to be aligned in order to support reforms. Otherwise, districts should not promote the adoptions of reform designs that are not workable in their particular environment.

- *Educators and design team representatives need to develop joint under-standings about how reforms can be successfully co-constructed*

This issue is particularly crucial for schools using more prescriptive, speci-fied reform models. No doubt, some degree of adaptation is inevitable and also necessary to engage local teacher support and program sustainability. But just how much adaptation is too much? At what point do local adapta-tions, particularly among teachers, compromise the quality of the change effort school-wide? Addressing these questions on a continual basis will depress frustration on the part of both the design team and local educators.

- *Educators' ideologies and the culture of the school need to be addressed in reform efforts, along with technical and/or curricular considerations*

A school may contract with a design team for support in curricular or organizational change. However, at the same time, educators' need to con-sider their own ideologies and the culture of the school and how these may impact the implementation of reforms. Many reform designs do not build in opportunities for these types of issues to be addressed through open dis-cussions. Moreover, design teams are often not aware of the normative and political issues in a school site. Thus, it is up to local educators to take charge in bringing them out in the open, before they constitute a hindrance to what might on the surface look to be a simple technical change. This is true whether the reform is a specialized program or a program that aims for whole-school reform. Technical changes alone are insufficient to ensure reform success.

While these lessons provide a starting point, gaps remain in our knowledge of how, where, and why some external reform design teams succeed at sustained school improvement and others do not. It is also important to understand which factors might facilitate or hinder the sustainability of external reforms. These topics will be considered in subsequent chapters. But first we turn to an examination of the changing activities and relation-ships among teachers, principals, and students that occurred in the process of reform implementation, and how educators' agency interacted with the structure and culture of which they were a part.

4   Change Agents in the School Reform Process

School reform introduces new activities for teachers, administrators, students, and parents. Principals are often called upon to be instructional leaders, teachers are called upon to help develop plans for change to adapt new curricula and/or methods, parents are expected to become active participants in schools, and students are to take active responsibility for learning. All participants are held increasingly accountable for the success or failure of reform.

For reform to be successful, Fullan (1993: 4) states that, "Educators must see themselves as experts in the dynamics of change. To become experts in the dynamics of change, educators – administrators and teachers alike – must become skilled change agents." Fullan defines change agentry as being self-conscious about the nature of change and the change process. In this chapter, we take up the issue of what it means to be an agent of change from both the principal and the teacher perspective. Broadly speaking, we define *agency* as the capacity to change the existing state of affairs – a capacity which all people have regardless of how they choose to exercise it. The agency of principals and teachers can take various forms: some push or sustain reform efforts, whereas others resist or actively subvert these efforts. Additionally, teacher or principal agency may be passive or active. Therefore, we believe that all forms of teacher agency must be recognized as shaping forces of reform efforts.

However, when we speak of agency, we do not mean to imply that individual principals and teachers can single-handedly change whole schools. That is, teachers and principals are not unbridled agents. Instead, their agency must be understood in terms of its interplay with the larger context in which it is embedded. The agency of teachers is part of a complex dynamic, interwoven with the structural and cultural features of their school environment and the larger societal structure and culture of which they are a part. Structural features of the school include organizational arrangements such as the track structure, the governance structure, the scheduling of time, and rules and regulations. The culture of the school includes general norms of behavior, beliefs about authority, habits of deference and resistance, and basic knowledge about how things work (Cohen and Spillane 1993). Various teacher subcultures often co-exist within schools as well (Hargreaves 1994; McLaughlin 1994; Siskin 1994).

Structure and culture on a societal level – the large scale institutional forces that arise from social relations, politics, and the economy – also interact with principal and teacher agency. Here, "structure" refers to how society is organized in terms of distribution of resources and class, gender, and race stratification. "Culture" on a societal level is the set of belief systems, norms, and ideologies that exist in the broader context outside the school: it is how people make meaning of the world and how they live out and make use of these meanings. However, while culture may be characterized as serving a dominant ideology, one must not overlook the fragmentation of competing ideologies produced by diversity and social differentiation.

In this chapter, we foreground the agency of principals and teachers in shaping the reform efforts we studied. In doing so, structure and culture are backgrounded – and are taken up in other chapters. Yet, as we will show, in the agency of teachers, we see structure and culture operating; in culture, we see structure and agency; and, in structure, we see agency and culture. This conceptualization shares a similarity with the school change theorists' belief that school structure and culture are mutually reinforcing (Hargreaves 1994). However, importantly, we must recognize the actions of principal and teacher agents in sustaining the school structure and culture. Educators' actions interplay with societal level forces through the structure and culture of the school and within other institutional structures at the community level. We are suggesting that structure and culture at the societal level become translated through educators' agency and with structure and culture at the school level (Datnow 1995). Such theorizing avoids the problem of leaping from the micro level of teachers' actions to the macro level of societal forces and creates a bridge between these two important levels, yet preserves the notion of reflexivity.

While this sociological theorizing is particularly helpful in making sense of the interplay of agency, structure, and culture, the education literature focuses on the important elements of principals' and teachers' roles in reform. It is important to incorporate this literature on teachers, principals, and school change so as to avoid building an abstract theory that does not take into account educators' lives and the day-to-day realities of schooling. Additionally, because the relevant education literature addresses intermediary processes and structures in schools at what Hargreaves (1985) and Hall (1997) call the "meso" level of analysis, it creates an important link in a theory that encompasses both the micro level of teacher actions and the macro level of societal level forces. Thus, we begin the subsequent sections on principals' and teachers' agency in reform with frameworks derived from the education literature.

In particular, we explore the agency of teachers and principals that was evident in the implementation of externally developed reform designs. Therefore, this is a story about how reforms changed educators' actions and relationships, and how the educators' actions and relationships in turn shaped the implementation of reforms. We discuss principals, classroom teachers, and teacher leaders occupying the positions of reform facilitators or coordinators. We explore the changes, tensions, and ambiguities that arise in schools as principals and teachers make meaning of their agency in reform. We illuminate the power relations and structural and cultural constraints that influenced their actions and the constructions of their role definitions. In the conclusion, we present ideas for how the findings from our studies can be applied to improve policy and practice.

Principals in the School Reform Process

Most of the literature that helps us understand the agency of principals in the school reform process discusses the changes in the principal's *role* that occur in reform. It is well established that reforming schools requires both restructuring and reculturing (Hargreaves 1994; Fullan 1999; Sarason 1996), in which the role of the principal is reshaped (Carlin 1992), and teacher leaders are developed (Miller 1998). The role of the principal as an active and ongoing supporter of reform is critical to the success of a school-wide change effort (Muncey and McQuillan 1996).

For principals to be effective at guiding change, they must play an instructional leadership role, create and maintain a sense of trust in the school, use positive micro-politics to negotiate between managerial, technical, and institutional arenas, and create a professional community and networks for communication within the school (Murphy and Louis 1999; Wasley 1989). Engaging in school change requires principals to move from being managers of the status quo to facilitators of reform (Frederick 1992). For principals, this involves a balancing act of knowing when to be directive and when to step back and allow teachers to direct reform efforts (Leithwood and Jantzi 1990; Muncey and McQuillan 1996).

Reform is often accompanied by role ambiguity or overload and loss of a sense of identity for principals (Prestine 1993; Murphy 1994). Principals often must spend increased time promoting the school's image and working more closely with parents, school boards, and other external agents (Goldring and Rallis 1994; Murphy 1994). This is a role in which some principals are uncomfortable (Hallinger and Hausman 1994; Murphy 1994). Even when principals are supportive of reform, their ability to provide effective leadership may be hampered by their own experience, training, or beliefs (Hallinger, Murphy and Hausman 1992; Murphy 1994) or their lack of understanding of the reform itself (Neufeld 1995).

These findings about the impact of reform on the role of the principal illuminate some of the issues that principals in the schools we studied might face. However, much of the research on principals and school reform is discussed in terms of more general school improvement initiatives (e.g., site-based management, and standards-based reform). There has been a dearth of research on how the new generation of externally developed school reform designs impact principals and their leadership in schools.

With specified curriculum and implementation plans, some of these designs raise a new set of issues for principals, who must learn to manage and guide teachers in the use of new instructional models and learn to interface with design teams.

Principals' Agency in School Reform

Not surprisingly, studies of externally developed reforms have found that strong principal support for reform and strong leadership are important to the successful initiation of reform and subsequent implementation (Bodilly 1998; Desimone 2000; Smith *et al.* 1998). Principal support could be described as one form of agency that we see in reform – agency directed at supporting reform efforts. As we discussed in Chapter 2, many principals in the schools we studied introduced reform designs to their schools or at least convinced their staffs that the reform was worth engaging in. It is not surprising, therefore, that we found active, reform-minded agency among principals in many of our schools, at least at the outset. Principal support for reform was so important that in most cases, the existence of a reform hinged upon the principal. Reforms were less likely to be implemented fully, much less institutionalized, when principals did not actively support them, or were more "passive" in their actions with respect to the reform. Some whole-school reforms died out when principal support was not present. In the case of AVID, passive support by principals did not necessarily threaten the existence of the program, but in these instances, the program limped along and was less successfully implemented. The following examples serve as illustrations of the need for active agency on the part of the principal in supporting reform.

AVID delineates what principal support for reform means and it includes selecting staff, attending meetings, supporting coordinators, garnering financial support, acting as a liaison with the district, among other things (AVID Center Guidelines 1996). Eight of the 12 sites that implemented AVID had principals who were active change agents and supportive of the reform. Active support is different from the passive acceptance or mere approval extended by some principals at the other four sites. Two examples will illustrate the difference between active and passive support. In the case of Madison High School, the school's capacity to support reform was built by an enthusiastic and supportive principal, working alongside the energetic and committed original AVID teacher of the school. Over a period of six years, the principal and the AVID coordinator bolstered the AVID program such that AVID grew from a class of 30 students to a program with six classes serving almost 200 students. They succeeded in training three-quarters of their faculty in AVID methodologies, and they were recognized as an AVID demonstration site "with distinction." The supportive principal with her savvy grant writing skills brought money to the school and directed that a significant portion of it pay the AVID coordinator's salary. This money released the coordinator from the majority of her teaching responsibilities and allowed her to provide staff development to the other AVID teachers at the school. The principal's financial and ideological support for the reform allowed the AVID coordinator to hold school-wide site team meetings, offer counseling to AVID students, conduct data collection and help with the expansion of AVID to other schools in the district.

The Madison High School educators brought AVID to the attention of the district. They brought AVID students to a school board meeting to convince them of the merits of the reform. The students' efforts had remarkable results. As the principal explained, "Well, all of a sudden . . . two weeks later the president [of the Board] called a special meeting saying that it was top priority of the Board to put AVID in every single school. And there is now an allocation of the budget for every school to start up AVID. . . ."

The story of Madison contrasts sharply with those at other high schools. AVID programs are weakest in schools where the principals' agency regarding reform could be described as passive or lacking in interest. In these schools, principals often selected the newest and least skilled teachers to teach the AVID classes. One AVID educator explained that "many schools do not have the support of the principal for AVID and therefore, in these schools, principals do not elevate AVID to a priority position." At one school in Virginia, the principal professed his support for AVID, "I have a special interest in AVID kids. They look like me and my sons and daughters and I know they face difficult odds." He offered ideological support for the reform but when faced with teacher selection decisions, he chose a teacher who was clearly struggling to learn how to teach.

Despite discussions with AVID Center administrators who recommended a teacher change, the principal kept the inexperienced teacher in place and thereby undermined the success of the program. Later, when the principal took a leave of absence, he was replaced by a new principal who knew very little about the reform and was not interested in becoming involved. The AVID class continued to be taught by an unqualified teacher and the program failed to expand its influence school wide. Very few teachers were interested in joining the AVID site team because there was no one to promote professionalism and networking among the faculty. The program showed no signs of expanding. Moreover, AVID students at this site continued to be disadvantaged as they took AVID classes that lacked academic rigor.

As was the case with AVID, principal support was key to successful reform in Sunland County. At most of the schools that continued reform for five years or more, the principals made efforts to support implementation wholeheartedly. Principal leadership for reform meant somewhat different things, depending on the reform, but active agency in support of the reform was the common ingredient. As an educator in one Success for All school commented, "This program is certainly a program that requires a very strong principal's support." In some schools, the very presence of the reform was also contingent on the principal. This was often the case in schools that had not institutionalized the reform and where staff engagement in it was relatively low.

In sum, active agency on the part of the principal in supporting reform was critical for its success. Active support meant not only speaking out in favor of the reform, but also organizing school structures and resources to support it, and creating a school culture in which the reform was not only seen as a given, but one in which it could grow and thrive.

Changing Principals' Activities and Perspectives

Across our schools, particularly those implementing whole-school reforms, principals' actions shaped and were shaped by the demands of the reform or the change process that accompanied its implementation. The areas in which this was most notable were in the relation between leadership styles and the reform (including whether they were comfortable sharing power with teachers, as some reforms demanded), their level of involvement in instruction, and the professional development they personally gained. Each of these issues is discussed below.

Reforms in Relation to Principals' Leadership Styles

The whole-school reforms varied in the degree to which they called upon principals to change the structure of governance and the way decisions were made in the school. Some designs, such as Comer SDP, Modern Red Schoolhouse, and Coalition of Essential Schools (CES), specifically called upon principals to share power with teachers. Other reform designs did not explicitly include this as a primary feature of their reforms, but by introducing a new set of opportunities and demands for principals and teachers they changed the context for leadership.

The principals and assistant principals in CES and Comer schools tended to use these reform designs as a vehicle to help them promote their goal of shared leadership throughout the building. These reforms fit with the principals' beliefs about teacher empowerment. At Holly Elementary, a Comer school, the principal said that before she took the helm of the school, she heard that "the teachers . . . run the school." And I said, "That's great for me. Let them run the school." The Comer model, which was already in place, fit with her leadership style. She explained that when she first learned about Comer, she responded, "Oh. I do that. That's the way I always run the school. I didn't call it Comer. But it's like school-based management. And that's fine with me. And then I'm Comer too."

At one Modern Red site, the change in principal in the third year of the reform allowed us to examine how conflicting views of leadership (between the reform and the administration) can hinder change efforts. The former principal's willingness to "promote the notion of leadership throughout the building" made it possible for Modern Red to come to the school initially. Because of Modern Red, teachers at the school purportedly took on new leadership roles in the first two years. However, when we returned to the school in year three, we found a new administration in place, one with a rather more top-down management style, in contrast to the former principal's shared leadership style. One problem the new administration had with Modern Red was that "a ship can only have one captain." That is, principals must lead, and teachers should not. Not surprisingly, the reform faltered under the new leadership and was soon dropped for these and other reasons.

Success for All does not seek to radically transform leadership structures in schools. However, the program does set forth specific functions for principals, which include ensuring resources, arranging the schedule, supporting the facilitator, monitoring progress, and keeping staff focused on the goals of the reform (Madden, Livingston and Cummings 1998: Role-1). While the scheduling and resource functions are fairly concrete, the functions of the principal as "keeper of the vision," as helping staff focus on the essential goals of SFA, and as supporting the facilitator are much more open to interpretation. As a result, the principals' ideologies and leadership styles influenced how they interacted with teachers and facilitators with respect to SFA, which in turn, influenced implementation (Datnow and Castellano 2001).

The principals varied in the flexibility they allowed teachers with respect to the SFA curriculum – with some requiring more stringent fidelity to the model and others approaching it with a more lax attitude. One principal approached SFA with a rather strict approach. He described himself as "a strong, military-type" principal. The teachers confirmed this, explaining that complaints about the lack of flexibility in SFA were simply not tolerated by the administration.

Most other principals tended to be willing to allow for at least some flexibility in how teachers implemented the SFA curriculum. For example, one principal felt he was as strict as he could be with regard to implementation, considering his own leadership style, "People come back from . . . these school visits, you know, these fascist regime SFA schools, which I would never . . . , I'm not going to ever have them. It wouldn't be me. . . ." He also felt that flexibility was required to engage teacher support for SFA: "You have to make it palatable." However, the facilitator at this school thought that the principal "tries to accommodate teachers – almost too much."

As these examples illustrate, the implementation of reforms required that principals question their leadership styles and interactions with teachers with respect to the reform. While some principals reported adjustments in their leadership stance as a result of reforms, others tended to fall back on their preferred style, whether or not this matched well with the demands of the reform.

Principal Engagement in Teaching and Learning

In some cases, the reform reshaped the activities of the principal to include more involvement with teaching and learning. This appeared most likely for designs that were specifically targeted at teaching and learning and for those that had clear principal expectations. For example, several of the principals in Success for All schools acknowledged that the implementation of SFA increased their involvement in reading instruction. Previously, when teachers were using eclectic methods to teach reading, principals had much less of a leadership role in this area. Now they were knowledgeable about the methods and curriculum teachers used in reading. This was in contrast to previous years in some schools where, as one teacher explained, "We had no language arts program really . . . it was kind of like 'do whatever you can do.'"

For some principals, the implementation of SFA also meant much more involvement in classrooms than in the past. It was during classroom observations that principals performed their monitoring function set forth by SFA. One principal explained, "I check lesson plans. I observe teachers' teaching. I observe students' reading to me . . . I have stickers and things I give to students when I go out and I hear them reading." In another case, the aforementioned "military-type" principal explained that since the adoption of SFA, "I go in every day. The kids used to be afraid. The teachers used to be afraid. Now they expect it." This was a clear change in role for him that was brought about by the reform. On the other hand, some teachers were not comfortable being monitored, and some were openly resistant, teaching other subjects when the principal stopped by to observe reading.

Success for All was the reform design that solicited the greatest change in terms of principals' roles in instruction. The design focuses squarely on the processes of teaching and learning (with respect to reading) and it is clear in terms of its expectations for principals in monitoring and leading the reform effort. We did not find that the other reform designs necessarily got principals more engaged with instruction. To be fair, some of the reform designs focus less on instructional issues, leaving these details to the teachers. Some reforms (e.g., Modern Red Schoolhouse) did not get off the ground fully in the schools we studied, in part because of waning support for external reforms at the district levels and competing demands resulting from new state and district requirements. Therefore, we were unable to see how they might have changed principals' involvement in instruction. In some cases, principals also delegated instructional leadership to the reform facilitators or AVID coordinators, as we describe in the last section of this chapter.

Principals Expand Professional Networks

In several cases, involvement with reform designs offered principals professional development and provided them opportunities to expand their networks. The AVID, Core Knowledge, Success for All, Comer, and the Coalition of Essential Schools design teams, hold annual national conferences for educators. Most of these design teams also employ educators as professional developers or coaches to bring along new schools. These opportunities proved useful for the principals in the schools we studied, who were able to expand their repertoire of skills and connect with other administrators working with the same design in schools around the country. AVID offers an Administrative Strand during their Summer Institutes specifically designed to train principals and other administrators in strategies that will provide effective leadership that supports the reform. Some principals also become instructors for Summer Institute sessions and train administrators throughout the country. This involvement contributes to their own professional growth as well as the growth of the reform.

As we mentioned earlier, the principals of both of the Comer schools in our study received distinctions from the national design team as a result of their embodiment and commitment to the Comer principles. About the principal at Forest Elementary, the integrated services coordinator remarked: "[Our principal] is now a facilitator out of Yale and she has gone a few summers and she actually does training for them. So we couldn't get anybody better." At the annual SDP Principals' Academy, principals learned how to better implement the Comer model and worked together. As the principal of one Comer school explained: "[You] get a broader perspective. You don't become as parochial as you can become when you are just in your corner."

The principals working in the two Coalition schools also gained professionally, mostly through the Annenberg Principalship Program that was connected with the Coalition. According to one principal, this program involved, "talking about the need for reform, networking, seeing how others have met the challenge, trying to come up with common denominators of what are effective in schools to bring about change, and what the leadership role is." Unfortunately, her participation in the program only lasted a year after which the funding dried up. According to the principal, "Annenberg was very generous with the money in the beginning, I mean it was fabulous. And then . . . it was well 'now you have to assume this cost and this cost and this cost.' And our district is very restrictive." While it was a valuable experience, she did not think that one year of the principal training was sufficient.

In conclusion, some principals expanded their leadership skills and professional networks as a result of their involvement with external reform designs. As we have shown, principals' actions were shaped by the reforms, and the principals themselves in turn shaped reforms through the development of new roles and relationships or by continuing with their existing activities. In any event, strong, active principal leadership was critical to the ongoing implementation of the reform. The same was true for teachers, whose agency in reform also took various forms, and whose relationships also changed as a result.

Teachers and School Reform

Teachers are considered by most policymakers and school change experts to be the centerpiece of educational change. Therefore, not surprisingly, many current reform efforts are directed at teachers, and the involvement of teachers in school reform is seen as critical. Teachers' receptivity towards reforms depends to a large degree on their level of involvement and buy-in to the change effort (Fullan 1991, 1993; Sarason 1990, 1996), which is obviously critical for the successful implementation of an externally developed reform design.

A series of imposed change is believed to create a "culture of compliance" among teachers such that when teachers are informed about a new initiative, "all they want to know [is] how to do it as painlessly as possible" (Blackmore 1998: 472). Instead, teachers need to "own" the process of change, and reform efforts need to be grounded in an understanding of teachers' professional lives and development (Fullan and Hargreaves 1996; Helsby 1999; Hopkins and Wideen 1984). If teachers are involved in planning and implementing reform, they are more likely to assume responsibility for it, rather than attributing it to others. Furthermore, when teachers are involved in the change process, it is more likely that novel ways of illuminating and solving problems will arise (Sarason 1996).

Consistent with these findings, recent research on externally developed reforms has found that indeed teacher involvement in the change process and active support for the reform is important (Bodilly 1998; Datnow *et al.* 1998; Desimone 2000). However, there is an inherent tension that exists here. On the one hand, some teachers have argued that externally developed reforms, namely those that are prescriptive, inhibit teacher creativity and active engagement in the reform effort (Ross *et al.* 1997). On the other hand, in schools using more loosely specified models, some teachers complain about time required for preparation of materials (Bodilly 1998; Desimone 2000).

A recent survey research study by Berends (2000) lends further support to the variability of teacher opinions towards externally developed reforms, finding that variation exists even more within schools than across schools. In some cases, patterns of reform support related to teacher characteristics. Berends found that teachers over 40 were less likely to support reforms, as were teachers in high minority teaching staffs. However, he did not find a correlation between teacher characteristics and implementation levels. Further in-depth investigation of teacher agency in schools using externally developed reforms is needed to better understand how and why teachers support or resist reforms and the impact of reforms on their professional lives.

Teacher Agency in School Reform

As we explained in Chapter 2, teachers acted in a variety of ways in response to the initiation of reform efforts in their schools. Over time, some teachers embraced reform efforts and were actively supportive of them. Other teachers passively accepted reforms, while perhaps grumbling about them on occasion, whereas a number were openly resistant towards reforms. In a number of schools, these varying forms of agency in response to reform created factionalism among teachers, but in other cases, teachers adopted a "live and let live" attitude about their colleagues. We provide some examples of how these dynamics played out in particular schools.

While the lack of teacher support was often connected to a school's decisions to abandon a reform, some schools managed to sustain reform even in the presence of some resistant teachers. In fact, according to one teacher in a Core Knowledge school, teacher support for the reform was "50–50," and there was an "I-hate-it group," as well as a group who embraced it. The two groups were sometimes at loggerheads, as the teachers who were supportive of the reform were seen as allied with the principal, whereas the others were not. The teachers who were supportive of the reform had attempted to bring the resistant teachers along by telling them that Core Knowledge content is something that they probably teach anyway, "They don't realize that they are doing Core every day of the week." Even so, six years into the implementation, these teachers were still complaining about Core.

Sometimes, teachers' agency in reform related to whether they found an ideological fit between the reform and what they considered good teaching. For example, teachers in Success for All schools who fell into the "strong supporters" category were very positive about the structure of the program, agreed with its approach to teaching reading, and were favorably outspoken about the program at their school sites (Datnow and Castellano 2000b). As one experienced teacher stated: "You don't know how long I've been teaching and it's the first time that anyone's . . . [made] teaching almost as a science rather than, 'Well, I think I'll do this today, or that today . . .'" On the other hand, teachers who were resistant to the program complained about its "one size fits all nature" of SFA with respect to expectations for teachers: "Okay, the teacher is absent. We can just put the lesson plan in and anybody can do it. . . . And I give myself more credit than that." While these teachers sometimes had philosophical complaints with reforms, their colleagues often viewed them as resistant to change of any sort. At one school, teachers who were resistant to reforms were described as simply "the complainers" or as teachers who "loathe to learn a new program."

In our research on the AVID program, we found that the gender identity of educators played heavily into who "bought into" the program (Hubbard and Datnow 2000). In spite of the fact that most secondary schools are comprised of equal numbers of male and female teachers, it is striking to note that the overwhelming number of AVID teachers (as well as coordinators and regional directors) are women. Women in schools routinely volunteered or were sought out to become the teachers and the leaders of the AVID program.

Understanding the structure of the AVID program provides some insight into the reasons behind the reform-minded agency of the women teachers. AVID is organized to address both the academic and social needs of students. AVID teachers repeatedly discussed their support for AVID because it included opportunities to extend mothering and care taking. One teacher said, "I can't adopt 120 kids. But by being an AVID teacher I can give them the help and support they need." Another teacher expressed her feelings regarding the needs of the AVID students this way, "I feel so fortunate to have these students. This is the something decent in [their] indecent world." To meet students' needs, this AVID teacher called or visited students' homes, sought professional help for them when they needed it, and interceded on their behalf with other teachers to negotiate grades and poor attendance. The commitment of AVID teachers to their students extended well beyond the academic world. Nurturing attitudes and practices seemed pervasive among the AVID teachers.

In sum, the eagerness of women to take on the role of AVID teacher was influenced significantly by their positionality as women. Early socialization as nurturers and caregivers led these women to see their role of teacher as someone who extends beyond offering academic information. Many of the AVID teachers spent as much if not more time acting as advocates and counselors rather than as simply teachers of subject matter. Overwhelmingly, these teachers were women.

Teachers' Professional Lives and School Reform

Some teachers experienced improvements in the quality of their professional lives as a result of the reform efforts at their schools. They engaged in continued learning, enjoyed their craft more, increased collaboration with colleagues, became involved in new professional opportunities beyond the school, and were more empowered in school decision-making. On the other hand, some teachers found that reforms constrained their professional lives by making teaching less enjoyable, adding stress and pressure, and causing division among their colleagues.

Changes in Teachers' Relationships

In the schools we studied, there were clear examples of where reforms were accompanied by genuine as well as what Hargreaves (1994) calls "contrived collegiality." A true collaborative culture among teachers can be a powerful force for school improvement (Lieberman 1990). On the other hand, contrived collegiality often means that teachers are administratively regulated, directive, implementation-oriented, fixed in time and space, and predictable. Collaboration among teachers who have these characteristics does not generally lead to meaningful change (Hargreaves 1994).

A teacher explained that as a result of Comer, ". . . we're more aware of having a support team around us. We don't feel isolated." This support team involved not only other teachers, but also administrators, other adults on staff, and parents. At another Comer school, the teachers pointed out the "ombudsmen's group" which was established at the school to address adult problems, as most of the other committees focus only on students. The group's job is to resolve issues among faculty or within teachers' classrooms before they escalate and become divisive. The teachers thought it was "a wonderful idea" that was "working beautifully." Positive instances of teacher collaboration were present in some other Sunland schools using different reforms. A teacher at Limestone, a Coalition school, explained that meeting in grade clusters (not just within grade levels) had helped increase collaboration: "It's good because you know so much more about your colleagues, and you get to interact . . . I think I know every single teacher here, meanwhile at my previous schools, if I said 'hi' to a teacher from a different grade level, it's because I maybe saw them after three months."

The AVID Design Team requires that all schools implementing AVID form a "site team." This group is comprised of the AVID coordinator, AVID teachers, academic teachers from each discipline, administrative staff and counselors. The purpose of the site team is designed to, "help set goals, make action plans, and [help teachers] feel ownership of the program, to improve the academic performance of the students and the teaching satisfaction of teachers" (AVID Research and Information, 1996–1997: 65). Collaboration is built into the organizational structure and encourages more school-wide involvement and support for the program.

At one school, the efforts of the AVID coordinator in forming a site team has led to increased collaboration among subject-area teachers, who were formerly isolated in their own departments, as is often the case in secondary schools (Siskin 1994). Sixty-three of the 90 teachers on the staff of one California high school were trained in AVID methodologies and became part of the AVID site team. The AVID coordinator believed that one of the reasons the site team had grown so large is that the initial teachers she recruited were the most credible teachers on the faculty. AVID led to increased collaboration among teachers, and teachers were now able to discuss the students they have in common. Because AVID teachers are trained to teach note-taking skills, critical thinking and other strategies, faculty were able to work together to help students school-wide. One teacher stated: "I look at the AVID program as a way of bringing our faculty together . . . first you have teacher isolation, then you have department isolation, then you have school isolation. [AVID] is helping us to break out of that. It's been a real positive."

On the contrary, there were examples of schools where collaboration among teachers was definitely contrived or almost non-existent. In one AVID school in Kentucky the site team existed in name only. Although the AVID teacher and guidance counselor worked together to support the reform, they were unsuccessful in getting the faculty involved. The AVID teacher complained that when it came time to choose people to be on the team . . . "it was almost like we sort of kind of *forced* people. We went around and asked . . . after we got [a few] teachers in, they hardly ever came to a meeting." One of the teachers had some bad experiences with AVID students and that "turned him off." Similarly, in a school in Virginia, the site team meetings became more infrequent when the AVID teacher who had spearheaded the program resigned. Generally speaking, forming and sustaining an active site team is one of the most difficult aspects of AVID implementation due in large part to the various levels of leadership and commitment to the reform.

In schools where the professional culture did not support collaboration, issues relating to the reforms sometimes resulted in factionalism or conflict among teachers. In one school, there was conflict between white and black AVID teachers. The racial identity of the AVID teachers informed their perceptions regarding the needs of the students in the program and it shaped their pedagogical strategies. Teacher differences were often profound and resulted in very different instantiations of the program. In some cases their differences resulted in conflict and finger-pointing to ascribe blame for student failure. This finger-pointing was racially informed. For example, a black AVID teacher criticized a white teacher for not being able to relate to the students' racial and socioeconomic background. She said, "He's a white teacher and he can't relate. You know, I have several students who live in public housing . . . I can understand. I lived there."

The conflict that resulted among these AVID teachers ultimately led to teacher turnover in the program and caused other faculty and even students to question the strength and merit of the program. Disappointingly, this debacle occurred in the presence of a committed and well-meaning district administrator who had personally selected AVID staff. "We wanted to build bridges that were built of *positive* steel . . . ," he explained. Little did he realize that the strong-willed, equity-minded teachers he hired would have rather different, racially- and experience-informed teaching philosophies, and difficulty coexisting in the program, much less working together.

As these examples illustrate, there were some school cultures that could be described as anything but collaborative. Reforms often brought underlying tensions among teachers to a head. Yet, we also observed positive examples of teacher collaboration in, not surprisingly, some of the schools where important changes were taking place. This did not mean the end of reform, necessarily, but it appeared that the reform's impact in the school was certainly blunted or at least hindered by these problems. It is important to note that the changes in teachers' relationships that we observed are not always directly attributable to the reforms themselves. Often, schools have long histories of isolation or collaboration that are hard to change, or are not principally dealt with in the implementation of a particular reform.

Teacher Empowerment and Learning

Often connected to the collaboration among teachers was the teacher learning and empowerment that was present in some of the schools undertaking reforms. In some cases, the empowerment derived from a greater role in school decision-making, whereas in others it came from the use of a new instructional model that opened doors for teachers, both in their schools and more broadly. At the same time, there were teachers who felt disempowered by reforms, as well as by the leadership in their schools.

At one Comer school, teachers were allowed – and adopted – an active role in school decision-making and this in turn increased their empowerment and commitment. "We have a lot of good leadership in this school that has been developed with the Comer program," explained the principal. All of the teachers talked about the fact that their voices were heard and said that they could bring up "pretty much anything" in "cadre" meetings. They describe the increased commitment as a result of the changes at their school. Despite the fact that the union says teachers must be allowed to leave at 3.20 p.m., many worked voluntarily until 6.00 p.m. and beyond. The teachers' union had an unusually collaborative role in school management, which the principal also attributed to the consensus-based decision-making at the heart of the Comer model. However, it should also be noted that teachers were handpicked when the school opened. "Many of them are strong leaders," explained the assistant principal. Yet, teacher satisfaction with the school – of which Comer SDP was a big part – led to a very stable faculty.

Opportunities for leadership and empowerment occurred for some AVID teachers, but in a rather different way, often occurring for individuals rather than groups. In some cases, participating in AVID gave teachers increased status at their school. AVID Center asks teachers to become leaders of a school-wide team. They gained recognition, validation for their efforts, and were given a chance to affect a greater number of lives. Their work often extended and impacted the whole school. Because the principal often chose AVID teachers, they gained status and were distinguished from other teachers. Some were even recognized by district officials who looked to them to create the change in academic performance promised by the reform efforts. Along with their newfound status, AVID teachers improved their structural position. They could now lobby for special consideration from the principals or from counselors on behalf of their students. Not only did it improve their structural position in the school, but one AVID teacher actually made a career leap to AVID Regional Director and another was appointed to a district position as a result of her involvement with AVID.

At one Core Knowledge school, teachers also attributed their increased personal learning and career development to the reform. In a focus group, the third grade teachers said that "Core Knowledge gave us the freedom to be creative, [and] I think we really took it and ran with it." This was a lively group of teachers, who admitted that when the reform was first initiated, "they caught us at a good time" in terms of their lives: they were still single and new to teaching, and "gung ho" to work late developing lesson plans. They were not paid extra for this extra work. Most staff viewed the curriculum development as establishing conditions for continual learning among them. Teachers sometimes use the common grade-level planning time that they have to instruct each other on different topics. At another Core Knowledge school, many teachers also reported that Core Knowledge had prompted them to research topics that they would not have done ordinarily, increasing their personal learning. One teacher explained, "It also makes me a smarter person. It increases my knowledge as well." These findings are consistent with those from a national study of twelve Core Knowledge schools (Datnow, Borman and Stringfield 2000).

Professional Opportunities Outside the School

As a result of their involvement with reform designs, teachers in some schools had enhanced professional opportunities in and outside their schools. These experiences were contingent, of course, on whether such opportunities existed with the reform design, whether local funding permitted for it, and whether administrators promoted teachers' involvement in these types of activities. Again, like teacher empowerment, the presence of professional opportunities was the result of a joint interaction of conditions and actions at various levels.

AVID Summer Institutes are the major source of staff development offered to AVID participants nationwide. These week-long institutes are held each year throughout the country. The AVID Design Team recruits some of their best veteran AVID teachers to staff these training sessions. Many AVID teachers enhanced their professional lives by teaching at these institutes. They were able to network with AVID educators, exchange ideas and problem solve with others around common issues they faced in their schools. Teachers reported that their own enthusiasm for the program grew. Several AVID teachers subsequently led on-site staff development on AVID methodologies to their entire faculty and some AVID teachers even went on to help market AVID in districts and states outside of their own.

Teachers in the schools implementing whole-school reforms also derived benefits from national conferences related to the design. This was especially true for teachers in Core Knowledge schools, many of whom had attended the annual conference. Teachers volunteered to attend the conference, local funding permitting. A major benefit of attending Core Knowledge conferences was the opportunity to learn about how teachers in other Core Knowledge schools teach Core topics and sometimes to make lasting connections with them. It was also a chance for experienced Core Knowledge teachers to share their expertise. The teachers who attended the conference presented ideas at faculty meetings when they returned, thereby increasing communication among teachers.

While the Coalition of Essential Schools, Comer SDP, and Success for All also hold conferences or summer institutes of their own, the teachers in the schools we studied did not typically attend them. Administrators and reform facilitators at these schools sometimes did attend, however, but this opportunity was not afforded to teachers as well, due to funding constraints. Teachers in these schools sometimes had the opportunity to attend local professional meetings related to the reform, but these did not appear to have a major impact on their professional lives in the way that the AVID and Core Knowledge conferences described for the teachers who were involved.

Teacher Stress in Reform

In some of the previous sections, we have highlighted the positive changes in teachers' actions and relationships that occurred as a result of reforms. We described teachers willing to expend extensive personal time engaged in activities related to reform, in part because they felt so committed and empowered. These teachers saw benefits in the innovations over current practices and thus were willing to expend the effort necessary to get reforms off the ground and keep them afloat. Not surprisingly, this was not always the case. When teachers were not committed to the reforms or found fault in the reform designs, they saw the additional demands associated with them as increasing the stress and pressure of their already difficult jobs teaching in urban schools.

In the case of AVID, new teachers experienced the most difficulty in implementing AVID because neither were they experienced teachers nor had they achieved a reputation among the faculty that inspired support for the program. A teacher's status in the school made a big impact on their ability to be effective with AVID. Teacher stress and time constraints were also apparent at two schools that implemented the Audrey Cohen College System of Education model, in part because they did not have ample resources or support. While some teachers were enthusiastic at the outset, they found some elements of the reform rather time consuming to execute, and thus their commitment waned. As one teacher explained:

> Some teachers spent Saturdays just driving around to do things that they had to do and making contacts with people and gathering information, gathering materials that they had to do because the kids at this age level, they can't drive themselves around. And parents don't have the time.

In order to write the curriculum, they felt they would have had to take time away from their own lives, families, and so forth. This was not something they were willing to do.

At a school that implemented the Modern Red design ostensibly for three years (but never fully got it off the ground), the demands of the reform seemingly frustrated teachers early on, causing them to lose interest. Teachers stated that ensuring that students moved through the various

Modern Red units and that all parents were informed of their children's progress would be time consuming. They believed they would need extra people-power if they were to do this well. Their regular workload, never mind the reform, already caused them to work long hours at school and at home. "It's not like we walk out of here at 3:20 with a pocketbook," said one teacher. "You're now talking to teachers who take work home." Teachers saw Modern Red and, in particular, its emphasis on community and parent involvement as placing additional constraints on their time, which were too much to bear. Teachers felt tired, worn out, and uninterested.

This was in large part because when new district and state mandates were layered on top of reforms, as we explained in Chapter 3, teachers experienced considerable stress. The Sunland district's new reading program initiated in 1998 and the push for increased accountability on state tests that preceded it added pressure to teachers work. According to one teacher:

> The big thing this year is the whole revamping of the reading program and that has been just incredible – a nightmare because it was sort of thrown on us over the summer and we really didn't get properly trained. And now they're trying to train us on Wednesdays and introducing workshops. And there really is a lot to be done. There's really a lot that they expect of you – and then testing, just testing, tons of tests.

Needless to say, the amount of time and energy they could expend on school-level reforms was downscaled significantly.

In conclusion, the findings of our investigation of the agency of classroom teachers engaged in reform are fairly consistent with the extant research. Teachers' support for reform was largely dependent on their buy-in to change efforts. No doubt, when teachers were involved in planning and implementing reform, they were more likely to assume responsibility for it, become empowered by it, and engage in continual learning. These teachers became change agents. On the other hand, when teachers are not fully committed to the change effort, or do not see its value over current practices, they resist the reforms and the time and effort that are required to make them work. In other cases, teachers were passive in the face of reform. We have highlighted how teachers' responses are interactive with structure and culture, both of the school and of the reform.

The Teacher Leader in School Reform

In the prior section, our focus was on what change means for the classroom teacher. Here, our concern is the teachers who occupy positions of leadership in schools. There is a plethora of research describing the development of teacher leadership, as this is generally thought to be a precondition for school improvement (Smylie 1997; Wasley 1989). Much of this work focuses on how teachers' roles might be redefined to include the responsibilities and decision-making powers related to instruction, assessment, procedures, and governance that are typically reserved for administrators. The hope is that "teacher leadership and administrative leadership work in collaboration to create more democratic and participatory school organizations" (Miller 1998: 531).

Opportunities for teacher leadership have also recently arisen from policies that designate master teachers to direct school improvement (Smylie 1997). However, the agency of teachers who are out of the classroom, occupying the position of full-time reform facilitator or coordinator, has gone relatively unexplored. The few studies that do exist suggest that the facilitator role is important for reform efforts and involves a tricky balance of multiple, sometimes conflicting, activities (Muncey and McQuillan 1996; Neufeld 1995; Nunnery *et al.* 1997; Smylie and Denny 1990; Smylie and Brownlee-Conyers 1992; Wasley 1989).

Teacher leaders are often reluctant to challenge the norms that characterize the professional lives of teachers for fear of separating themselves from their colleagues (Smylie and Denny 1990; Smylie and Brownlee-Conyers 1992; Wasley 1989). They tend to be cautious about their relationships with principals and their impact on the leadership terrain. In one study, the teacher leaders who served as reform coordinators were uncertain in how aggressively they could or should promote change. Teachers also saw coordinators as occupying an ill-defined role that constituted a "no-man's land" between teacher and administrator (Muncey and McQuillan 1996: 59).

As some of the aforementioned studies point out, power relations and status issues come into play in considerations of teacher leadership and the changing role of the principal in reform (Evans 1996). Gender is one of the most important variables in changing power relations within schools (Lieberman 1999), as traditionally men have held administrative positions and women, particularly in elementary schools, constitute the bulk of the teaching force (Apple 1994). Yet, the impact of gender on the roles and relationships of teacher leaders and administrators in reform has yet to be fully explored.

Overall, despite a growing research base on teacher leaders in some areas, there are still questions about how they work with teachers and principals to achieve school improvement (Heck and Hallinger 1999; Smylie and Brownlee-Conyers 1992), particularly in the context of externally developed reforms.

The Agency of the Teacher Leader

The teacher leaders who function as "facilitators" or "reform coordinators" occupy a position critical to the successful implementation of reforms and appreciated by principals and most teachers. Yet, as we will show, the jobs are often characterized by work overload, inadequate compensation, and tensions related to role ambiguity. The demands of the positions often do not gel with existing school cultures and policies that do not provide formal space for a position that combines evaluation, administration, and coaching. These findings reinforce prior studies, yet we provide new insight into how externally developed reform designs, some of which are rather explicit, contribute to these dynamics.

In this section, we examine the activities and relationships of teacher leaders in some of the reforms – AVID, Core Knowledge, Audrey Cohen, and Success for All – for which facilitators/coordinators were present in some of the schools in our studies. We begin first with a discussion of what these jobs look like for the persons involved. The day-to-day functions of the facilitator or reform coordinator varied somewhat according to the reform design; however, in all cases, the job was seen as critical to the functioning of the reform, as well as rather difficult and taxing.

AVID specifies a range of activities for those in the coordinator position, including selecting students, hiring tutors, arranging field trips and guest speakers, calling parents, leading the AVID site team, managing the reform and the budget, and assisting teachers with the AVID methodologies, among other things. The AVID coordinator's job has been described as simply "mammoth." AVID coordinators are often stressed because of the amount of work they must do to oversee the AVID program. Susan Graham at Redwood High coordinates the activities of 11 sections of AVID. Graham teaches AVID all day and in addition must staff the other AVID classes, arrange for fieldtrips and guest speakers, hire and coordinate tutor schedules. All the AVID teachers assume extra duties, which include AVID student recruitment, course planning and additional meetings and staff development.

Graham complained that maintaining the quality of such a large AVID program has created an enormous stress on those involved. According to Graham, she could not devote the time she should to run the program effectively because of her teaching responsibilities. Graham was given two prep periods a day to help her accomplish her AVID duties but she claimed that she desperately needs secretarial help. Financial concerns prevent hiring her the kind of assistance she needs. Graham's experience is not unique. In schools throughout our study, AVID coordinators were burdened by many additional hours of work. Clearly, the job of the AVID coordinator was taxing.

So, too, the Success for All facilitator's job was expansive. The SFA Foundation requires that SFA schools employ a facilitator and the functions of the facilitator are carefully spelled out. The principal's and facilitator's training manual for SFA (Madden, Livingston and Cummings 1998: Role-3) states that the facilitator's responsibilities are to: 1) know the progress of each teacher in implementing the program and to provide support accordingly; 2) know the progress of each student and ensure that no student falls through the cracks; and 3) manage assessments and regrouping efficiently. The manual further states that "the facilitator must be a mentor, and not an evaluator," and that the relationship between the facilitators and teachers should be "respectful and supportive." By laying out the functions for facilitators and principals, SFA helps to set the foundation for success, making it more likely that educators will know how to lead the reform.

One SFA facilitator explained her mission as she saw it: "You have to make this program work as easily as possible for the classroom teachers because they have so many other responsibilities." By and large, teachers believed that the facilitator really did make their teaching of SFA easier. About her school's facilitator, one teacher explained: "She runs everything off for us . . . We don't have to do anything. We go up there, we get our materials, we come back, and we teach it. That's half the reason it [the planning] takes ten minutes . . . Then she does, you know, all the testing, and she'll sit with you and talk with you . . . She's great." Similarly, about a facilitator in another school, a teacher remarked: "I can't ever imagine it running without her." In fact, one school where the facilitator was clearly not as strong as those in the other five schools struggled with implementation.

Facilitators and their colleagues described them variously as "taxed," "overburdened," and "swamped." Yet, despite these hardships, most of the facilitators remained very committed to their jobs and felt that the success of the reform hinged to a large degree on their function as the facilitator. They felt needed. Still, one facilitator admitted that she would return to being a classroom teacher immediately, if she had the opportunity. Two facilitators stated that the experience had taught them that they would never want to be administrators.

Success for All and AVID differ from other reforms in directly specifying the functions of the facilitator. The Core Knowledge Foundation, for example, does not require that schools employ a facilitator, much less specify the functions. However, some schools saw the facilitator function as essential and organized funding to provide for one. For example, at Jetty Elementary School, a woman served as the Core Knowledge facilitator. In her role as Core Knowledge coordinator, she gathered and organized materials for teachers, wrote grants to support the reform, and assisted in teachers' classrooms. She also worked as a teacher-consultant for the Core Knowledge Foundation, providing training for new Core schools.

The job of the facilitator in an Audrey Cohen school is also complex, involving not only work with teachers inside the school but the coordination of community members as well. The Audrey Cohen College System of Education requires that all elementary schools initially employ a full-time reform facilitator in order to "support and facilitate the implementation of the system" (Cohen and Jordan 1996: 49). Their functions, as compared to SFA, are a bit less specific. They include maintaining regular contact with the College and "assist[ing] teachers both in implementation and in developing community networks" (ibid.). These facilitators, or "resource specialists," as they are referred to by the College, are required for only one to three years, at which point it is presumed that "the resource specialists functions will be taken over by faculty and other staff" (ibid.). In Sunland

County, the facilitators were initially paid by College, as the schools were chosen as demonstration sites.

At one of the Audrey Cohen sites, the facilitator performed the functions of her position by meeting with grade level teams twice a month, offering assistance to teachers in incorporating the AC curriculum, helping teachers plan constructive actions for their students in the community, and training new teachers. She appeared overwhelmed by the support teachers required, and even developed a form that teachers could complete to request her assistance. Teachers found her involvement helpful, but argued that perhaps there was enough work for two lead teachers, as they often had to wait for the support they requested from her.

In sum, the job of facilitator combines administrative and curricular activities, in and sometimes outside the school. The most successful facilitators were those that saw themselves as change agents and who organized their activities to fully support the reforms. While many teachers and principals appreciated their efforts, facilitators understandably often found it difficult to perform their myriad of duties and keep teachers, principals, and design teams satisfied at all times. In this regard, whether or not the structure and culture of the school and the agency of other educators supported their activities was critical.

Facilitators' Relationships with Teachers

Reform facilitators worked in various ways to forge positive working relationships with teachers. Invariably, they encountered some obstacles due to the power relations existing in the schools, or due to the anxiety that the reforms induced among teachers. In some schools, developing relationships was particularly difficult at the beginning because facilitators had no more experience with the reforms than the teachers whom they were expected to mentor and/or monitor. A teacher in one school described this stage as "the blind leading the blind." Whereas principals had their institutional position of power to rely upon in their dealings with teachers, facilitators had to establish themselves as a trusted authority.

The relationships the Core Knowledge facilitator at Jetty Elementary had with teachers are revealing of the ambiguities of the facilitator position. Some teachers reported that they found her classroom visits helpful and neither intimidating nor threatening. "I see her as an equal," stated one teacher. On the other hand, a few teachers complained that she took the place of a classroom teacher when her position was no longer grant funded. One resentful teacher felt that while "she was pulled out of the classroom to be the Core resource," she was now "basically private secretary to the principal." As these statements show, some teachers saw her as classroom teacher, whereas others saw her as not even an administrator, but more nearly as an administrative assistant.

Some facilitators tried to portray themselves as teachers who were simply not engaged in classroom teaching. For example, one SFA facilitator said that she reminded herself that she was "just a teacher," and that she couldn't tell other teachers what to do. But regardless of how facilitators viewed themselves, teachers consistently viewed them as quasi-adminis-trators more than as teachers. This was compounded by the fact that the SFA facilitators were required to monitor teachers' implementation of the curriculum, as well as mentor them. The teachers in one school referred to the facilitator as the "SFA boss" or "Mrs. SFA." She found such attitudes from her long-time teacher colleagues upsetting: "It's kind of hurtful when teach-ers say, 'Oh, you're Mrs. SFA. Better do it your way.'"

The facilitators in a few schools had more difficulty in their relations with staff, in part because some teachers used them as scapegoats for their problems with the reforms. The principal at one school explained, "Teachers blamed her personally when things didn't go well. She was an easy target . . . It became a struggle between her and the staff." The same was true at another school where the facilitator was also blamed for not doing her job properly, thus contributing to the demise of the reform. These incidents are evidence of how the ambiguities of the role placed facilitators in the middle of staff micropolitics related to the reform.

Facilitators' Relationships with Principals

Not only did the quasi-administrative status of facilitators raise questions about their authority in dealing with teachers; it also led to ambiguities in their relationships with principals. We found variation in how closely prin-cipals and facilitators worked together. The nature of their relationship was influenced by how each person conceived of the boundaries of his or her role and the context for leadership in each school. Again, relations of power came into play as principals and facilitators negotiated ways to jointly lead reform.

In two Success for All schools, it seemed that the principal and facili-tator worked in very close partnership with each other. Both of these principals were women, as were the facilitators. The facilitator at one site remarked about the principal, "I can have her ear anytime I want. I mean, I have no qualms about walking in and talking to her anytime." The prin-cipal and facilitator at this school shared the leadership for the reform in the following way, as the principal described, "[The facilitator] and I have worked out a real nice system where she's the good guy and I'm the bad guy." She felt that her position as principal allowed her to enforce the implementation of SFA with more power than the facilitator had. Also, whereas the facilitator's relationship with teachers was somewhat fragile, the principal could bear the brunt of teachers' criticism without losing institutional power. This arrangement worked well for this pair.

At Madison High School, the AVID coordinator also jointly led the reform with the principal as described earlier. Under these conditions, the program thrived at the school, as well as district wide. However, when in 1998, the principal left the school, the context for leadership changed. While the new principal was supportive of AVID and of the coordinator's efforts more generally, he had his own reform agenda, and a much more directive leadership style. He expected her to not only lead AVID, but other new initiatives as well.

Some principals wanted to more nearly delegate the leadership role to facilitators, expecting the facilitator to adopt a position of power with respect to reform implementation. The principal at one Audrey Cohen school relied so heavily on the facilitator to lead the reform efforts at the school that she did not feel the reform could continue without him. When the district decided to no longer fund the reform facilitator in the school's third year of implementation, the principal was devastated. She remarked, "I don't have time to do this. I'm a principal . . . Without a facilitator, it's just not going to happen." And it needed to be that facilitator in particular. As she explained, "He *was* the program. Literally." The facilitator had come to embody the reform. She saw the facilitator as leading the reform – and herself as leading the school.

The constraints of the facilitators' own definitions of their roles and school structures created tensions for some facilitators. In one school, the facilitator worried that if she were to adopt a role that assumed more power in enforcement of implementation, the strong teachers' union, of which she was, ironically, a member, might intervene. She said: "If I start going out on a limb and saying, 'This is what we'll do,' then it starts looking like I'm the administrator . . . So I've got to be very careful."

She worried that her position as facilitator was not only ambiguous in function, it was also ambiguous in form, "It's never been written up. I mean, I'm just out of the classroom doing this job, and nobody's ever written anything about it." Formal employment policies typically do not exist to function as safety nets for teacher leaders in these types of positions (Hart 1995). While some reform design manuals include written expectations for facilitators, these guidelines may not fit with the job descriptions set up by teachers' unions or school boards.

Overall, the facilitator or reform coordinator position involved considerable challenges in terms of roles and relationships. First, facilitators were expected to be instant authorities on a program developed by an outside group. Second, facilitators had the status and pay of other teachers, yet they were sometimes required to monitor teachers' implementation of the program and work in partnership with the principal in leading the reform. They needed to engender the trust and collegiality of the teachers, some of whom viewed them as administrators. Finally, facilitators had to delicately establish new working relationships with principals, who themselves were often unaccustomed to negotiating leadership responsibilities with a teacher leader.

Who are Facilitators and Why?

Being a facilitator or coordinator did allow for a teacher to assume a spot in the limelight and to work closely with the principal. These were also positions that provided new challenges for an experienced teacher who had mastered her craft. In some cases, being chosen as the facilitator was akin to being nominated as a mentor teacher, and thus it was perceived as an honor. However, while the position of facilitator brought with it a leadership role and added responsibility, compensation was on a teacher salary scale. This is unlike some other teacher leadership opportunities, such as mentor teaching or career ladders, which are accompanied by additional financial rewards (Hart 1995).

From a compensation-in-relation-to-stress standpoint, the job of facilitator was not necessarily appealing. Why, then, would a teacher choose to take on this position? Aside from the leadership opportunities described above, an examination of gender issues provides some insight. The overwhelming majority of the facilitators and coordinators were women – in fact, middle-aged women. Prior research shows that women teachers often pursue promotion, greater responsibility, and involvement in reform after age forty when their families are no longer as dependent upon them (Sikes *et al.* 1985; Hubbard and Datnow 2000).

Additionally, one might argue that because the large majority of elementary school teachers are women (Apple 1994), it is more likely that women would be found occupying the facilitator position at the elementary level. Yet, despite the small number of male teachers in elementary settings, these men are often encouraged to aspire to the leadership positions of assistant principal or principal. In fact, 57 percent of elementary school principals are men (Leadership 1993). The overrepresentation of women in teacher leadership positions (e.g. as AVID coordinators) is even more striking at the high school level, where men comprise approximately 50 percent of the teaching force and 81 percent of all principals (Leadership 1993). So why are men not also seizing these new leadership opportunities or being chosen to become reform facilitators or coordinators?

The fact that most of the facilitators and coordinators in our study were women may suggest that these teacher leadership positions are inadvertently gendered from both functional and compensation standpoints. As we explained earlier, the structure of the AVID program as one in which providing social supports to students is an explicit component also attracts women teachers to the position, as well as inspiring principals to look to women to fill these positions (Hubbard and Datnow 2000). Similarly, in the case of Success for All, many of the desired attributes of the facilitator that are listed in the facilitator handbook (e.g., people skills, a real love and concern for children, cooperative and understanding) are commonly associated with women, rather than with men (Datnow and Castellano 2000a).

To be sure, women teachers may have been chosen as facilitators and coordinators because they exhibited some of the qualities of successful women principals, such as emphasizing caring and collaboration (Regan and Brooks 1995) and giving primacy to teaching and learning (Restine 1993). However, these positions required persons willing to take on time-consuming and difficult jobs, yet without extra compensation as compared to a classroom teacher. Women have historically been more likely than men to occupy jobs that are inadequately compensated. The high representation of women as facilitators is thus significant in terms of understanding these teacher leadership positions and the functions they served in schools.

Conclusions and Implications

In this chapter, we explored the agency of principals, teachers, and teacher leaders in the school reform process. In doing so, we illustrated some of the often unexamined dynamics involved in scaling up reforms, especially how people's interactions with each other and with the reforms changed the professional lives of educators. We explained the range of actions taken by principals in response to reforms and the variation in how principals' leadership styles meshed with reform demands. In each case, principals believed that their approach, which was consistent with their ideologies, would lead to a better implementation of the reform and/or to school improvement. The implementation of reforms influenced the activities and relationships of some principals, who delegated leadership to teachers, spent more time involved with instruction, and developed networks outside the school. In other words, principals' actions shaped the implementation of the reform, and the reform in turn shaped principals' activities.

Not surprisingly, teachers acted in a variety of ways in response to reforms, often within the same school as well as across schools and reform designs. In some cases, teachers' ideological differences about education and the need for reform led to these different forms of agency in reform; in other cases, teachers' personal characteristics were important, such as gender or experience level. There was variation in the levels of teacher empowerment and teacher learning that took place in concert with reform implementation. To be sure, many of the reforms did offer opportunities for teacher empowerment or learning of one type or another, whether through leadership opportunities, learning new skills, or developing curriculum. All paths that teachers took, however, were joint products of the teachers and their ideologies and experiences, the structure and culture existing in the school, the context for leadership, and the reform itself. Not all teachers' experiences with reform were positive. Some teachers experienced feelings of stress as a result of their experiences with reforms.

The facilitator or reform coordinator position was essential for the successful implementation of many reforms. Yet, it is a difficult position that seemed to involve constant negotiation, ambiguity, and tensions with respect to their roles and relationships with principals and with teachers. The quasi-administrative status of facilitators meant that they lacked formal authority in dealing with teachers or with principals. Like other teacher leaders (Smylie and Denny 1990; Muncey and McQuillan 1996), the facilitators occupied a netherworld that was neither that of the administrator nor that of the teacher. This role ambiguity sometimes constrained their ability to mentor (and in some cases, monitor) teachers' implementation and do what their principals sometimes expected of them. This was compounded by the fact that principals had varied conceptions of the roles that facilitators would occupy as reform leaders, and they themselves varied in their skills at collaboration and reform leadership.

The findings from this chapter on the changing activities and relationships of educators engaged in the implementation of externally developed reforms yield the following implications for policy and practice:

- *Principals need to be instructional leaders of reforms, not just manage or support them from a distance, and design teams need to promote this vision of principal leadership*

For principals to effectively lead reform efforts, they need to know what is happening in classrooms. This dictum implies that principals have or develop knowledge of curriculum content and effective instructional practices. If reforms are not impacting what happens in the classroom between teachers and students, then they are not likely to lead to school improvement. Design teams would be well advised to assist principals in becoming instructional leaders in their schools.

- *Teacher buy-in to reform should be present at the outset or cultivated quickly. Teacher resistance to reform must be confronted, rather than ignored*

When teachers have not bought into the reform effort, they see little reason for it and resist the changes that are asked of them. No doubt, there are always teachers who resist reforms – whether created by groups inside or outside the school. At the same time, these issues need to be directly addressed, because unhappy groups of teachers, however small, can derail reform efforts or at least lower staff morale around the reform.

- *External reform designs need to build in ample opportunities for teacher empowerment*

Commitment to reform designs and to actual school improvement occurs when teachers feel empowered. As we have shown, teacher empowerment can be facilitated through a variety of means – new responsibilities for leadership, working with colleagues in genuine collaborative activities, planning new and exciting lessons. Design teams need to actively cultivate such opportunities.

- *Districts should formalize policy regarding teacher leadership positions and modify working conditions to account for the burdensome responsibilities of these jobs*

The hardworking individuals who devote themselves to facilitating or co-ordinating reforms need adequate compensation, removal of other non-academic responsibilities, and increased support. Raising salaries is one obvious way to do this. Providing extra time to handle additional burdens is another possible option. Unless the extra burdens and additional responsibilities are recognized formally, coordinators risk burnout, which would have dire consequences for reforms in the many schools that rely so heavily on these persons. While it will take school cultures some time to adjust to the new roles of teacher leaders, policy changes at the district level might impact the power relations between teachers, facilitators, and principals in useful ways.

5   Building the Plane While It's Flying: The Evolving Design Team

Those of us who study school change tend to presume that schools are the locus of change, and thus we often do not pay sufficient attention to the changes that occur in other arenas, near to and far from them. In previous chapters, we have foregrounded the actions and perspectives of individuals inside schools, connecting them to actions and events occurring elsewhere. As we have argued throughout this book, because contexts are inevitably connected to each other (Sarason 1997), contexts throughout the system must be considered. Here, we focus on the connections between design teams, schools, and state and local policies.

As our previous chapters make abundantly clear, reform efforts do not proceed in a linear fashion, fixed in time and space. The vector of change does not flow in just one direction. That is, educators' actions in schools are not just influenced "top-down" by the actions of design teams, but so too the actions of design teams are also influenced "bottom-up" by the actions of educators in schools, as well as by other forces existing in different spheres. These forces are cultural, political, and technical (Oakes and Lipton 1992), and may or may not occur simultaneously, as we will explain.

The Paucity of Information on Design Team Change

To date, there has not been much research on how design teams change over time, nor on how their metamorphoses might impact schools. The work that has been done about how design teams change has often been written by people inside the organizations, or by those with close affiliations (e.g., Hatch 1998a, b; Marble and Stephens 1999; McDonald *et al.* 1999; Slavin and Madden 1998). This is not surprising, as most organizations are reticent to expose themselves to outsiders. As Tharp (2000: 6) reflects, this reticence can extend to research groups as well:

> Some years ago, I led an educational research-and-development organization, and became interested in studying the development of the organization itself. I provided an anthropologist with access to all our staff meetings, consultations, and supervisory interactions so that we researchers were observed regularly as we worked, just as our teachers were observed in their classrooms. None of us would ever again underestimate the impact of being observed!

Because it is likely much harder to secure funding to study teams design-ing reform than to study schools implementing reform, design teams have often "studied" themselves. The ATLAS reform design team engaged in extensive self- and external study during the development of their reform model (see Hatch 1998a, 1998b; Hatch and White 1997; McDonald *et al.* 1999). The dynamics among reform leaders have been carefully docu-mented and serve as a very interesting eye into "*school reform behind the scenes*," which is in fact the title of McDonald and colleagues' (1999) book. This book also includes a cogent and insightful examination of the various reform organizations that came together to form ATLAS, namely the Comer School Development Program, the Coalition of Essential Schools, Project Zero, and the Education Development Center.

The inner workings of ATLAS have perhaps been examined in more detail than those of any other design team. However, other design teams have also described their evolution over a period of years. Slavin *et al.* (1996) and Slavin and Madden (1998) have documented their own experi-ences with the development and dissemination of Success for All, some of which are discussed below. They offer an open insider perspective, in con-trast to the inside–outside perspective offered by McDonald and colleagues. Similarly, Marble and Stephens (1999) reflect upon the challenges and suc-cesses they have encountered in disseminating the Accelerated Schools reform through "satellite centers." Despite these notable exceptions, there is a paucity of research on how design teams and their reform models change, and much less on how design team changes impact the schools engaged in reform.

In this chapter, we discuss how and why design teams change, draw-ing upon our observations of and interviews with representatives of various design teams in regional and national offices, as well as our interviews with educators in schools. To be clear, we conclude that the loci of change are *both* the design teams as organizations and the reform models associated with them. We examine how design teams evolve in response to growth in the use of their models, to school or district demands, and to political and market forces. In some cases, as we will explain, this evolution has meant that design teams must operate increasingly like efficient businesses. We discuss the consequences of these changes for the design teams and their work with schools.

We argue that design teams often change their organizational forms and their reform models even as they work with schools. Whether design teams (and their associated reforms) were founded five or twenty years ago, we have found that they are constantly evolving. For example, reflect-ing back to the early stage of the development of the AVID model, Mary Catherine Swanson recalled that, "there was no grand plan, no synthesis of the literature, nor formal hypothesis development or systematic collection of data." She was trying to figure out, in her own way, how best to help minority students who were stuck in low track classes (Hubbard and Ottoson 1997: 43). Change occurred incrementally and over time influenced by Swanson's observations of students' learning. Swanson's depiction of the moral origins and seat-of-the-pants developments of AVID reinforce Houle's (1980: 104) observation, "In times of change the practitioner learns by trial and error, relying on associates, seeking advice, reading . . . and using other available resources."

Indeed, several of the design teams described themselves as being in a state of continual learning, progressively refining their model and their approach to working with schools. "We're always moving . . ." explained a design team member at the Comer School Development Program, a model that has been in existence for over 30 years. As we will show, the dynamics of change within the design teams lend a "building the plane while it's flying" quality to the entire scale up process.

In the section that follows we discuss the organizational changes that took place in design teams as a result of interactions with schools, state agencies, and funding sources. We discuss only the changes that occurred during the time period of our studies, acknowledging of course that many other changes have undoubtedly taken place before, during, and after we were there. By virtue of the fact that design teams are in a constant state of change, much of what we report here may be out of date by the time this book is published. A look at each organization's web site from year to year gives a different way of seeing the rapid developments that take place in design teams. Alas, due to the nature of Internet technology and the need to be constantly up to date, these web sites often erase the history of development within these and other organizations.

Organizational Changes in Design Teams

The advent of the Comprehensive Reform Demonstration (CSRD) program has spurred tremendous growth in the demand for services from design teams. As we explained before, CSRD, based on the bipartisan Porter-Obey Amendments of 1998, provides for $145 million of federal funding to go to schools adopting "research-based reform" models. The majority of the funding is allocated for Title I schools. In 2000, Congress added an additional $75 million to CSRD so that 1000 more schools could be funded. As Hatch (2000: 342) points out, "the creation of the CSRD Program sent a strong message that the time is right to scale up comprehensive designs around the country."

We are just beginning to see the impact of CSRD on the scale up of reforms. Commenting on the potential impact of CSRD on the consequent growth in the number of schools adopting reforms on their own and other design teams, as Slavin and Madden (1998: 9) predict, "All existing programs will be struggling to add training capacity without reducing quality." This prediction has in fact been fulfilled. More schools wish to adopt reforms than most design teams have the capacity to serve. A member of one design team stated, "We've had a real increase in interest and in trying to support those schools, we've been careful about not taking on too many." In other cases, responding to interest in their programs before establishing the capacity to implement them has arguably led some design teams to scale up too fast.

The scale up of reforms to a greater density of schools, both through CSRD and other forces, has spurred organizational changes on the part of design teams. As we explain below, some design teams have evolved from university-supported or state-supported status to become separate non-profit organizations in order to allow their organizational capacity to keep pace with growth. Design teams have also developed increasingly complex organizational structures in order to serve an increasing number of schools in regions around the country, some of which may be far away from their home base. Design teams have also faced challenges in recruiting and orienting a qualified cadre of staff when more and more schools call for their reform models.

Shifting Funding Status from Public-Supported to Non-Profit Organizations

Success for All

Nowhere are the challenges of responding to the demands created by rapid scale up more apparent than with Success for All, which is perhaps the fastest growing reform model in the U.S. Success for All was first piloted in an elementary school in Baltimore in 1987, expanding to six schools the following year. In the past ten years, the number of schools using SFA has grown by 50–100 percent each year. As of 2000, there were over 1600 schools in 44 U.S. states and five foreign countries implementing SFA. In the period of 1995–1998, when most of the schools we studied took on SFA, the total number of schools using SFA quadrupled, having sextupled in the three years prior (Slavin and Madden 1998). The period of exponential growth of SFA nationwide was mirrored by the growth of SFA in Sunland County, which went from 6 SFA schools in 1995–1996 to 48 schools in the following year.

This rapid growth placed a tremendous strain on limited district resources and an already taxed design team, causing support at the pre-existing Sunland SFA schools to decrease. Administrators and staff at these schools complained that they received materials late. Others grumbled that they did not receive feedback at key points during their implementation or training for their new teachers. One SFA principal complained that he and his teachers felt like the design team's "adopted stepchildren" who were "left out of the loop" when the new schools came on. The lack of attention this school received so frustrated educators that it contributed to their decision to drop the reform two years later. An SFA trainer who worked with these schools acknowledged, "I don't think we were responsive enough. We just didn't have . . . You just couldn't be," given the large number of new schools requiring support.

As the developers of SFA humbly stated, "The problem we have faced is how to provide such an intensive level of service on a broad scale . . . We have had to continually restructure ourselves to accommodate this growth without compromising on quality, and will continue to do so for the foreseeable future. We still have a long way to go" (Slavin and Madden 1998: 8). The chief change in the design team's configuration was its move from the Center for Social Organization of Schools at Johns Hopkins University to a separate, non-profit organization, the Success for All Foundation (SFAF). The design team found that creating an efficient organization and securing operating capital were difficult to do within the university when the program grew to so many schools. Slavin and Madden (1998: 19) explain: "On our side, the University's salary scales, policies, and practices were constant impediments to growth . . . On the University's side, the size and complexity of our operation were very difficult and time consuming to manage, and the University was understandably uncomfortable advancing us ever-larger amounts of capital each spring," to cover the deficit until schools paid for their services in the fall.

Slavin and Madden (1998: 19–20) also indicate that while the lure of being a for-profit organization was the ease of raising capital through venture firms and other sources, they chose the non-profit route in order to maintain an "institutional ethos that focused on what is best for the children, not what is best for profits and investors." They were also concerned about public perceptions and wanted to make certain that profits "would go back into development, research, and quality control, not into investors or taxes." However, becoming a non-profit organization had some costs, as they explain, because banks would not loan the foundation money until they had substantial assets. Eventually, SFAF raised $3.5 million in grants and loans from two family foundations and New American Schools and then were able to get a line of credit with a bank. However, they remain "seriously undercapitalized" for an organization of their size and scope.

Adding to fundraising challenges presented by non-profit status has been the need to recruit individuals to fulfill functions formerly dealt with by university personnel, such as finance, accounting, insurance, technology, and space. SFAF brought people with these specialties on board and relocated offices at the same time that their number of schools increased by almost 50 percent. As of 2000, the foundation employed over 350 people. Overall, the move to a non-profit status has been challenging, but the SFAF directors believe that in the long run it will be the best way for them to effectively work with schools.

AVID

Like SFA, one of the most significant changes in the AVID design team was the move to become a non-profit organization. This organizational change occurred in response to the rapid growth of the program outside of San Diego County during the 1990s. Early dissemination efforts of the AVID program had been supported by professional development funds from the State of California and the San Diego County Office of Education. In fact, the program was based in the county office. When AVID expanded outside of San Diego County, the county superintendent recognized that the San Diego County Office could not provide support and assistance to school districts outside the county and, indeed the country, as the Department of Defense was adopting AVID for schools on their military bases.

The director of finance for AVID Center said AVID became a non-profit organization because they "had to find a vehicle to allow them [to benefit students]." As a non-profit and a public charity, AVID is able to take advantage of tax benefits that allow them to offer services at a lower cost. She said we are "not concerned with making money . . . We're concerned with keeping AVID healthy so we can continue to operate the program."

While this reorganization has been advantageous because it enables AVID to serve a national and indeed an international constituency, it has also presented a new set of contingencies. AVID needs a constant revenue stream, some of which comes from schools in the form of Certification, Consultation and Networking (CCN) fees and copyright and licensing fees for AVID curriculum materials. The CCN fee is designed to keep AVID schools connected to the AVID Center for program innovation and research, to fund the Center's costs in the certification process, and fund the cost of *Access,* AVID's quarterly newsletter. These new financial arrangements have created some misconceptions and misgivings among some long-time AVID "customers" inside of California who joined AVID at the outset, however, when these charges did not yet exist.

The change in AVID to its current non-profit status, although made in response to local and national needs, has created a very specific set of business practices that in turn have caused significant challenges for AVID Center. As AVID has grown, it has required expanded facilities and a larger staff. While unequivocally this growth is beneficial for the students it is designed to help, it has become in many ways a Catch 22. With expansion comes the need for additional revenues for salary support.

AVID has moved closer to a business status with all its accoutrements. AVID must now escalate its efforts in marketing, research, development, and face increasingly complex human resource issues. AVID, like SFA, must continue to negotiate the dilemma of appearing altruistic and benevolent while wrestling with the need to meet the costs of running a business. The extent to which externally developed educational reform design teams such as SFA and AVID can negotiate this dilemma will be instrumental in determining their long-term success.

Coalition of Essential Schools

The Coalition of Essential Schools, which in 2000 involved over 1000 schools at various levels of membership, also became a separate non-profit organization when it moved from Brown University (in Providence, Rhode Island), directed by its founder Ted Sizer, to Oakland, California in 1997, directed at that time by Amy Gerstein. The establishment of a governing board accompanied the Coalition's move to a non-profit organization. When CES was based at Brown, they did not have a separate governing board, instead, they utilized the university's own board of trustees. Thus, most decisions were made by the design team, without external monitoring. When CES became a non-profit organization, it established a large, active board comprised of educators from the regional centers, as well as representatives from businesses, foundations, and higher education institutions. A member of the CES staff explained the changes in how decisions are made:

> In the old days, people in Providence would say, "well, I think we need this kind of project, what do you think?" "Yeah, I think that sounds like a good idea. I think that's what people in the field need." Well now we actually have mechanisms in place for people in the field to say, "this is a priority for us. We need help with this." . . .

Another significant change was the establishment of a national congress of 75–100 representatives from across the country who are "a democratic body that sets the direction and the big priorities of the Coalition," stated a design team member at CES. However, as the CES team member went on to explain, democracy is hard work, even for an organization that is explicitly committed to democratic principles: "It's really challenging for us to keep the conversations going and to articulate the common good, and it's exhausting for everybody. But it's really the right thing to do."

Amy Gerstein, CES's former executive director, was reportedly very deliberate about modeling democratic processes among staff at the national office. Mirroring the types of difficulties school principals face, she grappled with which decisions should be made by the whole group and which should be made at the management level. Another change, in keeping with CES's commitment to equity, was the hiring of a staff that is fifty-percent persons of color, which was unprecedented in the organization's history. In another significant move, the Coalition has also devolved most of its work to regional centers, a change that is explained in the next section.

A member of the CES national staff commented about the organizational changes that have taken place in the past several years, "We had to morph in a way that I don't think any of these other groups have. Like totally change our stripes, which we have." Since our interviews took place in 1999, CES has morphed again – the national congress voted to disband itself and CES has a new executive director, Hudi Podolsky.

Modern Red Schoolhouse

The evolution of the Modern Red Schoolhouse design team into a non-profit organization is an interesting case in point as it occurred somewhat in response to the growth of the reform in schools, but also due to differences with the initial parent organization. A member of the design team explained that for the first five years the Hudson Institute, a conservative think tank in Washington, DC, served as the "incubator" of the reform design, which was initially funded through New American Schools.

In 1997, circumstances began to change when Hudson's president, who had been a major advocate for the reform, resigned. In addition, "cultural incongruities between a group providing technical assistance to schools and a think tank" began to emerge, explained a member of the design team. Beacon, a for-profit company that manages charter schools, agreed to provide capital to allow the MRSh design team to become independent and relocate. Due to problems with control issues, the relationship between Beacon and MRSh lasted only a few months. "So we struck out on our own," explained a member of the design team, into a non-profit organization, a move that she described as "fairly terrifying" at first. "We had all the traumas that a new organization would have," she added, such as cash flow. The Modern Red Schoolhouse Institute is led by Sally Kilgore and is now based in Nashville and serves more than 80 schools nationwide as of 2000. This number has doubled since the advent of CSRD in 1998.

In summary, moving to non-profit status has brought both benefits and costs to these design teams. In Chapter 3, we said teachers' cultural beliefs mediated reforms-as designed and reforms-as enacted. We also found that technical concerns such as efficiency, cost and the political perception of an organization as being for children and not for profit have influenced changes in organizational arrangements. The benefits included more autonomy and control for Modern Red, ability to efficiently serve a larger number of schools in the case of AVID and SFAF, and a more democratic form of organization in the case of CES. However, there were also costs to being a non-profit, including being responsive to governing boards, meeting payroll, developing technical specialists on staff. The design teams we studied were willing to bear these costs in order to avoid a corporate, profit-driven image.

In recognition of the challenges of non-profit status, in 2000, the New American Schools Corporation launched a fund of $15.7 million to provide loans and technical assistance to its design teams and to districts working with them. Contributors to the fund include private foundations, the U.S. Department of Education, and companies, such as Prudential Insurance, which on its own committed $10 million. "The fund was motivated to give nonprofits a level playing field in the market," said the vice president of the NAS fund, quoted in an article in *Education Week* (Olsen 2000: 8). Underpinning this rationale is the fact that for-profit groups will also be eligible for loans.

We should note that the Audrey Cohen System of Education is based at Audrey Cohen College in New York, and the Comer SDP project is still based at Yale University, after many years. In other words, these design teams have maintained their university affiliations. The Core Knowledge Foundation has also maintained its original form, operating as non-profit since its founding in 1986; though its director and founder, E. D. Hirsch, is a professor at the University of Virginia. While these design teams have not changed organizational forms as the others have, they have dealt with other organizational issues including the need to establish regional training sites and developing cadres of qualified staff, which we discuss below.

Developing Organizational Complexity

In addition to redefining organizations from public- or state-supported in order to enable organizational capacity to keep pace with program and site growth, design teams added layers of organizational complexity to efficiently and effectively serve schools located in states across the U.S. For design teams serving larger numbers of schools, this has meant the dispersion of the design team into regional divisions, due in some cases to local educators' demands and in other cases due to organizational capacity or constraints. Other design teams serving smaller numbers of schools, such as Audrey Cohen College and Modern Red Schoolhouse, have attempted to fund a local educator or a field trainer to support implementation in particular locales.

Establishing Regional Offices to Handle Growth

AVID is an example of a design team that has established a regional division, both as a response to growth in the use of the program far away from its home base and due to the influence of educators in those distant regions. In particular, educators in Kentucky and Virginia reacted negatively to design features required by AVID Center, especially the need to attend professional development institutes in California. They also resisted the curricular materials designed for the California audience. In response to these locally generated concerns, AVID Center made a significant organizational adjustment. AVID Center secured a multiyear grant from the Dana Foundation to establish an "Eastern Division" office in White Wake, Virginia. The Eastern Division Office assumed professional development, personnel, and recruiting responsibilities for 12 states from the AVID Center in San Diego.

One educator described the value of this new organizational arrangement: "AVID could blow up into the next best thing since sliced bread, I mean it really could. But if you don't listen to those in the trenches, you lose, you just do." Respectful of the potential for AVID and realizing the need to "listen to those in the trenches," the Eastern Division Office serves as a mediator between AVID Center and the school sites in its jurisdiction. One AVID official with the Eastern Division explains the benefits of this regional office this way:

> I think having an east coast center really helps the Eastern Division see the relevance of AVID. Sometimes when you go to a state like California or New Mexico, you see a different minority population and you wonder about the applicability of AVID in your division, whereas here what [minority population] they see in White Wake is what you would see in North Carolina, it's what you see in Georgia.

The regional office made AVID constituents feel that the program and its curriculum addressed their local needs. In strictly economic terms, this modification means AVID teachers can be educated less expensively. Educators from eastern states now attend professional development institutes in Virginia rather than California, which saves these educators a considerable amount of money. In more socio-cultural terms, this modification illustrates how a design team can transport its prototype program to additional sites while remaining sensitive to concerns in the local context.

Establishing Regional Training Sites for Quality Control

The top priorities for increasing organizational complexity by establishing regional training sites for Success for All have been quality control and consistency. Over the years, the design team has experimented with different ways to disseminate their program and serve local sites effectively. The most prevalent approach currently used by SFAF is regionally-based training sites staffed with full-time SFAF employees, some of whom work in offices and others who work out of their homes. There is also a regional training program for SFA based at the University of Memphis.

Slavin and Madden (1998) argue that unlike other design teams, such as Accelerated Schools and Reading Recovery, that have used universities as regional training sites, SFA has not lent itself easily to this approach. This is because SFA calls upon individuals to work with schools for extended time periods and in a prescribed fashion, a practice that does not fit particularly well with university norms and structures. Efforts to recruit universities as SFA training sites have not been fruitful, with the exception of the University of Memphis. The partnership between SFA and Memphis relies on the high motivation, skill, and commitment of two faculty members there, their close relationship with local districts, and their prior experience in conducting research on SFA (Slavin and Madden 1998).

Education Partners (EP), a company in California, formerly operated as the largest regional trainer for SFA, serving approximately 130 schools. In 1998, SFAF limited the further expansion of the Education Partners due to its for-profit status, believing it has led to political and legal problems: "It has led to concerns at the IRS in terms of our [SFAF's] not-for-profit status, and concerns in teachers' unions and policy circles about our motives" (ibid.). In 2000, SFAF ended its relationship with Education Partners completely. Here again, the SFA design team has chosen to resist an increased connection with a corporate form in order to continue to be perceived as operating for the benefits of educators and students.

The SFAF's concern for quality control in its regional centers is also exemplified through its dissolution of their partnership with WestEd. Until 1998, the design team engaged WestEd, a federally-funded regional educational laboratory, to serve as a regional training site in the western region. However, this relationship ultimately proved problematic. According to Slavin and Madden (1998: 12), "WestEd reinterpreted SFA policies, failed to implement various program elements, or otherwise insisted on its own approaches." In the end, SFAF reclaimed this region.

As a result of their experiences, SFAF's dominant approach to professional development is region-based, with full-time SFA employees in 8 regions housed within 4 areas. This arrangement, as Slavin and Madden (1998: 14) interpret, "gives us far more control and assurance to fidelity than does engaging regional training sites in universities or other existing agencies, which may have their own agendas and constraints." SFAF recruits trainers from schools, usually former SFA facilitators and teachers, who have expert local knowledge. This allows them to attract personnel who may not be willing to move to Baltimore, which the design team required in the past. The schools and districts now no longer have to pay trainers' travel costs; however, SFAF has to bear the cost of bringing the trainers to Baltimore for meetings and supporting their home offices. Despite these costs and the problems with coordination that sometimes arise, the regionally-based training staff approach is the only dissemination model that the foundation plans to employ in the future.

Using Regional Trainers to Advance Systemic Change

The Comer SDP design team, which is based at the Yale University Child Study Center in New Haven, Connecticut, supports implementation in school districts through Comer SDP centers, university partners, national faculty, and facilitators in school districts and/or in schools. More recently, the design team has also tried to support individual schools by moving towards what they call a "systems" approach. Since 1995, the design team has consciously attempted to enroll many schools in a particular district, instead of just one. This strategy was borne out of a belief that "the best way to sustain change in schools is to have input at the district level," explained a design team member. With a critical mass of schools, the design team hoped that the program would then matter to the district and they could "create change not only at the school level but at the district level." They encourage districts to appoint a Comer SDP district facilitator to serve as a liaison between schools and the district. The facilitator can then coach schools locally after having received training in the Comer process. The design team has been able to develop these relationships with numerous districts. In some places, the systems approach is working very well. In other cases, it has been more difficult due to administrative turnover or other external pressures, such as the threat of state takeover of low performing schools. Thus, Comer SDP sees itself as a mediator between schools and districts; using gains and successes won with schools and teachers to influence districts' policies; not so much top-down or bottom-up, but sideways or outside in!

The recent advent of CSRD has also posed a challenge to the Comer design team's systemic approach. The legislation is written so that individual schools can adopt reforms, not exclusively groups of schools within a district. Thus, while the design team would prefer to work with cadres of schools in particular locations, they now are adapting to find ways to support individual schools. They have recruited educators from schools that have been implementing Comer for a long time and who are interested in doing part-time consulting work. These people are called "national faculty members," and are paid a stipend to serve as implementation coordinators in locations around the country, where Comer design team staff are not located and where there is not a systemic change effort at the district level. In effect, this design team has adapted their support mechanisms as new political arrangements and circumstances have arisen. By using a variety of approaches, they address the needs of schools operating in different circumstances without diluting their theory of action.

Decentralizing to Achieve Local Control

Like the Comer School Development Program, the Coalition of Essential Schools now functions in a decentralized fashion, since the move from Brown University in 1998. The small national office in Oakland of 11 people focuses on public advocacy, research, development, fundraising, and management of the CES reform. Virtually all of the school support work takes places out of 20+ regional centers. The regional centers provide professional development, coaching, networking, and/or advocacy at the district and community levels for schools. However, in keeping with the Coalition's belief in democracy, they all work in slightly different ways to support schools and they are all locally, rather than centrally, administrated. Offerings from centers range from critical friends groups to peer mentoring programs or teacher-as-researcher projects, among others. Unlike AVID, Success for All or Comer SDP design teams, there is no "set" training that all regional centers provide, and no effort to systematize their activities.

The regional centers also vary in size and structure. Some regional centers, such as the Bay Area Coalition, are non-profit organizations, while others have their home in universities, such as the New Mexico Elementary Network Center. One regional center is housed in a district office. This is known as an "unofficial" regional center, however, because CES does feel it is prudent for a district to control a center. Some centers are staffed by 15–20 people, whereas another might have just one person working from home. The intent is for the centers to be "horizontal" in structure and "owned by the schools," explained one regional center director. A concern for some centers is not growing too large so they can continue to serve schools effectively. Stated one director, "We're really into less is more. We realize that we have to have our critical mass to maintain funding. But it's quality versus quantity, and deep work versus work. You can't do deep work with large numbers."

The CES national office is deliberately trying to remain small so that the regional centers can grow. The national office exists on grant funding alone and some of the regional centers also raise grants of their own. However, some of the regional centers are also partially funded through the fees some schools pay for coaching services. This fee-for-service arrangement has increased as a result of CSRD, as new CES schools contract with regional centers for coaching and professional development. While the fees do help support center work, it has also brought challenges. As a CES national staff member explained, "moving to fee-for-service changes the nature of your relationship with schools and changes the way you think about your work."

With the advent of CSRD, the Coalition has been careful to tell interested new sites that they can only serve schools in areas where they have regional centers. The Coalition has learned that it difficult for schools to thrive with the reform when they do not have this local, ongoing support. Approximately one-third of the existing CES schools are not affiliated with centers. This was true for those schools in Sunland which were not close enough to a regional center to receive ongoing support. The principal of one school spoke regretfully of this problem:

> We're not as networked. We're still isolated, due to demand and location. We don't really communicate. We're hoping, and there is a group that's working on getting a local coalition branch here . . . That's where we haven't done enough, we haven't gone outside of our building.

Whereas another district in the state has access to a strong CES regional training center serving a network of 80 schools, Sunland does not. This was largely attributed to differing levels of support at the district level. A principal in Sunland explained:

> We were one of the first to go in. It's not a well-known, you know, hallmark thing to be in the Coalition of Essential Schools in Sunland County. Whereas in [the nearby district], they promote it a little differently, and they get a lot more attention than we do.

Summary

Design teams adopted various approaches to serve schools in far-flung locations, notably changing their funding status and increasing organizational complexity. The strategies they adopted typically evolved over time as demand for the model grew. In each case, different organizational priorities were evident, such as context specificity in the case of AVID, quality control in the case of SFA, local control in the case of the CES, preservation of an educator-led approach in the case of Core Knowledge, and systemic reform in the case of Comer SDP. The illustrations reveal a myriad of cultural factors, political issues, and structural constraints influencing decisions about how to best support local sites. As we describe in more detail below, the constraints on the individuals involved also influenced decisions that modified design teams.

The Challenge of Developing a Cadre of Qualified Staff

The need to develop a cadre of qualified staff who can build positive working relationships with schools is a particularly daunting challenge associated with scaling up. We often found the energy of the leaders and staff in design teams to be remarkable. Most staff truly believe in their reform. They exhibited a deep commitment to helping schools, teachers, and children. As one design team representative remarked, "In terms of my own life journey, it's so nice to be here . . . In some ways I'm back to being a teacher again. I'm now teaching schools and districts and principals. . . ."

Yet, scaling up often occurs at a faster rate than design teams can bring on these sorts of committed staff to support the schools. Additionally, the work of being school trainers or coaches can be rather taxing and can lead to burn out, as it often involves extensive travel and continuous days in school. Moreover, uncertain resource bases sometimes mean that design teams cannot hire trainers or coaches full-time. As a result, design teams might hire people (e.g., graduate students, current teachers or administrators) who have other commitments and constraints on their schedules, making it difficult to be flexible in spending time assisting educators in schools.

The Comer SDP design team, for example, has attempted to balance several demands in their development of a qualified and diverse staff. The design team employed approximately 20 full-time staff at their New Haven home base in 1999. Even though they are now serving 500+ schools, SDP prefers to keep the staff small, so that grant money may be directed to districts to support implementation in schools. Explained one staff member, "When you're dependent on grants, you're not quite sure of the long-term viability of a large staff." And although the design team does charge fees for training services, they typically only receive the money after the services have been provided, and these fees do not cover the team's operating expenses. Because staff were spread so thin, in one district, the Comer team eliminated some schools that "weren't doing very well . . . because they [the local Comer staff] had to conserve their resources," explained a design team member.

The growth in the number of schools employing the Comer model continuously creates the need for more staff, particularly in certain locations where many schools are located. The Comer SDP chooses new staff very carefully and is committing to having staff as ethnically and racially diverse as the urban schools they serve (McDonald *et al.* 1999). The director of operations at Comer SDP explained that when a position was open for a school support person in New Jersey, "there were lots of people that were interested in doing it, but no school work, and none of those knew Comer." It took a year for them to hire and relocate a well-qualified individual who had experience implementing the Comer model and in working with schools.

The efforts of all of the design teams to recruit sensitive and qualified staff were likely well worth it, because in our interviews at schools, we often found that educators were quick to point fingers at trainers who did not appear well suited to the task. At best, educators acknowledged that it was difficult for growing or new design teams to have qualified staff to serve all of their schools. About one design team, the principal said, "I don't think their ducks were all lined up either. That's the feeling I got. Anytime you start out something new it's going to happen."

Educators at one Modern Red Schoolhouse reported that training sessions were scheduled and then canceled on short notice. "[The Modern Red design team] had somebody that was supposed to be stationed in Sunland and they took a while to get somebody to come, and at that point the teachers felt a little frustrated," the principal illustrated. A member of the design team explained that these problems developed not due to a lack of capacity or responsibility on the part of the design team, but due to the fact that the district withdrew monetary support for Modern Red after the first year. Understandably, the design team could not provide services if they were not going to be paid. The design team and the schools had different perspectives on the series of events, but what is clear is that educators often approach design team trainers with strict scrutiny, particularly when they feel that the trainers do not fully understand how to support reform in their locality.

Funding issues notwithstanding, the training strategy of Modern Red Schoolhouse Institute has since evolved, and the design team is now much better able to serve schools' needs. The design team has a staff of 22 full-time people, most of whom are based in Nashville, and some of whom are field managers. However, at least half of the implementation support is provided by consultants who are specialists in different areas, such as technology, organizational management, and curriculum. This "team approach" is used because of the expertise required in so many different areas. Unlike with SFA, "one trainer can't implement our design," explained a design team member. Thus, Modern Red will send in different consultants who can meet schools' very particular needs. The use of many staff members and consultants is all the more critical when one learns that the design team often provides up to 100 days of training over a three-year period, much more than most of the other reform designs.

Summary

The Comer and Modern Red cases serve as just two examples of the challenges faced by design teams in securing staff who know the reform model, know schools, and understand the circumstances of particular school districts. All of the other design teams we studied faced similar issues – and continue to face them as the demand for their services grows. "Even organizations like ATLAS, with access to staff members from four different organizations and over a thousand schools around the country, has struggled to find individuals with the relevant experience and with an understanding of the work of the organizations" (Hatch 2000: 399). The same is true for Success for All, which also in theory has a large number of educators to draw upon from the ranks of their 1600+ schools, but has been in a constant state of hiring in the past few years. Even once the individuals are hired at these design teams, training them for positions as school support providers, trainers, or coaches takes considerable time, effort, and resources. Developing organizational capacity is no easy task.

Design Teams Change Reforms

Design teams also change aspects of their reform designs, not just their organizational structures, in response to actions taken in other situations, both "above" and "below" them in the implementation system. In what might be termed "learning from the locals," many design teams have refined their models based on educators' experiences with them, or in response to schools' demands. In some cases, this meant adapting the reform model for use in particular contexts. Design teams also changed aspects of their reforms to suit new policies and political realities impacting education, as well as to stem competition from other design teams. Not surprisingly, these forces sometimes converged when, for example, schools implementing reform models demanded assistance in meeting new state accountability systems or standards. Changing with the times, as we will see in the following detailed example of AVID's change in response to local and state politics, appears essential to both the long-term viability of the reform and its acceptance in changing political climates.

Changes in Response to State and Local Politics

An interesting case of a design team changing in response to a combination of political actions initiated by the state and pressures from local constituents occurred when AVID redefined its student population. From 1980 until 1995, AVID said it recruited low-income students with high academic potential from ethnic groups historically underrepresented in colleges and universities. Materials from an AVID staff development in the early 1990s detail the criteria for "Who Belongs in AVID?'

- Underachieving students with four-year college potential;
- Students who are currently underrepresented in our University of California and California State University systems (primarily, but not limited to, African-American, Native American, Latino and low-income students);
- Students who can succeed in college preparatory courses with tutor assistance;
- Students who are motivated to work hard to become independent thinkers and learners.

In practical terms, this meant African-American, Latino, and Native American students with high test scores but average grades were targeted by AVID. To be sure, not all students in AVID were from these ethnic minority groups, but this was the operational definition of the AVID student. In its current literature, AVID now says that it recruits "students in the middle."

This official statement has been echoed in public discussions about AVID. Guthrie and Guthrie (1998: 1), in their comprehensive review of AVID's impact on California education, define AVID as a "college preparatory program for low-income and underachieving students – those unlikely to attend four-year colleges and universities." In a widely read educational magazine, Bushweller (1998: 16) reported AVID students were defined as "average kids," "in the middle of the academic pack, an educational no man's land . . . the unfortunate members of the forgotten majority of public education," the kids that are "more and more invisible." The article goes on to describe the "typical" AVID profile – a student with "a C average, no behavior problems, and parents who did not graduate from college. The students must show a desire to want to do better, and their parents must agree to help the school push the kids." Note that neither race nor ethnicity nor minority status are mentioned in these statements. This shift in representation to "forgotten students" invokes images of the "silent majority" which is much different than an "equity" agenda – conceived as affirmative action, or active recruitment or active preparation.

AVID changed its way of representing students partially in response to actions taken by the state of California, and partially in response to sentiments expressed at new school sites. In June 1995, the Regents of the University of California (UC) passed a resolution (Regents SP 1) forbidding the nine campuses of the UC system from using race, gender, and ethnicity as supplemental criteria in admissions decisions. In November 1996, the voters of California passed the so-called "California Civil Rights Initiative" (Proposition 209), which reinforced this position. Although these changes in California state law did not directly affect AVID, the leadership felt AVID would be on safer ground not mentioning race or ethnicity in its program statements.

An AVID design team administrator offered a profile of the students that AVID intended to help before Proposition 209 passed. She reported that in 1995 "the program was to help students who are traditionally underrepresented in post-secondary, and we used the word 'underrepresented.'" After Proposition 209 passed AVID began talking differently about the students they would serve. She said, "Now you're *not* supposed to use the word 'underrepresented.' We wouldn't want people to think that it's an affirmative action program because of the anti-affirmative action thing."

Local political pressures have reinforced AVID Center's redefinition. The change in language by AVID Center in response to California state law has influenced student selection at school sites in Kentucky, Virginia, and North Carolina. Educators at two Kentucky high schools confirmed that they recruited students without taking race or ethnicity into account and from their perspective this is preferable. One AVID teacher described that the AVID program at her school is for the "C" student:

The greatest number of students that we have are in the middle, the "C" student, and there are no programs for the "C" student. And that just hit me in the head, and I was thinking "My God, this is finally something for the mass of society," something that would be great for our kids . . .

This educator welcomes the redefinition of AVID's students, because it reduces tension among the faculty and between the program and parents concerning recruitment:

Now the mission has changed, so it's much easier now. Now you don't have to be underrepresented. You don't have to be on free or reduced lunches. You don't have to be a minority, and I even like the program more, because we were losing a lot of [voice gets quieter] white kids . . . because . . . you know . . .

Educators at another Kentucky school implementing AVID have taken similar steps. The counselor at this high school, when asked how she would define AVID responded: "I define it as a program to offer support for students who attend college or some post-secondary educational setting." This definition is remarkable because it doesn't mention students' ethnicity, minority status, or socio-economic status as features considered in student selection. Indeed, this counselor explained that her high school was more comfortable depicting AVID in non-racial terms because of faculty and parental concerns. A program presented in "majority/minority terms," she said is "perceived as negative" in her community.

These views expressed by educators in Kentucky were also echoed by educators in Virginia. An AVID teacher in Freeport, Virginia said that the way in which AVID Center describes the students eligible for AVID ("students in the middle") works in Virginia helps to appease the strong right-wing element in the state. Apparently, Virginia schools cannot have special programs devoted exclusively to minorities. Therefore, talking about AVID as "helping minorities" makes educators in Virginia nervous.

AVID may be resented in certain communities in the south if it is a program identified as specifically and especially for blacks. One North Carolina AVID educator stated that: "Now that our kids are having the opportunity to take the Princeton Review, I've even heard some jealousy amongst the faculty about that. 'Well, why can't this be an opportunity for others?'" The AVID teacher, who is black, justified AVID's original concentration on minority students because of the supports that black students in her district still need, long after civil rights legislation officially ended discrimination. She was critical of the shift in AVID recruiting and pointed to the often unspoken, unwritten affirmative action policies that have always benefited whites: ". . . If you ask me about affirmative action, then I will say that whites have always had affirmative action." The observations of these AVID educators are powerful for many reasons: their words reveal ambivalence about AVID's change in focus. Some educators perceive it negatively – as if it is "discriminatory." Others see it as a welcome shift in practice away from the quotas associated with affirmative action and toward programs emphasizing intensified academic preparation.

Local context has affected representations as well. The redefinition of the AVID student to one "in the middle" has a different meaning in California schools. Schools that had established AVID programs before the passage of anti-affirmative action legislation have not shifted their recruitment and selection practices. For one AVID teacher in California, "AVID is a program for underrepresented students." When asked how California's Proposition 209 has affected her AVID program, she indicated that it really hadn't. There is every indication, however, that California schools that adopt AVID after the passage of anti-affirmative action legislation may have a different ethnic profile than schools that adopted AVID before the passage of anti-affirmative action legislation, especially given the watchful diligent eye of special interest groups who monitor policies and practices that might single out benefits for minority students.

The demographics of the various schools implementing AVID also have a significant impact on who is selected for AVID and directly affects the number of minority students served by the program. At Palm Valley High, for example, the population is approximately 99 percent Hispanic and, therefore, almost all students in AVID are Hispanic. Conversely, in North Carolina, where there is only a 12 to 16 percent African-American population in East Oakwood High and Oakwood High respectively, one AVID teacher complained that the AVID classes are getting whiter and whiter.

In sum, AVID's decision to change the definition of students targeted for admission occurred in response to forces outside of AVID, specifically the political and social climate in California, Virginia and Kentucky. This redefinition of the target population is a particularly vivid case of a design team continuing to change in order to remain a vital educational reform. Educational reform is a process that requires continuous reevaluation and modification in order to remain responsive to the needs of policy makers, students, teachers and parents.

We worry, however, about the unintended consequences of the redefinition of AVID students. Declaring its target population to be "students in the middle" may satisfy needs to build constituencies in communities sensitive to racial politics. But it may also draw AVID away from its initial mission to close the achievement gap between minority and majority students. AVID must be careful of what might result from the change in its mission statement if it wants to stay focused on goals of social justice.

Changes in Response to New Policies and Market Forces

CSRD

As we just explained, AVID made adjustments to its model to keep pace with state legislation eliminating affirmative action and to appeal to a broader base of constituents in diverse communities. So too, in response to the Comprehensive School Reform Demonstration (CSRD) program funding at the federal level, several design teams are making changes, often enhancing the services they offer schools. In several cases, the design teams have further specified their reform models, or at least what is required to implement their models, in order to make them more marketable in the CSRD landscape.

For example, largely in response to CSRD, the Core Knowledge Foundation now offers professional development, sample lesson plans, and assistance in preparing grant applications for federal funds. This is a significant departure from even three years prior, when relatively no assistance to schools was provided. At most, the schools in our sample received short overview presentations from Core Knowledge Foundation staff, as was the case for the two schools we studied in Sunland as well as those in a national study of 12 CK schools (Datnow, Borman and Stringfield 2000). Now, as a response to CSRD, the Foundation has substantially increased its professional development offerings to include a series of four workshops. These workshops are required for any schools that contract with the Foundation as part of their CSRD grant applications. For CSRD schools, the Foundation requires a formal application process which includes a letter of commitment stating how buy-in of 80 percent of the staff was obtained. Schools must also submit a school-wide planning document that includes a year-long proposal for teaching Core and state and district standards, and sample lesson plans. They must also spend a minimum of $200 per teacher on Core Knowledge-related resource materials. None of these guidelines existed before CSRD, nor did most of the professional development offerings.

Although not all design teams have scaled up their offerings in response to CSRD, all of the designs we studied appear to have become more specified in one way or another. As a design team member from Comer SDP stated: "Obey-Porter really highlighted that we need to be more definitive in our program, what it is that we do, and what it takes to do this program . . . I think that was a good thing." The Comer design team has also recently developed a web site, as have most of the other design teams, to answer people's questions about the reform. The CES national office explained that they too have made efforts to think about how CES can "do well in the design fairs" that now occur as a result of CSRD.

In essence, CSRD has pushed reform designs further into competition with each other. Most of the representatives from design teams that we spoke with were intimately aware of this. One design team member spoke of Success for All as having the "market share . . . and once you have the market share, you never lose it." Breaking into the reform market was difficult for some design teams who were not accustomed to marketing efforts, or to how they might be seen by the outside world. The lesser-known reform designs had to struggle to establish a national reputation or "increase visibility," particularly if they were not affiliated with a well-known university. Some newer design teams worried about being "pigeon-holed" as having particular types of schools, such as suburban schools or charter schools, as their only "customers," when they were in fact attempting to appeal to a broader market.

Standards and Accountability

Design teams have also responded to the rising tide of academic standards and accountability, particularly with respect to reading and math, as well as to the competition from other reform designs that already address these issues. For example, the Modern Red Schoolhouse Institute responded by engaging in "product diversification" by developing "a targeted reading program that really addresses shifting scores on state tests." A member of the design team explained that this component of the design could be "unbundled" from the rest of the model for specific use in low performing schools, particularly those that needed to raise basic skill levels before they could begin the major work of reform through Modern Red. The Institute thought they could better market their services to low-performing schools that are often in need of quick fixes this way, and thereby deflect schools away from another model that can be implemented more rapidly. The Modern Red Schoolhouse Institute also engages all schools in a process of aligning the school curriculum to state and local standards, as well as the standards of the reform.

In order be more responsive to schools' needs and similar policy demands, the Coalition of Essential Schools formed a partnership with the Developmental Studies Center in Oakland to provide optional elementary school curricula and lesson ideas. CES has begun conversations about working with the National Writing Project in a similar fashion with respect to high school curricula. The CES web site now also includes a repository of "best practices" which teachers can use as resources. All the while, CES has been careful not to endorse a particular curriculum, yet as a staff member explained, there is concern that CES has not provided enough help to teachers over the years.

Also in response to similar demands, the Comer School Development Program has made its model more "academic" according to a member of the design team:

> I think we believe that schools were having dialogues about the curriculum and instruction and the more we worked with schools we realized that those conversations weren't happening, or they weren't happening to the degree that we thought they should be happening. And certainly as school reforms and different programs were focusing on special areas, literacy, math, social skills, etc. . . . And that if we didn't do that, that would be a gap, and people would see that as a weakness in our program, and so we got criticized in many instances for not having a stronger academic focus.

She described the "Essentials for Literacy" program, developed at SDP through a collaboration between a reading professor from Sacred Heart

University and SDP's current Director of the Child and Adolescent Development Unit. The design team does not require schools to use this literacy program, but they might recommend it after schools have undertaken the "balanced curriculum" process. This process involves staff development activities in which school staffs work together to align the curriculum with state and district standards, use assessment results to refine and improve the curriculum, and make connections to the development pathways that are at the heart of the Comer model (Squires 1998). This process has been refined in response to increased pressure for schools to address state standards and perform well on high-stakes tests. While schools that have been implementing Comer SDP for some time may not have participated in the curricular aspects of the model as of yet, they acknowledged that the reform was heading in that direction. A Sunland principal who attended the design team's leadership institute noticed this change, "The last conference that I attended, they were getting very much into the developmental pathways."

Like the Comer School Development Program, the Audrey Cohen College design team has adapted its model to help new schools correlate state and local standards with the "24 abilities" that are part of the reform model. Audrey Cohen College has also responded to the increased emphasis on accountability for reading and math, but to a much lesser degree, even if it meant slower growth, rather than swimming with the tide. As a representative from the college stated, "While we're trying to be more and more sensitive to the issues of reading, and we're trying to come up with recommendations for reading approaches that are complementary. And we certainly are working on math . . . But we're still . . . I think we just have all these additional pieces." She also added:

> Schools are sort of like in the literacy frenzy . . . and here we come along saying "yes, you have to develop reading skills and you have to develop math skills, you need to be oriented toward the world of work and to the future, but there's a whole lot more that has to be done if the children are going to be competitive for the next century." And what we offer you is a whole package to get to work on all of those issues. So when a superintendent or a principal looks at that says, "oh that sounds wonderful, but right now I've got to raise those reading scores" . . .

They might choose a structured literacy program instead. In fact, she pointed to an example of a district that wanted schools to implement SFA as well as the Audrey Cohen model, which was already in place. The design team chose to withdraw its involvement from those schools because they did not see the compatibility between the reforms. However, there is a cost involved in these decisions, as the design team member explained: "We're going to grow at a slower rate because we've got a good design, it's just that I view it as a little ahead of its time." In other words, the Audrey Cohen College design team has been willing to compromise their rate of growth in favor of working with schools that have goals beyond improving students' literacy and numeracy skills.

Even Success for All, which is naturally well aligned with the policy focus on improved reading achievement (and arguably helped to fuel the reform movement in this direction), has had to adjust its model in some localities to meet demands of state and local tests. In Sunland County, for example, the Success for All design team worked to supplement some features of their curriculum around the state test, as students were not showing expected improvements in reading comprehension. According to one SFA facilitator, Slavin and Madden themselves (the directors of SFA) visited the district and provided materials that would aid the school in preparation for the state assessment test. As these and the other examples make clear, design teams have been flexible in responding to changing policy and political climates in order to better compete in the reform marketplace.

Changes in Response to School Demands

Some design teams have adjusted their reforms in response to the practical needs and insights of school educators. For example, in two Sunland schools, not only was the Audrey Cohen College reform design molded by teachers to better suit their needs, in certain instances, the adaptations that teachers made were incorporated by Audrey Cohen College to further refine the design for use in schools elsewhere. An educator at one school explained this multidirectional process as it pertained to his school site, "Audrey Cohen is still being developed, and the development is taking place right here." A member of the design team triangulated this finding stating, "I got some really good advice about how to modify and improve our materials."

At one Audrey Cohen school, teachers complained about repetition in the purpose guides published by the College. The College responded in the following year with new purpose guides, eliminating much of the repetition in the program. One of the teachers praised the College, "I do give the College credit because we responded that the purpose guides were too long and too repetitious, particularly at the younger grades, and they drastically changed them." Another teacher added, "And they did it very quickly from one year to the next." This responsiveness is at the core of the Audrey Cohen model and its founder's philosophy, as a leader of the design team explained:

> That climate of constant refinement was created by Audrey. I mean nothing is perfect. She always used to say to us, it drove us crazy, "we're almost there." She said that for 28 years, and it kind of goaded us on to realize that we were not perfect by any means, and that we had to constantly be improving, and that's what our faculty members do here.

While a Sunland principal credited the design team for being responsive, she was careful to point out that in some areas they were less flexible. However, she was sympathetic to the design team's perspective that some aspects of the model had to be non-negotiable: "It's going back to the McDonalds and Burger King. If you want to have the franchise you've got to take it the way they want it."

Success for All is commonly perceived as a reform design that is less flexible than some others. This is a misperception, as the reform has been modified considerably over the years as a result of educators' experiences. During the course of our studies, we found that the SFA design team has changed aspects of the model to respond to the requests of local educators. First, they developed an ESL version of their reading program in response to needs of the linguistically diverse student population in Sunland County. Not surprisingly, this rather major adaptation took time to develop – too long in the minds of some educators, as we explained in Chapter 3. Smaller adaptations could be made more quickly. An SFA trainer explained that when Sunland teachers complained about the time required to write "meaningful sentences" for their lessons, "we kind of said 'we'll negotiate it.'" The responsiveness of the SFA design team met with praise from educators in Sunland. Explained the facilitator at one school, "We had so much on our plate that having the help of the pre-written meaningful sentences is just a boost." It was a great help in alleviating the amount of paperwork for teachers. The facilitator also knew that these adaptations were done to keep district schools happy, and that it wasn't a service provided to schools elsewhere, "It's only for Sunland . . . as a compromise for us to keep the program because we did lose some schools."

Not surprisingly, the evolution of the Coalition of Essential Schools "model" has proceeded rather democratically. In 1997, CES's National Congress, a group in which many educators from CES schools are represented, adopted a tenth Common Principle. The goal of this tenth principle was to make the organization's commitment to equity and democracy an explicit part of CES. The tenth principle states:

> The school should demonstrate non-discriminatory and inclusive policies, practices, and pedagogies. It should model democratic practices that involve all who are directly affected by the school. The school should honor diversity and build on the strengths of its communities, deliberately and explicitly challenging all forms of inequity.

As Simon and Gerstein (2000: n. p.) explain, "The drafting and adoption of this Principle was in itself a demonstration of democratic practice in which a diverse group of CES members were invited to deliberate upon a significant issue for the organization and to take action."

The Coalition of Essential Schools has also adapted to fit school demands in other ways. Historically, CES schools have been secondary schools, as the research upon which the CES model is based was conducted in high schools. However, beginning in the late 1980s, elementary schools expressed an interest in being a part of the Coalition. "They said, 'let us in,'" explained a CES staff member. Now the CES design team is adjusting the 10 principles in order to speak to elementary as well as secondary school circumstances. A CES staff member explained: "When we were redesigning the future of the Coalition, we said we have to quite deliberately be K–12. One of the things that we are working on that the congress pushed is one set of principles that is inclusive of K–12."

The Modern Red Schoolhouse Institute has also refined their reform design to adapt to needs that have arisen in their course of work with particular schools. For example, the design team has recently introduced a strand of leadership training. A member of the design team explained how the need for this new development arose:

> We had these explosions with these leadership teams. People didn't know how to hold meetings. My last straw was when one of our graduate students came back from a school . . . where for 12 hours on two different days, people were trying to decide . . . about where they were going to put the materials for Modern Red.

As a result, the Institute began to offer two to four days of training for principals in how to understand their strengths and weaknesses as leaders, how to build good meeting agendas, and how to resolve conflict, among other things. Training modules are targeted to the needs of a particular principal and his or her school and are "culturally and person-driven." In addition, the design team now also offers a principals' conference that is "targeted on tools to be an administrator of the Modern Red Schoolhouse," such as how to look for design implementation in classrooms, explained a design team member.

Summary

Design teams often responded rather quickly to the changing demands presented by schools, districts, and state and federal political events by changing aspects of their reforms accordingly. These changes were often made so that external conditions did not become structural constraints for the implementation of reform. In most cases, the evolution of reforms that resulted was seen as positive by design teams and schools alike. However, as some organizational sociologists (Hannan and Freeman 1989) who study markets might caution, it may be difficult and in fact risky for design teams to change their "product" too much in response to environmental conditions, which may themselves quickly change. On the other hand, flexibility and adaptability on the part of a design team imply a learning organization (Senge 1990), which is of course an attribute of organizations that presumably survive in constantly changing social conditions.

Conclusion and Implications

Our findings about the changing design team add credence to our argument that the scaling up of school reform is not just about school level change. As McDonald *et al.* (1999: 4) state, some might argue that investigations of what occurs within the design team "are somewhat removed from the heart of the matter" and that the "school is the real center of action." No doubt, the school is a center of action in reform, but it is not the only locus of action. Actions (or inactions) taken by the design team are inextricably connected to actions taken within schools. Design team actions are also bound up with actions occurring on the senate floor, in staterooms, in district offices, in the public domain, and in other design teams. The relationship between the actions in these various sites can be understood as a "thick chain or braid" (Star and Bowker 1997: 17; cf. McDermott 1980: 14–15), not a one-directional process emanating at the "top" or the "bottom" of the reform process.

The design teams' changes we documented included moves from small programs in universities or county offices to non-profit organizations complete with governing boards, a cadre of staff in charge of business and training functions, and significant cash flow in and out of the organization. These moves often were accompanied by challenges for design team leaders, many of whom were originally teachers or researchers and often not trained for the demands required to run large organizations of this kind. We also described the efforts by design teams to serve schools in a wide range of places, and the structural and cultural opportunities and constraints presented by various outreach approaches. Finally, we explicated how forces at the school, district, or government levels resulted in changes in reform models. In some cases, when one reform design changed or experienced more success, others followed suit with changes of their own.

In spite of their resistance to having for-profit associations, design teams have changed to become more and more like businesses. The *lingua franca* and the practices of the corporate world have increasingly come into play in the school reform arena. When we study educational reform in the current context, we hear about design teams "competing" with each other for space in schools, organizations "peddling" their models (Olsen 2000), of design teams awarding "franchises," of achieving "market share" among reform models, and of conducting "good business" with schools. It appears that as design teams evolve in ways that are responsive to political and local demands, they are pushed even more toward a business orientation. We still do not know what the rise of these "businesses" (Rowan 2000) and their increasingly private-sector style practices will mean in the long run for schools or school systems.

In the short term however, the evolution of design teams has important practical implications for design teams and the districts and schools who work with them:

- *Recognizing that reform designs change over time, educators must realize that reform design teams might have varying organizational forms and levels of support at different points in time and in different places*
Schools tend to underestimate the "building the plane while it's flying" quality of reform efforts, and often do not account for this when they make decisions to undertake reforms. Yet, dynamics within the design

team can be quite powerful for schools, as studies have found that the quality of communication and support between design teams and schools affected level of implementation and teacher support for reform (Berends 2000; Bodilly 1998, cited in Desimone 2000). Educators would be well advised to address representatives from design teams with the following questions: What major changes is your organization experiencing? How might these affect my school and the amount of communication and support we will experience? What type of support is provided to schools in my local area? How does this differ from the support provided to schools in other areas?

- *Educators choosing among reforms should attempt to gauge the level of flexibility of various design teams*

In addition to finding out how design teams might be changing themselves or their models, educators might want to find out how willing they might be to change aspects of the reform to suit teacher or school needs or state and district requirements. Reforms should be flexible enough to adapt to local circumstances, and design team members should be willing to work with educators to make certain that the reforms "work" in their locales.

- *Design teams should link their levels of scale up with the development of their organizational capacity*

Some reform designs have scaled up very fast, and support for local schools has suffered in the process. Design teams should manage their rate of growth until they are actually ready to work with schools on a grand scale. However, growing slowly could prove difficult, as design team success is often measured in terms of the number of schools served, and thus the imperative to grow quickly is strong. This is an issue we will address in more detail in the next chapter.

- *Design teams might wish to carefully gauge the consequences of becoming too much alike*

Dimaggio and Powell (1991: 70) propose, "Organizations tend to model themselves after similar organizations [that] they perceive to be more legitimate or successful." As design teams increasingly compete with each other for presence in schools (and mold themselves to fit achievement accountability systems), there is the risk that their reforms lose their distinctiveness and shift away from their original, often broadly conceived goals. The end result might be that schools have fewer choices among reform strategies to pursue, and that the visions of these reform designs no longer "break the mold" of traditional school organizations.

6   The Life of External Reform Models: Sustainability and Expiration

In this chapter we take up the issues of sustainability and expiration, that is the ability of educational reforms to endure (or not) over time. Cuban (1986) proposed that a cycle of exhilaration, scientific credibility, disappointment, and blame characterized the life of machine technologies (such as radio, film, instructional television, and computers) in the social organization of the school. Some more general educational reforms have traversed a similar cycle, while others have enjoyed a more happy accommodation. What factors, then, enable externally developed reform designs to last and what factors lead to their expiration?

Very few studies have actually examined the sustainability of reform or school improvement over long periods of time, in part because few fundamental reforms actually institutionalize (Tyack and Cuban 1995; Cuban 1986, 1992; Anderson & Stiegelbauer 1994; Kirst & Meister 1985). Additionally, such studies are costly and labor intensive, and the reward structures of universities can be antithetical to longitudinal research efforts (Sarason 1996; Yonezawa and Stringfield 2000).

In the Special Strategies follow-up study, Yonezawa and Stringfield (2000) took advantage of the unusual opportunity to document the sustainability of reform over an extended period. This study included eight schools that had implemented either an externally or internally developed reform model with at least moderate success in the early 1990s. Eight years later, they found that three schools had moved toward institutionalizing their reforms. In these schools, educators and design teams successfully maintained reform through: (a) the alignment of the "cultural logic" of the reform design and that of the local reformers; (b) securing political support (or, at least not acquiring powerful political enemies); and (c) integrating reform structures into the daily lives of the school community. Schools that simultaneously attended to these change processes – and more importantly, the interaction between them – were able to sustain reforms.

Also presenting a "multiple processes" perspective on reform sustainability, Hargreaves and Fink (2000) argue that only three issues matter in educational reform: *depth* – can a reform improve the important rather than superficial aspects of students' learning; *length or duration* – can a reform be sustained over long periods of time; and *breadth* – can it be extended beyond a few schools? All too often large-scale reform projects fail to achieve depth, length and breadth.

Researchers have pointed to a number of reasons why sustainability is so problematic. While the authors we review consider a wide range of variables when analyzing the reasons innovations aren't sustained, they emphasize certain points more than others. Calling upon the analytics we introduced earlier in the book, we find it useful to group these explanations according to their point of emphasis – culture, structure, or agency. Some explanations of the failure to sustain reforms emphasize the actions of educators, that is, their agency. Notable here are those explanations that blame educators in schools for not implementing the reform as designed and those explanations that blame the design team for not being sensitive to local circumstances. Other explanations focus on cultural considerations, suggesting that reforms fail because they do not touch or challenge cultural beliefs or core values – the "culture of the school." A third set of explanations emphasizes structural considerations, suggesting that the social organization of the school and district, the actions of the state, and the features of the reform itself enhance or inhibit attempts to sustain reform.

In the following sections we intersperse our findings and observations with those of earlier commentators. The study of diverse reforms in Sunland County provides an interesting opportunity to investigate reform sustainability or expiration. After three years of our study, only seven of the 13 schools were still continuing to implement their chosen reform designs, and two of the seven schools were implementing at low levels. Reforms expired in six schools. AVID, in contrast, was sustained in all of the 12 schools we studied over the three-year period of our study, but the reform's depth and breadth varied across contexts. We provide some explanations for why these varied outcomes occurred.

We attempt to demonstrate that reform sustainability or expiration is a joint accomplishment of multiple actors in the classroom, school, district, design team, and state government offices. These are not outcomes that result from individuals or institutions acting in isolation from one another, but rather forces in all of these settings shape the longevity of reform. We end the chapter with a discussion of how policy and political systems can be aligned with the interests of local educators and with reform models to support successful whole-school improvement.

Agency-Based Explanations of the Failure to Sustain Reforms

According to some commentators, the movement of innovative reforms to scale can be thwarted by actions taken in one of two domains, "on the street" or in the design team. In the first case, the design team encounters "resistance" and the like in classrooms. We will call this "failure by subversion."

Reforms Fail Because "Street Level Bureaucrats" Subvert Reform

One reason given for the failure of innovations is that the design team has good ideas but actors at the local level undermine them. This "subversion" explanation of the failure to sustain reform treats educators in schools as culprits; they circumvent well-intended reforms, either because they are irrational, or they are selfish, or they are protecting their own interests, or they do not understand the intentions of the design team.

According to Lighthall (1973), Smith and Keith's (1971) narrative of a school district's failed attempt to implement progressive reform is one of the earliest studies that identifies subversion as the reason why change is not sustained. The school district Smith and Keith studied hired a new superintendent and an architectural firm to develop a unique, novel and ultra-contemporary educational program. The new superintendent, in turn, hired high-level curriculum specialists to implement the new plan; thus, all the ideas for the innovation came from the top of the school organization.

While Smith and Keith, like all the other authors we consult, consider a wide range of variables when analyzing the reasons innovations are not sustained, they emphasize the actions of recalcitrant actors at the school site. The superintendent and the principal had tried to isolate the school from undue interference and outside pressure ("establish a protected sub-culture" was the expression that they used), build a school to facilitate progressive education, but, within a couple of years, the plan unraveled. According to Lighthall (1973), Smith and Keith's (1971: 366) emphasis upon reluctant teachers circumventing reform is evident when they describe their purpose in writing their book:

> We want our monograph to be useful to the educational administrator who is contemplating the possibility of innovation in his school. The theory we have been developing is one that will enable him to analyze his situation clearly, to anticipate hazards, and to create mechanisms and solutions to the problems that arise.

This statement of intentions clearly adopts the perspective of the school's leadership. Schools belong to administrators. If they act rationally, then they can anticipate barriers to innovation that may arise down the chain of implementation. Smith and Keith more explicitly blame the teachers for the failure of the school to sustain the innovation when they analyze the reasons why teachers expressed concerns about disciplinary issues in team teaching situations:

> My own guess is that this group will not go back to any systematic team teaching, except for the minimal kinds of things like music and maybe occasionally PE, because of the difficulty in implementing the curricular areas. . . . As it stands now, the total shift has been overwhelming and the people have *retreated*.
>
> (Smith and Keith 1971: 367, emphasis added by Lighthall 1973)

The teachers' "retreat" is presumably from progressive to traditional methods of instruction; that is, the authors' phrasing represents reform failure as the result of uninformed or recalcitrant teachers subverting the good intentions of a design team.

In the California study of three Success for All (SFA) schools, there were numerous examples of teachers who were seen as subverting the intentions of the SFA reform and the leaders who promoted it. For example, at one school the SFA facilitator believed that the SFA would work better "if the teachers modified it less." As this comment implies, she trusted that the SFA curriculum was "correct" as written and believed that some teachers were errant for not complying with it. A principal in another school contrasted the new teachers who were in favor of SFA as "just great" with the veteran teachers who were openly hostile towards SFA as "reactive." These resistant teachers constituted a barrier to sustaining the reform, one that the principal would try to overcome: "The bottom line is that the program is not going away."

As we explained earlier, the Success for All design team makes bi-annual implementation visits in order to make sure that the reform is being implemented as planned and that deviations from the model by local "agents" are not so extreme as to produce reform expiration. While some teachers complained about these visits, others viewed them as necessary to keep them in check. One teacher compared teachers' tendency to deviate if not monitored as "just like the state trooper on the highway. You know, if he's got radar, you're going to slow down. It's just human nature. And people will tend to do their own thing, if they're not monitored." In this context, "do your own thing" is equivalent to failing to properly implement the reform and reverting to traditional practice.

At Keys Elementary School in Sunland County, weak implementation among teachers was one of the reasons given for why the Audrey Cohen College System of Education expired. After four years of working with the model, the staff elected (by a vote of 48 to 18) to discontinue the reform. The vote was apparently carefully orchestrated by a small group of disgruntled teachers who were described by the principal as "vocal." The reform facilitator explained that the vote to finally drop the reform was "a relief . . . because it wasn't being done in the way it should be done," and towards the end, most teachers were not implementing the model at all. However, as we will explain in subsequent sections, subversion by teachers was not the only reason the reform expired there. There were other issues as well.

> *The Insensitivity Critique: Reforms Fail Because Reformers*
> *Do Not Understand Local Circumstances*

The subversion explanation of the failure to sustain reforms expresses sympathy for the change agents, and blames street level bureaucrats for any failure. A second agency-based set of explanations criticizes the reformers who work in design teams, state or federal offices for being removed from and not understanding or adapting to local circumstances (Sarason 1982; Lipsky 1982; Fullan 1991). From this point of view, reforms are not sustained because reformers in distant locations are not sensitive to the culture of the school or the perplexities of the daily life of educators, not because educators in schools openly subverted innovations out of hostility, indifference, slough, or resistance. We call this "failure due to insensitivity."

The great curricular reform movement of the 1960s is often cited as a case in point (Silberman 1970; Sarason 1982; Fullan 1991; Muncey and McQuillan 1996). This effort emerged from a combination of university professors interested in upgrading the quality of discipline-based teaching and government officials preoccupied with the importance of producing better scientists and mathematicians after the Soviet Union launched Sputnik. Sarason (1982: 56) analyzes the experience of the new math and concludes: "There were no grounds for assuming that any aspect of the impetus for change came from teachers, parents, or children. The teachers were not hurting because of the existing curriculum." Silberman (1970: 49) draws a similar conclusion. The curriculum reform movement failed, he says, because the well-intentioned, intelligent university professors and experts on education had abstract theories that did not relate to practice, had limited or no contact or understanding with the school, and failed to consider explicitly the relationship between the nature of the proposed innovations and the purposes of the schools.

An unfortunate sense of opportunism can also accompany reform mandates, in which success is measured in terms of programs started and funds secured, not results obtained. School site educators, always desperately in need of extra funding or outside resources, react opportunistically to new reform ideas, "polished by hope, unsullied by experience" (Fullan 1991: 24). Enabling legislation may provide some level of start-up funding, but local sites may not have the resources to sustain the effort. As a result, reform efforts atrophy or meet legal mandates on paper only. Because local sites often do not have the resources to sustain government-sponsored programs, they often don't last more than a year or 18 months. Worse, they are abandoned entirely when other similar programs become available. The net result of the opportunistic search for reforms that work and the funds that accompany them is often a hodge-podge of uncoordinated, disconnected programs at school sites.

Fullan (1991: 22–23) says that "hyperrationalization" – the assumption that reformers initiating reforms in state or federal offices know everything there is to know about educational goals, the means to achieve them, and the consequences of actions – has plagued many innovations initiated from outside the school system. It is impossible to manage social action by analyzing all possible alternatives and their consequences (Schutz 1962). Therefore, when educational outcomes are thoroughly prescribed – as in competency-based education, California's new Reading Instruction Competence Assessment (RICA) and English only provisions – there is the [misguided] belief that a technical change in procedures will lead to improvement. The "insensitivity explanation" of the failure to sustain reform raises questions about the very source or origin of innovation. The core belief supporting educational reform is that the design team is best suited to be the engine driving reform. But instead of facilitating reform, the top-down vector of change sometimes actually contributes to its very difficulties.

Similar Orwellian rhetorical reversals have been applied successfully to other lynch pins of liberal policy, notably welfare "reform," gun control, and the use of primary language in instruction. What had been seen as the solution to the problem becomes cast as the problem itself. Murray (1984) argued well enough to convince the Republican-led 103rd U.S. Congress that welfare was not a beneficial remedy or safety net for the poor, but actually contributed to slough, irresponsibility and government dependency. The National Rifle Association (NRA) has convinced members of Congress (if not the general public and public defenders) that more, bigger and more powerful guns in the hands of private citizens does not cause crime, but prevents it. Woolard (1989) shows how the supporters of the "English only" initiative in California reversed the prevailing wisdom about the educational benefits of the native language with the claim that continued use of the native language placed immigrants in a "language prison." Proponents of California's Proposition 209 (the so-called California Civil Rights Initiative) convinced voters that affirmative action was a cause of racial discord not a remedy for it (Chavez 1998).

In some of the schools we studied, educators came to believe that the reforms created by design teams did not address their local circumstances. When this occurred, the demise of the reform was not far behind. For example, in one school, the design team representative was described as "alienating" instead of open and "inflexible" instead of willing to adapt the reform to the school. At one school in Sunland, almost all teachers complained that the whole-school reform they had bought into did not provide the curriculum, pedagogy, or resources for students' initial acquisition of skills. This "major deficit" in the model, as the teachers saw it, was articulated by many of the teachers we interviewed. The model was strong on higher order thinking skills and authentic pedagogy and while important, these were not the areas of most pressing need, according to the teachers.

Dissatisfaction with the design team and the reform model was also apparent at Tupelo Elementary. According to the principal, the design model had not turned out to be what the principal had initially imagined, and thus she was now critical of it:

> I think I went in with the feeling that they were going to give us a program. And after we got into it we realized that we weren't going to get a program. . . . And I think it probably came because they were showing us installations, and we assumed that installation would be transported right over here.

The principal did not feel that the design team had delivered what they had promised. A teacher confirmed: "We were expecting an overhaul. I thought over the next three years we were going to really change the school." However, it is plausible that these educators had not sufficiently investigated the reform design before adoption and thus blamed the design team for the reform's expiration. In a three-year period, the only components of the reform that were implemented at Tupelo were block scheduling and the design's task force structure of committees to address technology, finance, and curriculum. The educators' unwillingness to expend the effort required to fully implement the model contributed to its expiration, as well as the waning district support for the reform, which we describe in an upcoming section.

Cultural Explanations For the Failure to Sustain Reforms

In the agency-based set of explanations, reforms are not sustained because of the misdeeds of social actors. Either educators at school sites did not implement the reform as designed, or the design team or district did not develop sufficient sympathy for the lived experiences and practical circumstances of the people asked to implement reforms. While these accounts are helpful in calling attention to the importance of individuals' actions, they tend to overlook cultural considerations that become practical and political constraints. With those concerns in mind, we now turn our attention to a set of explanations that focus more on social context than actors' intentions.

In these culturally based explanations, observers recognize that replication is rendered complicated because the conditions under which an innovation is implemented are always different than the conditions in the replication setting (Healey and De Stefano 1997; Fullan 1999). These "conditions" are influenced by the culture of the school and the political climate surrounding it. The difficulties of transferring innovations have been associated with the fact that design teams have not always recognized that the transfer of products is very difficult. Reformers assume that their model can be replicated because from their perspective the reform is explicit. But, according to Schorr (1997: 29), "what is essential, is invisible to the eye." In other words, the transfer of knowledge about reforms is not straightforward and is not always complete because it is dependent on the ability to impart the complexity, essence, and context-specific dimensions of the reform. As Fullan (1994: 64) suggests the "deeper reason that transferability is so complex is that successful reforms in one place are partly a function of good ideas, and largely a function of the *conditions* under which the ideas flourished."

As we explained in Chapter 3, popular reforms are adopted and as "they are implemented, undergo changes that transform them in ways that few designers of the original reform could predict or even claim ownership. Schools change reforms as much as reforms change schools" (Cuban 1998: 455). While some design team representatives might balk at how their reforms are changed, oftentimes this adaptation at the local level led educators to build commitment for the reform over the long term.

Practical Circumstances Constrain Reform – Adapting to "How We Do Things Here"

A case study of special education implementation emphasizes the power of local conditions to modify reform. Mehan *et al.* (1986) do not blame the failure to sustain educational reform on misguided designers or recalcitrant educators. Instead, they say educators' actions are constrained by "practical circumstances" in local schools. According to these authors, reform efforts are not implemented exactly as they were planned because educators adapt mandates to preexisting norms, routines, and standard operating procedures. These adaptations occur because schools are sites of pragmatic accommodation in which educators try to achieve multiple goals simultaneously.

When new reforms, such as special education mandates, place new demands on local educators, they work hard to maintain previous routines while conforming to the new demands. In the act of trying to balance new demands and established routines, educators cause educational innovations to undergo changes as they become institutionalized. Educators at the local level inevitably modify attempts to reform or change organizations, especially those introduced from above or from outside them. The innovations are absorbed into the culture of the organization and adapted to fit preexisting routines or standard operating procedures.

The history of the junior high school is another example of a reform absorbed into previously established routines by practical circumstances. Although designed to be a fundamental change in schooling, over time it has been revised to become only a modest addition to the high school (Cuban 1992). A more recent effort to correct the flaws in junior high schools through the middle school movement shows little change in the original design. Reforms of the junior high school curriculum and its tracking practices have been adapted to the "existing social architecture of the school," which has durable cultural and structural dimensions.

Machine technologies (radios, film, instructional television, and computers) have also been blended into the existing social architecture of the school, traversing a cycle of exhilaration, scientific credibility, disappointment, and blame (Cuban 1986). In each case, the cycle began with extravagant claims for the revolutionary power of the machine to transform teacher practice and student learning. Fervent believers in technology readily predicted that computers and radios would replace teachers, and motion pictures would render textbooks obsolete. Reformers, including public officials, foundation executives, school administrators, and machine sales representatives, fastened onto the innovation and promoted it as a solution to school problems. School boards and superintendents adopted policies and allocated funds to secure the machines. Soon after the machines appeared in schools, academic studies reported that the new technology was as effective as a teacher using conventional practices. Shortly afterward, the pessimistic phase of the cycle replaced the optimistic phase. Teachers started to complain about logistical difficulties in using the machines, reported problems in getting access to machines, and found new machines to be incompatible with existing programs. These scattered complaints marred the mantle of scientific credibility that had begun to settle over the innovation. Later, large-scale surveys conducted by university researchers documented infrequent teacher use of the machines. These results were then used by supporters of technological innovation to criticize both teachers and administrators for blocking the advance of technology and classroom improvement.

Similarly, in a school we studied in Virginia, the success of the AVID reform was undermined when the district implemented AVID solely as a 9th and 10th grade program, rather than offer it for four years because of conflicts with another reform designed to help minority and low-income students that was well-entrenched in the district. The "College Partnerships" program was perceived as "the GATE program for African-American kids." Apparently the two programs could only coexist at different grade levels because of the competition for students and prior agreements that protected the College Partnership "territory." Their turf battle resulted in minimizing the support available to AVID students.

In an elementary school in Sunland, we discovered that educators proceeded very cautiously in balancing of the new demands of the Modern Red Schoolhouse (MRSh) design and their existing routines. Administrators at Bay Elementary attempted implementing the Modern Red design very slowly with the intention of not bombarding teachers with too many changes at once. A year and a half after adopting the model, the assistant principal reported that the school was still "at the very early stages of adopting." Administrators defended their approach but acknowledged that they had "moved a little slower than the Modern Red [design team] had recommended."

This slow evolution towards reform – and indeed the clinging to old beliefs and practices that accompanied it – meant that teachers had invested very little into Modern Red even after two years. Teachers never thought deeply about the reform and they never were entirely sure what it was all about. Their consequent lack of ownership made the reform easy to abandon when district support wavered. The strained relations between the design team and the school accelerated the reform's expiration after three years. Teachers who were never committed to the reform were sensitive to any show of lack of commitment on the design team's part. These poor conditions for sustainability were compounded by a turnover in the principalship after the first year of reform, from a principal who advocated shared leadership (consistent with the reform) to one with a more top-down management style.

Other practical constraints on the sustainability of reform are related to the everyday practice of doing the reform. Hargreaves and Fink (2000) point out that such seemingly mundane issues as time to implement, change in leadership, staff recruitment and retention issues, the size of the institution, district and policy changes and detrimental relations with the community can inhibit or enhance the sustainability of reform. In effect, these issues turn out to be not mundane at all.

Reform flounders when there has been insufficient time or knowledge for implementers to understand whether the reform fits within their school, district or state's educational goals. Decision-makers are influenced by interests, ideology and information, past experience, education and training (Weiss 1995). As we noted in Chapter 2, educators who attended "reform design fairs" often lacked sufficient time to make educated choices among reform models. The short timelines for decision-making about reform were often compounded by hierarchical relations of power in which a district administrator or principal was pushing the choice of a reform. Even the best reforms suffer without adequate support or "buy in" from administration and faculties who do not interpret the goals of the reform as matching their own. Moreover, when teachers suffer from overload and burnout, reforms fail to motivate those most essential to its success (Fullan and Hargreaves 1992). All too frequently, teachers may not understand what they are getting into, have not really accepted the reform and thus plans for restructuring fail (Stringfield *et al.* 1996).

Cultural and Political Changes that Accompany Leadership Shifts

Problems of sustainability occur in part because of leadership and teacher turnover (Hargreaves and Fink 2000). District administrations impact the pace, quality, and form of school reform through their stability or instability of leadership (Bodilly 1998; Bryk *et al.* 1998; Desimone 2000). It takes three to five years to bring real change, yet we know that the average tenure of a superintendent is about 2½ years. Principals and faculty move and along with them goes the commitment to reform. For example, when Thomas Boysen left his position as Commissioner of Education in Kentucky, the AVID program lost much of its support. The new administration saw AVID as "Boysen's program." Anxious to put its stamp on the district, the new Commissioner invested in different programs. New people bring new ideas and new loyalties that often undermine efforts to sustain what is seen as somebody else's "baby."

No where was this more true than in Sunland County. In 1995–96, Sunland's then-superintendent was very much in favor of promoting the use of externally developed reforms. As one teacher explained, he was "very supportive." Under his tenure, the district created an Office of Instructional Leadership to support the designs' implementation. This office had six regional directors who were responsible for providing the various restructuring schools within their regions with training and support. The purpose of these regional directors was to provide information, practical assistance, and encouragement to the restructuring schools. "We help them, we support, and we give them technical assistance in reviewing the plan with them, and then identify what kind of support they need," explained one regional director. A principal of a Coalition school corroborated this point, referring to one of the directors: "If it weren't for Linda Baker, the Coalition of Essential Schools would not be in the county, because she promoted it and talked to her supervisor and said 'give these folks a chance.' This is the kind of thing we want going on."

The following year, however, the district leadership changed dramatically. First, the district, which had elected its school board members at large, moved to a sub-district-specific election format dramatically altering the make-up of the board. Second, industry leaders in the district and surrounding areas began to make their voices heard, and they published a high visibility report highlighting industries for which schools should be preparing their students. A culture and value shift had occurred. The focus on student employability intensified with the arrival of a new superintendent whose background was in vocational and secondary education. This superintendent's reform agenda matched the concerns of the new board and local businesses. His priority on school-to-work educational programs shifted the district's focus even further away from the restructuring models and towards the goal of helping students become "viable products" for industry leaders. He also emphasized ending social promotion, reading instruction and community schools (Yonezawa and Datnow 1999).

The new district administration eliminated the Office of Instructional Improvement in early 1997. District officials reasoned that the dismantling was a response to fiscal belt-tightening at the district level; however, many educators in the restructuring schools and other local observers saw the move as a priority shift. The director of the office was transferred to another division. Three of the six district regional directors were also transferred to other district offices and two retired. The last regional director was given a new position as the Director of Curriculum Support Services and Special Programs, where she was responsible for doing the same job that six directors had done the year prior. Not surprisingly, district support for many of the restructuring schools decreased dramatically.

Changes in leadership at the school level, both among teachers and principals, also had a tremendous impact on reform implementation and sustainability. As we explained in Chapter 4, in the initial stages of adoption and implementation, many principals have been active agents in bringing the reform to their school. In one school in Virginia, the AVID reform seemingly had a good chance of sustainability because a significant proportion of the school's faculty and administration supported the reform. Yet, just two years later, following the departure of the AVID teacher who was described as the heart of the program and the principal who had been actively involved in promoting AVID at the school and in the district, support for the program changed dramatically. The new principal, while claiming loyalty to AVID, knew little about it and was not involved in promoting it on campus. The new AVID coordinator was not only new to the program but also new to the school and had not yet earned the respect of his fellow faculty members. As a result, the reform effort atrophied.

Reforms that Neglect the Culture of the School are Difficult to Sustain

Every school has its own culture that is socially constructed by the members within it (Sarason 1982, 1996). As a result, Hargreaves (1996) claims that educational reform requires more than restructuring. It requires the "reculturing" of a school. This is a significant challenge because as Tyack and Tobin (1994) point out reforms often challenge the "grammar of schooling." Educational reform efforts often challenge the most fundamental beliefs of education and force educators to wrestle with age-old cultural beliefs. When reformers call for new practices that diverge too far from educators' common understandings about schooling, they do not sustain.

One such belief involves the tension between education as a public good and education as a commodity. In the Jeffersonian ideal of schooling, there would be no distinction between the common good and individual interests. Education would address both. Yet, as Oakes *et al.* (1999: 60) point out the "legacy of individualism" traditionally embedded in our educational system "does not present civic virtue as the principal engine behind good schools." Rather, "a competitive, merit-based approach to learning and achievement" dominates. Schools foster an emphasis on learning as "an individual activity rather than as fundamentally social." Schools act as sorting mechanisms and assert their ability to identify students who are best able to succeed. They premise their practices on notions of meritocracy that advantage students from well-to-do families. The result has been that many groups, including those from racial and language minority backgrounds, have not been adequately served by the educational system.

As we explained in Chapter 4, ideologies, values, and beliefs are fundamental constituents of the school culture. Competing ideologies are evident in many schools when educators who emphasize efficiency and productivity, and adhere to an authoritarian structure, battle those who advocate a "community of learners" structure. In these "mechanistic" models of teaching and learning (Kohlberg and Mayer 1972), teachers are assumed to hold all the knowledge and are in a position of control (Gee 1996). Most schools remain locked into "hierarchical and bureaucratic principles" (Oakes *et al.* 1999: 56). Gee (1996: 397) points out that the "core dilemma" of education is how to ensure that everyone will act in the best interests of the whole without exerting top-down power. Moreover, if schools did respond to the imperatives of what Gee (1996) has described as "new capitalism," it would reward collaboration among individuals, "distributive knowledge," people working as teams, and learning from each other. The school reform work of Brown and Campione (1994) exemplify this position. They have built "learning communities" in which knowledge resides in "situated activities." They stress that students learn not only from their teachers but also from each other. Such understandings offer potential in solving the public good versus self-interest debate. Schools that organize around "communities of practice" and "learning communities" allow for the mutual appropriation of thoughts, beliefs, skills and practices whereby the individual and the whole are respected. Yet, there is resistance to such strategies. Even when people acknowledge that such maneuvers would be more likely to benefit all students, they fall back on folk theories that stress knowledge should rest in the hands of a central authority.

Perhaps most importantly, change is sometimes not sustained because most of what has transpired in the process of implementation has not really changed the "core" of the culture of schooling, which is teacher–student interaction around subject matter (Cazden and Mehan 1989; Elmore 1996; Stigler and Hiebert 1999). In other words, reform has not influenced the way knowledge is constructed nor has it interrupted the division of responsibility between teacher and students. "There is no real change in the fundamental condition of teaching and learning for students, and teachers" (Elmore 1996: 3). Reforms that focus on general ideas and countless workshops but neglect the culture of teaching and learning encounter failure because they have not really changed the everyday practices and standard operating procedures of the school (Elmore 1996; Fullan 1991).

Gaining insight into educators' ideologies can help make sense of their agency in sustaining or constraining reform efforts.

As we described in Chapter 5, the success and longevity of the AVID program hinged on AVID teachers' convictions that their students were capable of success. However, the positive attitudes and support of AVID teachers were often in conflict with the ideologies held by other faculty members at their schools. As we have discussed, when AVID was implemented in a district in North Carolina, the reform confronted educators' entrenched beliefs about African-American students' inability to achieve.

To be sure, reform efforts that call for social justice, the blurring of hierarchies and the dismantling of centralized control of knowledge challenge traditional conceptions of education. When reforms threaten individuals' fundamental beliefs about education, they are diminished or unable to be sustained. However, when innovations do not fundamentally challenge the beliefs and values of the school or threaten the practices of a school or politics of a district, they can more easily be accommodated in the existing school culture.

The expansion policy of the AVID program illustrates this point well. AVID, which began as the idea of one high school English teacher in San Diego has grown to become a nation-wide program. From an activity in a single classroom in one school, it now serves students in more than 700 schools in 13 states and 11 foreign countries, enrolling more than 20,000 students (AVID Center 1997). Viewed in terms of Hargreaves and Fink's (2000) criteria of *breadth*, then, AVID has expanded considerably since its inception in 1980. And, AVID has sustained its implementation in all 12 of the schools in our study.

When we view AVID expansion in terms of Hargreaves and Fink's (2000) criteria of *depth* however, we get a different picture. There are, on the average, 3.2 sections of AVID students with 30 students per section at each of its schools. The number of sections ranges from 6.2 in schools with mature programs to 1.5 in schools with new programs. When viewed as a proportion of the school population, AVID has not penetrated deeply into the schools it has entered. When we studied AVID from 1990–1992, we found an average of 66 students in each of the 16 high schools in San Diego (Mehan *et al.* 1996: 25). Similarly, Guthrie and Guthrie (1998: 10–11) report an average of 50 students per program in the 152 middle and high schools in three California counties as of October 1997.

What accounts for the relatively small size of AVID's programs in school sites across the country? AVID appeals to schools, districts, states that have equity and achievement gaps and districts and states that are engaged in reform. AVID also appeals to low income, minority parents who want their children to achieve academically and to gain access to resources denied to them previously. But AVID encounters resistance when it challenges pre-conceived notions concerning race and intelligence and challenges schools to untrack all of their classes. Faced with political opposition to its efforts to achieve school reform, AVID has adopted an expansion policy that emphasizes breadth more than it does depth. As a result, AVID remains a small program – enrolling less than 10 percent of typical high school populations.

As the history of Oakes and her colleagues' research shows (Oakes *et al.* 1997; Oakes *et al.* 1999), institutionalizing a reform designed to detrack racially diverse students requires more than the technical tinkering with the organization of course offerings. Educational reformers attempting to close the achievement gap need to confront prevailing cultural beliefs about race, intelligence, and ability. Because AVID is forced to stay small at any one school, the program is not a serious threat to teachers of honors and Advanced Placement courses and privileged parents, nor to the tracking system in the school. As long as AVID is relegated to a safe niche, it offers hope and opportunity to a small number of low achieving students and their families, but does not seriously challenge the special privileges accruing to students and their families in high track classes (Hubbard and Mehan 1999b).

Structural Reasons for the Difficulty of Sustaining Reforms

To this point, we have considered the actions of design teams and educators and the cultural conditions of schools and districts as possible reasons for the difficulties associated with sustaining reforms deeply and over long periods of time. In this section, we shift our focus to structural issues. We acknowledge that structural issues at the school level influence reform sustainability, as our section on culture-based explanations makes clear. Many of the cultural issues we discussed were framed within structures, such as track systems, board arrangements, etc. Typical school-level structural reasons for, or barriers to, reform sustainability, such as the use of time, were evident in the schools we studied. Here, we examine the role of the district and the state as structural enablers or constraints to reform. Again, as we will show, these structures were intertwined with culture and agency. Studies of school change seldom document how actions at the school level interact with actions taken in a broader policy context – the district or state – to sustain or spell the demise of reform. Recently, however, researchers have begun to argue for treating the policy context as integral to school and district reform efforts, rather than simply as an "irritant" to local school change efforts (Hargreaves and Fink 2000).

The Role of the District in Sustaining Reform

District support for reform, or at least a commitment that the district will enable rather than hinder long-term implementation, is critical to sustaining reform at the school level. As we explained, a significant issue in the sustainability of reforms in Sunland was the dramatic change in district leadership and the change in beliefs and values that accompanied it. New mandates and priorities were introduced by the district administration, some of which did not mesh with the schools' chosen reforms. In general, educators felt that they had so many demands on their time that sustaining externally developed reforms was difficult, and thus often not a priority.

Marking a significant shift away from external reform models, in 1998 the district developed its own reading program, as we mentioned briefly in Chapter 4. The district gave schools the option to vote among the new Comprehensive Reading Plan developed by the district language arts department, the SRA reading program (an external program), or to stay with Success for All if they were already implementing it. Educators in most schools told us that the writing was on the wall – in other words, the district reading program was the best supported option by principals largely because it had the district endorsements.

Two of the three Success for All schools in our sample dropped the reform at this time in favor of the district's new plan. One of the 13 other sites we studied elected SRA, and the remaining schools went with the Comprehensive Reading Plan. The new reading program occupied two hours per day, which meant that schools had to restructure the organization of time and the curriculum to accommodate it. This often meant less time devoted to reform-related activities.

As one principal in a Coalition of Essential Schools site explained, "This year, with the district-mandated Comprehensive Reading Plan, we've kind of been swamped . . . and we really haven't looked at our Coalition work as closely this year." She added: "Our directions have been to deal more with the administrative changes and initiatives that are politically supported by the school board . . . Once we get through this initial change, we plan to go back to some of our Coalition activities." Despite the best of intentions, this had not yet occurred. Teachers in a Core Knowledge school voiced similar statements about having to put Core Knowledge "on the back burner" while they learned the new reading program.

Educators in Sunland reacted to the lesser emphasis or expiration of reforms in their schools with a mix of glee and disappointment. Some teachers and principals who heartily embraced the changes reform had brought to their schools felt a profound sense of loss. They also complained that this was yet another example of where support for change received no follow-through from the system. On the other hand, some teachers and principals were relieved that they no longer had to implement reforms that they felt were ill matched to their schools from the beginning.

The Power of the State in Sustaining Reform

Like districts, states play an active role in and sustaining reforms (Fuhrman and Fry 1989; Lusi 1997; Ross, Alberg and Nunnery 1999). Comparing the circumstances in California with those in Kentucky offers us an example of the power of the state in providing structural support for the AVID reform. Efforts to implement AVID in California are helped considerably by permanent state funding. In 1980, under the auspices of the "Tanner bill," AVID received $50,000 from the Department of Education to develop programs that supported under represented students' participation in post-secondary education. Between 1996 and 1997, AVID was awarded $1,000,000 to establish eight regional centers in California and to establish the position of AVID State Director. This state fiscal support has been key to the sustainability of AVID in California. While schools do not directly receive money from the state for implementing AVID, they receive assistance from their regional directors and coordinators whose salaries, or at least a portion of them, are paid by the state.

Whereas AVID in California is a budgetary line item, AVID in Kentucky never achieved that status. The former Kentucky State Commissioner explained the importance of a program being part of the state budget; or else it is subject to the fragility of leadership:

> It was *never* viewed as a state grant [in Kentucky]. One of the differences in having it be a legislative line item vs. an administrative priority is that the administrator changes more often then the legislator. And as soon as you get something in there as a line item you have a constituency and it's hard to get it out.

The director of a Kentucky education advocacy group reinforced his observation about the importance of permanent state funding: "AVID in general doesn't have any champions . . . I don't think it is on anybody's radar screen politically. . . ."

The Kentucky State Department of Education reduced funding for AVID to $7,000 per school for the 1998–99 school year, and $3,000 for the 1999–2000 school year – the last year of state support. From that point on, if districts and schools want to continue AVID, they must do so with their funds. Without state directors to provide professional assistance to school sites, local schools and districts must contract directly to AVID Center for services. Some AVID programs are limping along without tutors, field trips, guest speakers and curriculum, which raises the specter of decertification by the AVID Center. AVID's longevity is precarious when state funds dry up and local sites must scurry for money.

Reform sustainability was impacted by a different set of structural issues at the state level in Sunland. In particular, the state's new high stakes accountability system – a powerful external structure – had the unintended consequence of destabilizing reform efforts in most of the schools. Beginning in 1999, schools received ratings based on student performance on norm-referenced and criterion-referenced tests. Many educators believed that their scores were not a reflection of school quality, but rather had more to do with the mobility, ethnicity, and language status of their student populations. The state's new grading system proved demoralizing to teachers in the schools that received low ratings, particularly given the extensive effort they had expended on reform in the past several years.

Almost uniformly, teachers admitted to putting reform-related activities aside in order to prepare students for "the test." The presence of the high stakes testing program invariably meant that test-preparation activities, often unconnected to any previous or ongoing instructional activities, took precedence over reform activities. One Success for All (SFA) school chose to spend 90 minutes one day per week taking practice tests instead of complying with the SFA reading curriculum that day. The principal explained the reason for this adaptation: "I'm in a dilemma because I've got to have that test score." That is, while he believed students were learning to read, their test performance did not improve. After three years of implementation and with increasing pressure from the state and the district, the school dropped SFA. Another SFA school stuck with the program, even though their scores were low, by adding 30 minutes a day of reading instruction devoted specifically to the types of comprehension questions asked on the state test.

Educators lamented that test scores were not the proper measure of success for their reform efforts, but they realized the constraints under which they operated. Schools scrambled to improve outcomes on the state test and implement the district's new reading program with high fidelity, so that at least they could point to strong district-sanctioned efforts if their state test scores did not improve. We found that the only schools that did not suffer or experience conflicts in the face of these state and district demands were those that had reforms well institutionalized and obtained high marks on the state report cards. Two of these schools were implementing the Comer School Development Program and one was implementing Core Knowledge – reforms that could be adapted around test preparation activities and which did not have contentious histories in the district, nor did they require funding to sustain them. These reforms had become taken-for-granted features of daily life at the schools, and these schools enjoyed strong reputations and protected positions in the district. They were flagship schools that had sustained effectiveness on traditional measures for long periods of time. Teachers at these schools were told by administrators to simply "continue doing what they were doing because it seemed to be working."

The situation in Sunland is not unique. Prior studies of externally developed reforms have documented that in schools where state accountability demands were high, reform strategies were abandoned in favor of test preparation (Bodilly and Berends 1999; Datnow, Borman, and Stringfield 2000). As Desimone (2000) points out, design teams often market their models on the basis that they will help schools improve test scores. Yet reforms may not align with standardized tests. A design team member we interviewed lamented the focus on test scores as the only measure of reform success. She stated:

> I think there was a strategic error made in not realizing the public pressure that was going to come on producing high test scores. . . . The practicalities and the politics of education were not factored in. And we were just almost heading like to the edge of a cliff and almost ready to go over, and then everybody realized and said, "oh, we've got to get those test scores up just to survive as a reform movement." And that was really unfortunate. There probably should have been more dialogue around . . . at the national level for encouragement of new ways of thinking about student performance; the climate wasn't built to really allow some of these things to happen.

Standardized tests have become the primary measure of school and reform success. District and school administrators are increasingly making decisions about whether to continue reforms – and their contracts with design teams – on the basis of this single, rather narrow reform "effectiveness" standard (Cuban 1998). Meanwhile, teachers, like reformers, seek improvement in student performance, but what "counts as" success or results are seldom test scores, but attitudes, values, actual behavior on academic and nonacademic tasks in and out of the classroom. Moreover, "[w]hat becomes especially important for teachers is how they can put their personal signature on the mandated reform and make it work for their students and themselves" (Cuban 1998: 459). This debate illustrates the perspectival differences of teachers and policymakers and the differing values about what sustains a reform.

Conclusion and Implications

In this chapter, we have discussed reform sustainability and expiration in terms of the agency, cultural, and structural forces that shape it. Studies of school change that focus on the school as the unit of change either praise or blame local educators for the outcome of reform efforts. But school-level factors do not tell the complete story. Our research shows that reform sustainability or expiration does not result from individuals or institutions acting in isolation from one another. Forces at the state, in districts, design teams, the school and classrooms all interact to shape the longevity of reform.

We attempted to show that structures and cultures do not exist "out there" but rather are the contingent outcomes of practical activities of individuals. As we have shown, real people – confronting real problems in classrooms, school board meetings, and reform design teams – interacted together and produced the texts, the rules, and the guidelines, that are part and parcel of the school change process. In sum, educators in schools, policy makers in districts and states, and personnel in design teams "co-construct" reform success.

In many ways, it is not just this chapter that is about sustainability, but rather the whole book. The themes we raised in previous chapters – how schools choose reforms, the influence of the local context, the importance of leadership, the changing design team – all profoundly relate to reform sustainability as well. The collective wisdom we have gathered results in the following implications for practice and policy:

- *Reforms that have an inauthentic beginning almost surely will not be sustained*

The schools that dropped their reforms almost always exhibited an absence of staff buy-in initially. Staff in these schools were often hurried to make decisions or coerced to go along with the choice of reform, regardless of their true wishes. In contrast, in some of the sustaining schools, educators were more likely to have chosen a reform with which they could engage with integrity and for which there was substantial teacher and principal support.

- *Reform sustainability requires building ideological commitment and ownership among teachers*

No doubt teachers need to have substantial interest in attempting reform at the outset. However, establishing ownership over the long term requires that teachers understand and commit to the theory behind the reform. Just as we have concluded that students have to construct their own meaning for learning to occur, people in all change situations must construct their own meaning as they go about reform. Teachers need to wrestle with what the reform model means for them and their students (Yonezawa 1998). Some level of local development or adaptation seems necessary in order to create this ownership, particularly when teachers are implementing a highly structured model (Datnow and Castellano 2000b).

- *Reform models with more flexibility are more sustainable in the face of changing district and state constraints. Flexible reforms more easily mold to local circumstances, but they can potentially have less of an impact in the short term*

The reforms that lasted in Sunland were those that helped educators meet local district and state demands, or at least did not come into conflict with them. These tended to be less structured reforms, whereas reforms that included more demands on the system and its resources faced greater difficulty. So, too, successful AVID programs were those that adapted to local circumstances. In addition to the discontinuation of district support and the changing political climate at both the state and district levels, frustration with the lack of workability of some reform models caused them to expire. Some reform designs appeared more naturally suited or better equipped to work in this multilingual, multicultural context than others. Their ability to adapt to local circumstances impacted their longevity in the schools.

- *Resource-hungry reform models are at greater risk of instability*

Some school reform designs require substantial funding to implement and to sustain over time. In the face of budget cuts, reform models that require a continual financial outlay might find themselves at risk of expiration or at least instability. Yet, the reforms that are the most comprehensive are often the most expensive. As we well know, school change is resource hungry (Fullan 1991).

- *High stakes accountability systems may inhibit dramatic, sustainable change in schools*

Prevailing measures of reform effectiveness run counter to school change, serve to hold in place existing structures and practices, and do not fit with teachers' realities. Reform success needs to be more broadly measured. Few would argue with the fact that students should benefit academically, but not only in terms of the narrow measure of standardized achievement tests. Understanding the value of school, the development of civic virtue, and critical thinking are other possible valuable goals for students. Moreover, the interests of those responsible for implementing the reform – teachers – and whether the change serves their interests are also of utmost importance in measuring success. Finally, measures of reform success should address whether the implementation of a reform design leads to long-term school improvement and the development of a school culture that is ripe for change, or whether it hinders such efforts.

- *Policy systems need to be aligned to support school reform efforts*

Already over 1800 schools have received federal funding for reform through the federal Comprehensive School Reform Demonstration (CSRD) Program. Meanwhile, many states are simultaneously implementing high stakes accountability systems. Districts are also promoting their own change efforts. In other words, change vectors are coming at schools from three, often ill-aligned directions. Districts promoting the use of externally developed reforms (and the seeking of federal CSRD funds) often believe that the reforms will produce better outcomes on state-mandated assessments. Meanwhile, many reform models are not necessarily aligned toward these outcomes, nor can they produce desired results in short periods of time.

- *Reform strategies that seek a "safe niche" may have limited impact on school improvement*

Although programs that do not seek to change the whole-school improve their chances of sustainability, the goal of offering an excellent education to all students will not be achieved by limited reform efforts that impact only part of the school. As long as such programs only occupy a safe niche, inequities will remain in place and low income and minority students will continue to be disadvantaged because they are not placed in rigorous and demanding courses. Educators must actively confront deep-seated values and cultural beliefs as well as modify institutional practices to achieve educational equity and excellence. This transformation will not happen automatically or naturally. A concerted effort must exist on the part of design teams and school-site educators to accomplish social justice goals.

7   Prospects for Educational Change

What can be learned about school change from our investigation of how numerous reforms in varied contexts tried to "go to scale"? One might argue that we compared apples and oranges. We presented examples of reforms that are aimed expressly at changing entire schools and one that is aimed at changing schooling for a group of students, with the intention that change might then germinate in a more wholesale fashion. We studied principle-driven reforms and those that are more nearly prescriptive programs. We documented reforms that were fully and successfully implemented in schools and those that hardly got off the ground even after several years. While there are certainly major differences between reforms in terms of their goals, purposes, and how they manifested themselves in schools, there are common themes that we found in almost all efforts to scale up educational reforms. This book is about those common patterns that arise when reforms are scaled up, transplanted, or replicated.

These themes, we have argued, are best illuminated through a theoretical framework that views the implementation of externally developed reforms as a co-constructed process. Below we briefly summarize our major theoretical and empirical findings. For more detailed policy implications, we refer you to the summaries at the end of each chapter. We then proceed with ruminations on what the externally developed reform movement suggests for the prospects of educational change and for the changing nature of the public educational system in the U.S. In doing so, we raise questions and suggest directions for future research in these areas. We conclude with a brief examination of the politics of research and practice in the reform scale up movement.

Overview of Theoretical and Empirical Contributions

In this book, we illuminated the dynamic process that occurs when school reform models are transplanted into new locations, often far away from where they were initially designed, first implemented and where they experienced their initial success. We examined reform implementation as a dynamic, multidirectional process in which educators' actions in schools shaped and were shaped by actions simultaneously occurring in diverse contexts, including the classroom, school, district, reform design team, state, and federal levels. For example, in Chapter 2, we discussed the way in which educators who moved to other districts convinced their new district administrators of the merits of a particular reform. As a consequence, the reform grew and this growth in turn impacted the amount of district support educators received for implementation.

We showed how interactions in one context (e.g., at the design team level) generated events and outcomes, which in turn potentially conditioned the interactions of other actors in other contexts. Recall that when the AVID design team established their Eastern Division, schools throughout the east saw the reform as their own and subsequently many more schools adopted the reform. We also demonstrated the possibilities enabled by and the constraints imposed on school reform by conditions in these various settings. For example, as we explained in Chapter 6, state systems of accountability influenced reform sustainability in significant ways. Similarly, the presence of students with special language needs raised new demands for design teams, who were called upon to help educators mold reforms to fit local conditions and respond to policy constraints in the form of state policies regarding the education of these students.

Our work supports Hall (1997) who asserts that field research can address "macro issues." We have shown that interactional studies do not have to be preoccupied with local sites, activities, and individual actions. Our research does not relegate structure, social forces, and power to the background or preliminary literature review. As is often the case, these elements are not studied, but constituted through secondary literature. Our study addresses these elements with empirical data.

We emphasized the relationship between structure, culture, and agency and illustrated how the interrelationship between these forces worked in the implementation of school reform. We adopted the premise that social structures are the contingent outcomes of practical activities of individuals. As we have shown, real people – confronting real problems in classrooms, school board meetings, and reform design teams – interacted together and produced the texts, the rules, and the guidelines, that are part and parcel of the school change process. Recall how a Virginia superintendent's chance encounter with an AVID teacher led to district- and subsequently statewide adoption of the program. Yet, as we explained, reform did not proceed in a smooth fashion in all cases, as AVID was not received by educators in a uniform way – some embraced the reform, others resisted, and still others passively complied.

Reform implementation is not an exclusively linear process by which design teams or districts "insert" reforms into schools. Rather, educators in schools, policy makers in districts and states, and design teams in places often far from the sites where their reform is being implemented reacted in various ways and thereby co-construct reform adoption, implementation, and sustainability. We illustrated the various actions (and inactions) teachers and principals took in the school reform process, as well as how decisions were influenced by beliefs, histories, school cultures, as well as their interactions with the reform and its design team and the level of district and state support. Educators' beliefs about the naturalness of ability and its uneven distribution across racial groups became structural barriers to educational reform in some of the schools we investigated.

As demonstrated throughout this book, we believe it is important to pay attention to the role of power and perspective in shaping reform implementation. Put simply, educators in schools had to respond to decisions made by more powerful people who interacted in board rooms, legislatures, or design teams. Reform efforts are suffused by politics in various ways. In numerous instances, particularly in our discussions of how schools adopted reforms and how they fit them to local contextual demands, we have shown that the meaning of reform – and how it was implemented – varied according to a person's or organization's perspective.

We have shown how schools, districts, design teams, and states successfully worked together – or did not work well together – to implement an externally developed reform model in their particular local contexts. Our empirical findings about the process of transferring externally developed reforms germinate from this theoretical framework. We believe that the strength of these findings is the complexity they have exposed about the reform process and the contributions they make to social theory. Very few, if any, studies of school reform, much less studies of the current generation of externally developed reforms, attempt to integrate theory in a meaningful way. The educational reforms described in this book offer the following contributions to our understanding of the educational change process:

1 Relations of power and politics within and outside the school, serendipitous events, and differing perspectives among teachers, administrators, and policymakers are characteristic of reform adoption processes, regardless of where the push for reform originates.
2 Local educators helped to "make" educational reforms, regardless of whether a reform had well-defined elements. Educators modified reform design features in various ways to fit with sociopolitical and cultural factors, their local needs, practical circumstances, and their own ideologies. In some cases, reform implementation was enhanced. In other cases, reform implementation was constricted.
3 In many cases, externally developed reforms changed educators' activities and relationships. In turn, educators' actions and relationships shaped the implementation of reforms. Changes, tensions, and ambiguities arose in schools as principals and teachers made meaning of their roles in reform in the context of existing cultural, structural, and political arrangements.
4 Just as schools changed, design teams changed. In some cases, design teams metamorphosed into different forms, often to serve increasingly large numbers of schools effectively. Elements of reform models themselves were sometime changed to reflect market and accountability

demands. Several design teams found tensions in offering schools business-level efficiency when it came to training, materials, and support, but yet attempting not to appear profit-oriented and thereby maintaining their integrity as organizations aimed towards educational improvement.

5   Agency-based explanations that praise or denigrate actors on the "top" or the "bottom" of the school system do not adequately explain reform success or failure. Rather, the sustainability or expiration of externally developed reforms is a joint accomplishment of multiple actors in the classroom, school, district, design team, and state government offices, existing within a particular set of cultural, structural, and political arrangements.

Prospects for School Improvement

What are the prospects for long-term, genuine school change and improvement through externally developed reforms? This is not a question that we set out to explicitly address in this book, however our findings do allow us to posit some conclusions. We believe that school reforms can be a vehicle for school improvement, but how they are used determines in large degree how likely they are to succeed. An analogous case is computers in education – they can be an instrument for instructional change or they can be yet another stratifying practice. The resultant outcome depends on how they are used, not any of their intrinsic properties.

Yet it is important not to overemphasize instrumentality when considering the effectiveness of various reform designs. In addition to the reform itself, so many factors influence whether the reform will lead to school improvement, including the actors involved, the politics, differing local capacities for change, to name just a few. Reform designs should be thought of as part of an *overall* school change effort grounded in the local context and values and goals of local educators, not the sole school improvement activity. Fullan (2001: 268) succinctly describes this tenet of school change in what he calls the 25/75 rule: "Twenty-five percent of the solution is having good directional ideas; seventy-five percent is figuring out how to get there in one local context after another."

School reforms are certainly being adopted, implemented, and sustained or abandoned in schools across the U.S., but creating "buy in" from all teachers and administrators is difficult and makes the likelihood of school "improvement" very much dependent on local context. Oakes *et al.*'s (1999) discussion of the "reform mill," is echoed by Hess (1999), who found that "school boards and superintendents consistently engage in a kind of hyperactive policy dance – a phenomenon he calls 'policy churn' in which relative unstable political factions advance new 'reforms' as ways of satisfying their electoral constituencies . . . with no attention being paid to the institutionalization or implementation of previous reforms" (cited in Elmore 2000:19). Reform instability has created passivity or resistance among some educators. Motivations become suspect as educators wonder why they should jump on the bandwagon when the reform may well expire when there is a change in leadership or political tide.

In their exuberance to make schools *change*, there is concern that some educators might lose sight of the goals of education. Educational change is not isomorphic with educational improvement. Change implies reorganization, doing things differently, but it doesn't necessarily mean that a school is moving in the direction of particular goals or that these goals are fundamentally valuable for all segments of society. School improvement involves movement towards some overarching goal or purpose of education, such as commitments to an educated citizenry, social justice, and participatory democracy (Oakes *et al.* 1999). Studies of externally developed reforms that have an explicit equity agenda would help us answer some of the most important questions concerning the way in which reforms enhance or constrain the possibilities of educational change aimed at these sorts of goals. In other words, are reforms working for all students, and if not, why not? Moreover, are particular reforms being implemented exclusively in some types of schools (e.g., urban, suburban) and not others, and how might this reduce or exacerbate race and class stratification in the educational system?

Over the long term, how will externally developed reforms, particularly those that are more prescriptive, influence educators' sense of professionalism and orientation towards continual school improvement? In order for change to be "improvement," Elmore (2000: 13) points out that it must "engag[e] people in analysis and understanding of why some actions seem to work and others don't." Educators must understand not only what they are doing, but why they are doing it. Fullan (2000) has expressed concerns about how large-scale, state-driven reforms that are focused primarily on numeracy and literacy will influence teachers' communities of practice in the long term. Similar concerns exist with some externally developed reforms. Longitudinal studies are needed to determine what various reforms mean for broader goals of education, for teacher creativity, and for teachers' engagement in crafting future change efforts at their schools. These studies would be wise to consider what school reform means for teachers on an emotional level (e.g., Hargreaves 1998) as well as how reforms are embedded in teachers' life histories (e.g., Goodson 2001).

Prospects for Reshaping the Educational System

How do the roles of school districts, states, teacher education programs, and professional organizations change in this era of externally developed reforms? The increased reliance on external organizations, existing outside what has commonly been thought of as the school system, suggests a change in the nature of governance and management in education and new roles for entities that schools have traditionally relied upon (Fleisch 2000, personal communication). This is not simply a question of decentralization or centralization, as has formerly been the case (Tyack 1990). Therefore, these changes in educational governance and management systems must be examined within a historical perspective.

Investigating the marketization and in some cases, privatization, of school reform is an important piece to this puzzle of the changing nature of school management systems. As we have shown, reform designs are increasingly placed into competition with each other for space in schools. To our knowledge, the influence of these types of market forces on school systems has not yet been studied extensively. Recent studies have primarily focused on the privatization of education that occurs through school choice policies or voucher plans (e.g., Witte 2000). In the future, schools may find themselves in competition with each other, marketing themselves on the basis of their chosen externally developed reform models.

This shift towards the privatizing of school reform and an increased reliance on external organizations for reform services is likely to have a dramatic effect on the definition of schooling as a public good. Historically, education has been kept separate from business so there would be "no interference with the development of a business-like system of hierarchical control and direction" (Mitchell 1990: 154). Because Americans have seen education as a "public good" and not a commodity to be purchased, the education system is in theory run by individuals who "take public service as a moral duty rather than an economic opportunity" (Mitchell 1990: 154). Though reform design teams eschew profit-making connotations, in fact they have economic imperatives of their own, separate from the public school system. Moreover, some reform designs, such as Edison Schools, are explicitly profit-driven.

But just how far is the marketization of reform likely to go? Will this competition among reform designs produce better, more refined models for schooling? Tyack and Cuban (1995) suggest there is an ideological rigidity that surrounds what education and educators should look like. They claim that departures from customary school practice are difficult at best because change disrupts popular opinion about what a "real school" should look like. Will the increased presence of external reform design teams in schools fracture ideologies about what education is and who is in charge? These are questions we cannot answer, but can merely suggest for future inquiry. The next few years offer a timely opportunity to address some of these issues, particularly given the exponential growth in the number of schools implementing reforms as a result of the Comprehensive School Reform Demonstration Program.

The Politics of Research and Practice Concerning Externally Developed Reforms

As is the case with many studies of educational change, our research causes us to ponder the relationship between research and practice and, in particular, the politics that arise concerning externally developed reform models. First, we concur with Muncey and McQuillan (1996: 81–82) when they say "if change is to take root, those involved must confront the political dimensions of change . . . the initial apolitical stance of reform advocates (for example, focusing on classroom centered change) left many unprepared for political disruptions that arose, tensions that overwhelmed pedagogical, curricular, and structural aspects of change." Second, there is the dilemma of bringing research "news" to design team members. It is not difficult to imagine a scenario in which design team members would be reticent to hear information about reform implementation that they perceive as negative, or studies of reform that place them in unfavorable comparison with other nationally recognized models. In fact, in one instance, we have encountered tensions with the members of a design team over whose definition of what was occurring in school sites and within the design team would prevail. The mutual agreements that were negotiated early on can be forgotten in favor of protectionist principles. In other cases, we have found that design teams have approached our research findings with a more academic mindset, seeking to learn from our findings about reform at the school level and valuing our perspective as third-party researchers.

Another issue related to research and practice involves what counts as research. As we explained in Chapter 2, reforms that carry the label "research-based" and those that have "statistics behind them" receive greater consideration in reform adoption decisions. At the present time, design teams are under pressure to produce (or preferably, have external evaluators conduct) quasi-experimental studies on reform that compare the achievement results of experimental (i.e. reform) and control schools longitudinally. Many nationally known reform models were critiqued in the *Educator's Guide to Schoolwide Reform* (Herman *et al.* 1999) and *Show Me the Evidence* (Slavin and Fashola 1998) for not having a strong research base according to these criteria.

On the other hand, ethnographers brag that their rich descriptions provide us insight into the process by which schools implement, modify, or even resist design team principles (see, for example Muncey and McQuillan 1996). These observers would echo the sentiments of some reform design teams who have argued that their models have led to students seeing a purpose in their education, increased levels of professional community, or more equitable school settings, among other less tangible but important outcomes. In some cases, ethnographers or design teams point to emotional testimonials from students or teachers about how the reforms made a difference in their lives. While these testimonials might convince some teachers on the "adaptability" of a reform effort, it is increasingly the test score indicators (what Cuban 1998 calls the "effectiveness standard") that policymakers and administrators are concerned about.

The recent RAND study (Klein *et al.* 2000) that compares the performance of Texas youth on the Texas Assessment of Academic Skills (TAAS) with their performance on the National Assessment of Educational Progress

(NAEP) should give policy makers pause about using a single high-stakes test when evaluating educational reforms, however. Even though the Texas students did show progress on TAAS, the size of their gain was less than on NAEP. The stark differences reported caution against making decisions to sanction teachers or students or schools on the basis of test scores that may be inflated or misleading.

Compounding the politics of defining what counts as research are the battles that have recently ensued in education publications over who should conduct research on reform and whether the findings, if not conducted by an "unbiased evaluator," are in fact valid (see Pogrow 1998; Slavin 1999). The *Phi Delta Kappan, Education Week,* and *Educational Researcher* have each published debates of these kinds, mostly involving Success for All. Other scholars have discounted the claims of skeptics of Success for All, defending the research of SFA and the genuine motives of its developers (Joyce 1999; Stringfield 1998).

A final issue in the relationship between research and practice is the degree to which strategies associated with reform designs become taken-for-granted features of American schools. In some cases, it appears that design teams want to receive credit for the use of their reform strategies and/or curricula and in fact would be upset to know that they were being used without their official sanction. On the other hand, some design teams view the natural proliferation of their practices as significant of the reform's success and are content to see their practices spread in an organic fashion, without their explicit involvement. Who "owns" or invented particular reform strategies is another issue that is open to question, as some reform designs are deliberately an amalgamation of best practices used in educa-tion. Questions of ownership are also raised when the reform is significantly changed, modified or subverted.

Final Remarks

Our hope is that this book has suggested new ways of thinking about the transferability of educational reforms. However, as we have described, much remains to be learned about this process and the outcomes of the scale up of reforms. While research on school reform can become tricky political terrain, it is a worthy enterprise as we consider the prospects of change in schools and school systems that might result from these reforms. Understanding the social and political realities that shape reform is impor-tant if we are to find ways to improve education for students in schools where change has long proved to be difficult.

Appendix: Description of Reform Designs

AVID

The Achievement Via Individual Determination (AVID) program is fairly unique in its origin, having been founded within the K–12 sector, rather than outside the system. AVID was developed in 1980 by English teacher Mary Catherine Swanson at Clairemont High School in San Diego. AVID was developed to help educate minority students bussed to the predominantly white school under a court ordered desegregation decree. Unwilling to segregate African-American and Latino students into a separate, compensatory curriculum or "low track," Swanson and the Clairemont faculty placed the minority students in college preparatory classes with their white peers and provided them with additional academic and social supports to assist their development.

The program was founded on the educational philosophy that students who had previously been poorly served by our educational system deserved the opportunity to achieve success. AVID supports the goal that:

> All students, but especially students in the middle with academic potential, will succeed in rigorous curriculum, enter mainstream activities of the school, increase their enrollment in four-year colleges and become educated and responsible participants and leaders in a democratic society.
>
> (AVID Center 1996: 1)

We found in our earlier research that AVID students benefit from academic and social supports in the form of study skills, test taking skills, explicit instruction in the hidden curriculum of the school and the intervention and advocacy of institutional agents (Mehan *et al.* 1996).

AVID grew from one classroom in one school to all high schools and middle schools in San Diego and now 850 middle and high schools in 13 U.S. states and Department of Defense schools in 13 foreign countries (http://www.avidcenter.org/). When AVID spread across San Diego, the design team moved from Clairemont High School to the San Diego County Office of Education. In order to serve schools better in diverse locales, AVID Center, still based in San Diego, has since become a not-for-profit organization and has established an eastern division office.

Strictly speaking, AVID is not a "whole-school" reform design. Rather, the AVID program typically directly involves 30–120 students in a school, with the intent of provoking a school-wide restructuring effort. Middle and high schools that implement AVID agree to: (1) identify high potential students "in the middle" and place them in college-prep classes; (2) offer the AVID elective class within the regular school day; (3) identify a teacher to serve as AVID coordinator who will teach the AVID elective class; (4) use AVID curriculum materials and AVID pedagogical practices (writing, inquiry and collaboration); (5) participate in ongoing staff development activities; and (6) use a sufficient number of tutors, trained to use the AVID methodologies, in AVID classrooms. These are known as the "AVID Essentials."

AVID Center has established several mechanisms to export these program standards to school sites. Foremost among these practices are the creation of a specific AVID organizational structure at the school district level, an extensive mandatory staff development system, a certification process, and a data collection system to maintain program quality. Each school is to have a site team that is typically composed of academic teachers, the principal, counselor and AVID teachers. While there is some latitude for local program variation, the AVID Essentials are non-negotiable and "implementation of these essentials is a condition for use of the AVID™ trade name, trademark and logo" (AVID Program 1997). AVID Center has instituted a certification process whereby all AVID programs are evaluated based on the extent to which they incorporate the essentials. If a program does not meet the AVID criteria it can lose the right to the AVID trade name and license.

Staff development is another mechanism that AVID Center has established to export program standards. District directors attend extensive training sessions to learn how to help AVID coordinators with problems and how to conduct training in their regions. Staff development also includes opportunities to visit "demonstration schools." AVID coordinators, teachers and site team members also participate in ongoing staff development activities. AVID Center intends that each site send a new group of teachers to week-long summer institutes so that incrementally more people in each school could learn about how to use AVID methodologies, how to work as a site team to plan and implement the program, and how AVID can be a catalyst for a school-wide restructuring effort.

Audrey Cohen College System of Education

Visionary educator Audrey Cohen founded Audrey Cohen College in 1964 in New York in order to meet the demands of a changing global economy. At the College, undergraduate and graduate students take courses oriented around purposes and meaningful learning, rather than traditional academic subjects. In 1983, Audrey Cohen College was given funding by a local foundation to try its "Purpose-Centered System of Education" in a middle school in New York City (Cohen and Jordan 1996). This experiment proved successful and in the early 1990s, the Hasbro Children's Foundation committed funding the K–12 schools project, allowing the College to attempt implementation at the elementary level in four new geographic areas, San Diego, Phoenix, rural Mississippi, and Chicago. In 1995, the Audrey Cohen System was selected as a NAS design, and for several years, NAS provided funds towards the development of the College's K–12 reform design; however, the design is no longer part of NAS. As of July 1999, there were approximately 27 rural, urban, and suburban schools nationwide implementing the design. The College's vice president, Janith Jordan, serves as director of school programs.

The Audrey Cohen College System of Education for K–12 schools is predicated on the belief that the traditional educational goal of transmitting discrete pieces of knowledge is severely limited and unlikely to prepare students for responsible citizenry and productive work in a rapidly changing world. Absent from most education approaches, the developers argue, is the larger mission of teaching people how to use their knowledge (Cohen and Jordan 1996). Thus, "the Audrey Cohen College System of Education is based on the premise that students learn best when they use their knowledge and skills to achieve a meaningful and complex Purpose that makes a positive difference in their lives and the lives of others" (http://www.audrey-cohen.edu/).

The Audrey Cohen College System of Education is a whole-school reform model that can be implemented at the elementary, middle, or high school level. School learning is focused around purposes, instead of traditional subjects. The Audrey Cohen College has established 24 developmentally appropriate purposes, one for each semester at each grade level. For example, first grade students work on the purpose "We Work for Safety" and tenth graders work on the purpose "I use science and technology to help shape a just and productive society."

Focusing on their purpose, Audrey Cohen students are encouraged to work with each other and with community members, in and out of the school, to plan, prepare, carry out, and evaluate a project. Each semester, students work toward a defined goal, showing their accomplishment of a "purpose" by performing a "constructive action" such as the creation of a videotape on their community's environmental situation. Each semester, students must also work towards achieving a set of 24 "abilities," which can be aligned with state and local standards.

In order to organize teaching and learning around purposes, the curriculum is organized not around traditional academic disciplines but around five "dimensions of effective learning and action" (Cohen and Jordan 1996: 37): purpose, values and ethics, self and others, systems, and skills. The content from traditional disciplines is maintained, but not the subject-oriented framework. For example, the values and ethics dimension uses perspectives from history, literature, and philosophy to help students understand the ethical consequences of their decisions and actions. The systems dimension draws upon social and natural sciences to explore the systems of which students are part and which they hope to affect, such as family, community, and the world at large. The self and others dimension involves using reading, language, and literature so that students improve their skills of communication and in working with others. The skills dimension builds students' mathematical, technical, linguistic, and physical abilities (http://www.audrey-cohen.edu/). In order to facilitate these changes, the College asks that schools avoid structured curricula or programs that do not allow for subject integration.

The Audrey Cohen College System of Education calls for teachers to develop certain skills and qualities: teamwork, comfort with the switch from disciplines to dimensions, a new web of contacts with community members, and a willingness to shift their role from directing to facilitating learning (Cohen and Jordan 1996). Though the reform design provides the framework and some materials for students, the curriculum development is left to teachers at the local level. Teachers' manuals are deliberately not provided. Trainers from the College provide staff development to help facilitate the shift to these new roles and tasks.

School districts pay licensing and annual participation fees for the program. In return, the school receives five days of orientation training, up to eight on-site visits in the first year of implementation, and up to six on-site visits in the subsequent two years. During on-site visits, trainers conduct demonstration lessons, meetings with school and district staff, and program quality reviews. Schools also purchase "Purpose Achiever" record books for each student. Audrey Cohen College also requires that each elementary school hire a school resource specialist for the first one to three years of operation. The tasks of these resource specialists include collecting materials, coaching teachers, and maintaining contact with community members and the design team. Middle and high schools are not required to hire a resource specialist to support implementation.

The Coalition of Essential Schools

Brown University Professor Theodore Sizer's research on American high schools and the publication of his landmark book, *Horace's Compromise: The Dilemma of the American High School* (1984), led to the creation of the Coalition of Essential Schools (CES). In 1984, a group of 12 schools in seven states agreed to restructure their schools according to Sizer's ideas and formed the Coalition. A team based at Brown was established to support these schools' reform efforts (Simon and Gerstein no date). Since that time, the Coalition principles have spread and as of early 2000, there were over 1000 CES schools. These schools are located in 38 U.S. states and four foreign countries and are situated in a mix of urban, rural, and suburban communities. Approximately 75 percent of CES schools are secondary schools, and 25 percent are elementary schools.

At the heart of the CES is the belief that traditional American schools, particularly high schools, are fundamentally misdesigned. Their compartmentalized structure promotes impersonal environments for students, passive models of learning and student apathy, fragmented curricula, teacher-centered pedagogies, isolated teaching environments, and the measurement of superficial and static skills, among other things (Simon and Gerstein no date; Tucker 1999). Offering a wide array of courses and tracks in an attempt to gear learning to students' needs, the comprehensive high school in fact "failed to focus on their ostensible central purpose – helping students learn to use their minds well" (Simon and Gerstein no date: 2).

CES advocates a total restructuring of traditional school organizations, practices and beliefs. "Given the dismal historical record of major 'top-down' reform initiatives over the past 50 years, Sizer chose to approach reform not with a new and improved 'model' to be imposed but rather with a general set of nine ideas or common principles which a school could fashion in ways that made sense to their community" (Simon and Gerstein no date: 1). CES advocates "Ten[3] Common Principles" that should be used as a framework for schools to provide "personalized education" to all students. A summary of the principles is listed below (for details see http://www.essentialschools.org/aboutus/phil/10cps.html):

1 Schools should be intellectually-focused and learner-centered, addressing students' academic, social, and emotional development.
2 Academic goals should be simple and universal; "less is more."
3 The school's goals should apply to all students.
4 Teaching and learning should be personalized.
5 The guiding metaphor should be "student as worker, teacher as coach."
6 Teaching and learning should be assessed according to student performance of real tasks. Schools should not be age-graded or evaluate students based on time spent in class.
7 Families should be vital members of the school community. The tone of the school should stress values of unanxious high expectations, trust, and decency.
8 Administrators and teachers should be generalists first and specialists second.
9 Administrative and budget targets should allow for collective teacher planning.
10 The school should demonstrate non-discriminatory and inclusive policies, practices, and pedagogies.

Schools that specifically commit to redesigning according to these principles join the Coalition of Essential Schools (Simons and Gerstein no date). The principles are deliberately general to allow for adaptation to local requirements and priorities. Practical applications of the principles recommended by CES include: reduced class sizes; curriculum based on interdisciplinary questions; school policies based on a system of trust and shared values as well as belief and expectation that students can succeed; teachers' functioning in several roles (such as counselor, advisor, or manager) and shifting from didactic methods to facilitating independent learning; and modified scheduling, including block scheduling and double periods to spend more time on fewer subjects and an extended school day and year. However, these are only suggestions, as each school approaches the principles in unique ways. CES is not a "cookie cutter" approach to reform, and instead is "intentionally messy" (Tucker 1999: 3). CES is also not a territorial reform, and often one finds a CES school that is implementing numerous efforts under the CES umbrella. Moreover, many of the CES principles have filtered in to the education community and now form the lingua franca of school restructuring (Tucker 1999).

In the past five years, CES has evolved from a centrally run organization at Brown to a decentralized network of regional centers. The CES National Office is now located in Oakland, California and serves as a coordinating body. CES schools' primary source of support is regional centers. Schools that are located near one of the 24+ regional centers receive local support that is sensitive to their context. These centers attempt to build networks among schools in their regions and offer ongoing professional development and coaching services to schools on a fee-for-service basis. Educators in CES schools also have the option of attending the annual CES Fall Forum, the inspirational national conference dedicated to fostering professional development and strengthening the CES network. However, none of these activities is required and some CES schools exist more or less independently, while others take full advantage of the opportunities provided by CES's national and regional centers.

Schools involved with CES, engage in a three-stage membership process. First, schools enter the "exploring" stage, during which time members of a school community gather information and attempt to reach consensus on whether they want to commit to the ten principles. If consensus is reached, schools enter the "planning" stage and begin to develop a vision and an action plan for restructuring. To reach the "membership" stage, schools need to show evidence that they have met CES standard. The school undergoes a review by regional center staff and constituent member schools with site teams. To maintain membership over times, CES schools must continually self-assess their growth and also engage in peer review (http://www.essentialschools.org/schools/becoming/3stagesmem.html).

Comer School Development Program

Professor James Comer and his staff at the Yale Child Study Center developed the Comer School Development Program (SDP) (Comer *et al.* 1996) over thirty years ago. Among the oldest school reform designs still in use today, the Comer School Development Program began in two schools in 1968 and as of early 2000 was being implemented in 388 schools in 18 U.S. states and three foreign countries. SDP can be adapted to the elementary, middle, and high school levels, though it is implemented most commonly in elementary schools in urban areas.

The SDP reform design is guided by Comer's belief that the academic struggles faced by many low-income and minority students are rooted in their unmet developmental needs. "To compound this problem, many school staff members, lacking adequate knowledge of child development and the children's home culture, are unprepared to deal appropriately with these students and their families" (http://info.med.yale.edu/comer/overview2.html). According to Comer, schools need to meet students' social and emotional needs before they can expect students to be ready to achieve high academic standards and become productive citizens. All school decisions should be based on students' needs, and teachers, administrators, and other school staff, counselors, parents, social workers, and psychologists must mobilize to become part of the learning process.

The goal of the Comer SDP is to restructure entire schools to address the needs of the whole child. Improving home–school relations and educating staff in the physical, cognitive, psychological, language, social, and ethical developmental pathways of students are two central priorities. Incorporated into the program are three mechanisms (the School Planning and Management Team, the Student and Staff Support Team, and the Parent Team), three guiding principles (collaboration, consensus decision-making, and no fault problem-solving), and three operations (comprehensive school plan, staff development, and periodic assessment and modification).

The School Planning and Management team is the central organizing body in the school and is usually led by the principal and includes teachers, parents, a mental health specialist, support staff, and sometimes students and community members. This team develops the Comprehensive School Plan. On-site professionals and community members determine the specific shape of the program. The Student and Staff Support Team attempts to improve the social climate of the school, and also engages social workers, counselors, and other staff with mental health backgrounds to manage individual student cases. The Parent Team attempts to engage parent involvement in many ways in the life of the school (http://info.med.yale.edu/comer/overview2.html).

Until recently, SDP has not dealt with curriculum and pedagogy, leaving these decisions to local educators. Specific additional reforms, such as cooperative learning, and Reading Recovery, have all been implemented at a single school under the SDP umbrella. The design team's new Learning, Teaching, and Development Unit is now working with new SDP schools to improve their literacy programs, align teaching, learning, and assessment, and improve transitions from pre-school to elementary school (School Development Program no date).

Schools wishing to adopt the Comer SDP model must make a commitment to the program after extensive discussion at the school and district levels. A staff vote is not required. Recently, the SDP design team has agreed to only accept new SDP schools in districts that commit to having a sizable number of SDP schools. As such, they no longer support implementation of Comer in a single school, recognizing the need for strong district support and systemic coordination.

SDP offers national academies to support implementation. Before beginning implementation, schools send a district facilitator and a principal to the Leadership Training Academy at Yale. District facilitators and principals then train their own local school staffs. They also return to Yale to attend the Academy for Developmentally Centered Education and the Principals' Academy. Upon request, SDP staff from the national office or from regional training centers in Maryland, Detroit, or Chicago can assist with staff training. Trainers from the national and regional SDP centers visit districts at least twice a year to assess the quality of implementation. SDP also administers questionnaires to schools to document their progress with reform efforts and to assess school climate.

Core Knowledge Sequence

E. D. Hirsch, Jr., a professor of English at the University of Virginia, first presented the thesis behind the Core Knowledge Sequence in his controversial bestseller, *Cultural Literacy* (1987). In *Cultural Literacy*, Hirsch provided an appendix listing "what every American should know." The book was criticized as promoting arbitrarily decided elitist forms of knowledge. Some saw Hirsch as among a group of academic traditionalists who treat "curriculum as the repository of society's dominant values about worthwhile knowledge" (Elmore and Sykes 1992: 208). Responding to these criticisms, Hirsch convened an advisory board of experts in multiculturalism and consulted an independent group of educators, scholars, and scientists to attempt to make a master list of content topics for grades K–6 that included diverse perspectives. This list became the Core Knowledge Sequence. It was first piloted in 1990 in a Florida elementary school and as of 2000 was being implemented in over 800 schools nationwide. Most of these schools are elementary schools, though recently some middle schools have implemented Core Knowledge since the development of the middle school Core Knowledge Sequence. This reform design now finds its home in the nonprofit, non-partisan Core Knowledge Foundation, directed by Hirsch, and located in Charlottesville, Virginia.

Following the premise that individuals must find common ground in order to interact, Core Knowledge's goal is to provide disadvantaged students equal access to knowledge, and thus to a base of common experience enabling them to fit in and to communicate with other members of society (Hirsch 1998). Core Knowledge is based on the beliefs that: (1) there is lasting knowledge that should form the core of a Preschool-Grade 8 curriculum; (2) that children learn new knowledge by building on what they already know; (3) that important knowledge in language arts, history and geography, math, science, and the fine arts should be specified in school curricula; (4) that all children, regardless of background, need to be included "in our national literate culture" (http://www.coreknowledge.org/CKproto2/about/index.htm).

The Core Knowledge Sequence provides a planned progression of specific topics, designed so that students build on knowledge from year to year in grades K–6 (e.g. Hirsch 1993). The most distinguishing feature of the Core Knowledge Sequence is its content specificity. Intended as 50 percent of a school's curriculum, the Core Knowledge sequence provides grade-level specific topics to be covered in history, geography, mathematics, science, language arts, and fine arts. Material in subsequent years relies on knowledge and skills learned in previous years. Elements from the Core Knowledge curriculum are carefully chosen to reflect an "inclusive multiculturalism" (Core Knowledge Foundation 1998), balancing lessons that increase knowledge of mainstream culture (such as American History or science) with others that encourage students to respect and celebrate cultural diversity (such as units on modern-day Egypt or ancient China).

While the Core Knowledge sequence specifies content, it does not specify classroom process or implementation procedures. It does not try to change the structural arrangements of schooling, such as the schedule, the grouping of students, or staffing arrangements. It does not provide guidelines, materials, pedagogical strategies or lesson plans for how to teach the material, and it provides only general guidelines about how a school might implement the sequence (Core Knowledge Foundation 1998). There is no Core Knowledge teacher manual, nor are there textbooks or other materials for children. However, teachers share lesson plans at a national annual conference, and some plans, developed by teachers in Core schools, are posted on the Internet.

Core Knowledge historically neither required nor offered professional development. Until recently, the only professional development available was an overview presentation from a Foundation consultant or a workshop in writing Core Knowledge lessons. In the past several years, the Foundation has substantially increased its professional development offerings. However, none of the workshops is required, unless schools contract with the Foundation as part of their federal Comprehensive School Reform Demonstration Program grant applications.

Modern Red Schoolhouse

The Modern Red Schoolhouse (MRSH) reform design originated in 1992 as a project of the Hudson Institute, a conservative public policy research organization in Indianapolis. MRSH was one of 11 reform projects funded by New American Schools. Now, MRSH is housed at the non-profit Modern Red Schoolhouse Institute in Nashville and is directed by Sally Kilgore, a sociologist of education and the reform design's chief architect and founder. In 1993, six schools began implementation of MRSH. As of late 2000, there were 72 Modern Red elementary, middle, and high schools in 23 states in urban, rural, and suburban locations (http://www.mrsh.org/is.html).

The Modern Red Schoolhouse whole-school reform design is premised on the belief that most American public schools are neither preparing students for work in a global, technologically driven marketplace nor preparing them for democratic citizenry. As schools have become more diverse, the developers argue, expectations for students have been lowered. The goal of MRSH is to raise expectations for all students through a common set of academic standards and assessments. In the MRSH design, the common culture, character development, high expectations and community support evident in the "little red schoolhouse" of yesteryear are infused with the technology and informational resources of the 21st century (Modern Red Schoolhouse Institute no date).

Six tenets embody the goals of the MRSH design (see Heady and Kilgore 1996 for a more detailed description of these principles):

1 All children can learn and attain high standards in core academic subjects. Children simply vary in the time they need to learn and the ways they learn best.
2 Schools should help transmit a shared culture that draws on the traditions and histories of our pluralistic society and the principles of democratic government that unite us all. At the same time, children should understand the histories and cultures of other nations and peoples.
3 Principals and teachers should have considerable freedom in organizing instruction and deploying resources to meet the needs of their students.
4 Schools should have greater flexibility in deciding how best to accomplish their mission and, at the same time, should be held accountable through assessments of student progress.
5 Advanced technology is a critical requisite to attaining high quality education in cost-effective ways.
6 Schools should be places where students and staff choose to belong. Students should attend a school by choice, not by assignment.

A school that adopts the MRSH design has great flexibility in how they meet these tenets. Decisions take place in six "task forces" oriented around standards and assessment, curriculum, school organization and finance, technology, community involvement, and professional development. In each area, MRSH provides technical assistance in helping schools identify their needs and develop plans for action. For example, MRSH provides comprehensive performance-based assessments and provides schools with assistance in developing their own school and classroom assessments. Curriculum development also takes place locally, but the MRSH provides some assistance and recommendations, such as the Core Knowledge Sequence for the elementary grades. Teachers can continue to use the instructional strategies and curricula that already address state and MRSH standards (Modern Red Schoolhouse Institute, no date).

The MRSH Institute requires that 80 percent of a school's teaching staff vote by secret ballot to adopt the reform design. Schools vary in the amount of time that they need to implement the design and the costs that they can anticipate, depending on the degree to which various elements of the design are already in place and the size of the school. Generally, though, it takes between three and five years to complete the initial implementation phase (http://www.mrsh.org/i.html).

Ongoing professional development is a major component of the MRSH design. During the first several years of implementation, a school staff might receive as many as 100 days of on-site training, depending on their needs. Training modules focus on the change process, redesigning management structures, designing and implementing standards-driven curriculum, instruction, and assessment, and establishing a computerized instructional management system. MRSH consultants who have expertise in each area provide these training modules. While some training modules are provided to entire staffs, other modules are provided for particular task forces or individuals. Training is ongoing for as many years as needed, and is provided on a fee-for-service basis.

Success for All

Developed by researchers Robert Slavin, Nancy Madden, and a team of developers at Johns Hopkins University, the Success for All (SFA) reform design is now headquartered at the Success for All Foundation in Baltimore. The research and development behind the SFA program began in the 1970s with Robert Slavin's influential work on cooperative learning. SFA, as a whole-school reform design, was first implemented in an elementary school in Baltimore in 1987. Since then, SFA has experienced exponential growth. As of early 2000, SFA was being implemented in over 1600 elementary schools in 48 states in the U.S. and in five foreign countries (http://www.successforall.net/about/sfafschools.html).

According to Slavin (1996), success in elementary school is based largely on success in reading. When children do not learn to read well in the early elementary grades, they often begin a downward cycle of failure in which poor achievement, poor motivation, and low self-esteem become mutually reinforcing. Typically, schools attempt to provide remediation for these students, which is often too little and too late. Instead, Slavin believes that schools should shift from remediation to prevention and early intervention so that no students fall through the cracks.

The Success for All program is built upon the belief that through prevention (e.g., high quality pre-school and kindergarten programs, effective curricula, instructional tools, and professional development for elementary teachers) and intervention (e.g., early supplementary instructional services provision), all children, regardless of home background, will learn to read (Slavin 1996). Major components of SFA include a 90-minute reading period, the regrouping of students into smaller, homogeneous groups for reading instruction, eight-week assessments, cooperative learning, and one-to-one tutoring. The Success for All reading curriculum is comprised of an Early Learning program for kindergarten students; Reading Roots, a beginning reading program; and Reading Wings, its upper-elementary counterpart (Slavin *et al.* 1996). There are both English and Spanish versions of the program; the Spanish version of SFA is called *Exito Para Todos.*

Success for All is a reform model that takes an aggressive approach to changing teaching and learning. As a result, the program is highly specified and comprehensive with respect to implementation guidelines and materials for students and teachers. Almost all materials for students are provided, including reading booklets for the primary grades, materials to accompany various textbook series and novels for the upper grades, as well as workbooks, activity sheets, and assessments for all grade levels. Teachers are expected to follow SFA lesson plans closely, which involve an active pacing of multiple activities during the 90-minute reading period. Each activity has a particular time allotment as do particular lessons, which are intended to last two to three days in Roots and five days in Wings (Madden, Livingston, and Cummings 1998).

The SFA Foundation requires that the majority (80 percent) of a school's teaching staffs vote to adopt the program before it will provide the materials and technical assistance. The SFA program also asks that schools employ a full-time SFA facilitator, organize a Family Support Team, and organize bi-weekly meetings among Roots and Wings teachers. The principal of an SFA school is responsible for ensuring staff motivation and commitment for the program, as well as adequate resources. The role of the SFA facilitator is to ensure the quality of the day-to-day implementation of the program by monitoring and supporting teachers, monitoring the progress of all students, and managing assessments and regrouping efficiently (Madden, Livingston and Cummings 1998).

Implementation of the program is supported through ongoing professional development from SFA trainers and through local and national networks of SFA schools (Slavin and Madden 1996; Slavin *et al.* 1996). When a school adopts SFA, full training is provided. This initial training is in the form of a three-day session that typically takes place in the summer before implementation begins. Each year, SFA schools receive follow-up "implementation visits" from two SFA trainers who monitor the progress of implementation, help schools solve problems, and provide feedback. These visits typically occur twice annually. Every year, the SFAF holds annual SFA conferences in several regional locations in order to maximize the attendance of personnel from schools around the country.

Notes

1 In accordance with our confidentiality agreement with this district, the names of this school district and individual schools discussed in this book are pseudonyms.
2 Snyder, Bolin, and Zumwalt's (1992) extensive review of these approaches informs our understandings. They also review a third approach, curriculum enactment, but we do not include it here, as it is not as relevant to our work.
3 The Tenth Principle was added in 1997.

References

Acker, S. (1994) *Gendered education: Sociological reflections on women, teaching, and feminism*, Bristol, PA: Open University Press.

Anderson, S. and Stiegelbauer, S. (1994) "Institutionalization and renewal in a restructured secondary school", *School Organization* 14(3): 279–293.

Apple, M. (1985) *Education and power*, Boston, MA: Routledge and Kegan Paul.

Apple, M. W. (1994) "Is change always good for teachers? Gender, class, and teaching in history", in K. Borman and N. Greenman (eds) *Changing American education: Recapturing the past or inventing the future?*, (pp. 71–105), Albany, NY: SUNY Press.

Austin, J. L. (1961) *Philosophical papers*, Oxford: Oxford University Press.

AVID Center (1996) AVID Tutorial College Studies Guide. San Diego, CA: AVID Center.

AVID Program (1997) *Implementation essentials*, San Diego, CA: AVID Center.

Bailey, B. (2000) "The impact of mandated change on teachers", in N. Bascia and A. Hargreaves (eds) *The sharp edge of educational change*, (pp. 112–128), London: Falmer Press.

Bakhtin, M. (1981) *The dialogic imagination*, Austin, TX: University of Texas Press.

Ball, S. J. (1987) *The micro-politics of the school: Towards a theory of school organization*, New York: Routledge.

Bascia, N. and Hargreaves, A. (eds) (2000) *The sharp edge of educational change*, London: RoutledgeFalmer Press.

Berends, M. (2000) "Teacher-reported effects of new American schools designs: Exploring relationships to teacher background and school context", *Educational Evaluation and Policy Analysis* 22, 1: 65–82.

Berends, M. and Bodilly, S. (1998) *New American schools' scale up phase: Lessons learned to date*, Santa Monica, CA: RAND.

Berger, P. and Luckmann, T. (1967) *The social construction of reality*, New York: Doubleday.

Berliner, D. and Biddle, B. (1995) *The manufactured crisis*, Reading, MA: Addison-Wesley.

Berman, P. and McLaughlin, M. W. (1978) *Federal programs supporting educational change*, Vol. VIII. Santa Monica, CA: RAND.

Bird, T. (1986) "Mutual adaptation and mutual accomplishment: Images of change in a field experiment", in A. Lieberman (ed.) *Rethinking school improvement: Research, craft, and concept*, New York: Teachers College Press.

Black, I. (1997) *Dictionary of economics*, New York: Oxford University Press.

Blackmore, J. (1998) "The politics of gender and educational change: Managing gender or changing gender relations?", in A. Hargreaves, A. Lieberman, M. Fullan, and D. Hopkins (eds) *International handbook of educational change*, (pp. 460–481), Norwell, MA: Kluwer Academic Publishers.

Blackmore, J. and Kenway, J. (1995) "Changing schools, teachers, and curriculum: But what about the girls?", in D. Corson (ed.) *Discourse and power in educational organizations,* (pp. 232–256), Cresskill, NJ: Hampton Press..

Blase, J. (1989) "The teachers' political orientation vis-à-vis the principal: The micropolitics of the school", in J. Hannaway and R. Crowson (eds) *The politics of reforming school administration,* (pp. 113–126), Philadelphia: Falmer Press.

—— (1993) "The micropolitics of effective school-based leadership: Teachers' perspectives", *Educational Administration Quarterly* 29, 2: 142–163.

Bodilly, S. (1998) *Lessons from new American schools' scale up phase,* Santa Monica, CA: RAND.

Bodilly, S. and Berends, M. (1999) "Necessary district support for comprehensive school reform", in G. Orfield and E. H. DeBray (eds) *Hard work for good schools: Facts not fads in Title I reform,* (pp. 111–139), Cambridge, MA: Harvard University, Civil Rights Project.

Borman, K. and Cookson, P. (1996) "Sociology of education and educational policy: When worlds collide or happily ever after?", in K. Borman, A. Sadovnik, P. Cookson, and J. Spade (eds) *Implementing educational reform: Sociological perspectives on education policy,* (pp. 3–20), Norwood, NJ: Ablex Publishing.

Bronfenbrenner, U. (1979) *Ecology of human development: Experiments by nature and design,* Cambridge, MA: Harvard University Press.

Brown, A. and Campione, J. (1994) "Guided discovery in a community of learners", in K. McGilly (ed.) *Classroom lessons: Integrating cognitive theory and classroom practice* (pp. 229–270), Cambridge, MA: MIT Press.

Bryk, A. S., Sebring, P. B., Kerbow, D. and Rollow, S. (1998) *Charting Chicago school reform,* Boulder, CO: Westview Press.

Bushweller, K. (1998) "The forgotten majority", *American School Board Journal* March: 16–21.

Carlin, P. (1992) "The principal's role in urban school reform", *Education and Urban Society* 25, 1: 45–56.

Carlson, R. (1965) *The adoption of educational innovations,* Eugene: Oregon Press.

Casey, K. (1993) *I answer with my life: Life histories of women teachers working for social change,* New York: Routledge.

Cazden, C. B. and Mehan, H. (1989) "Codes, culture and context: Principles from anthropology and sociology", in M. Reynolds (ed.) *Knowledge base for beginning teachers* (pp. 47–57), Boston, MA: Peragon Press.

Chavez, L. (1998) *The color bind: California's battle to end affirmative action,* Berkeley, CA: University of California Press.

Cicourel, A. V. (1973) *Cognitive sociology,* London: Macmillan.

Clune, W. (1993) "The best path to systemic educational policy: Standard/centralized or differentiated/decentralized?", *Educational Evaluation and Policy Analysis* 15, 3: 233–254.

Cohen, A. and Jordan, J. (1996) "The Audrey Cohen College System of Education: Purpose-centered education", in S. Stringfield, S. M. Ross and L. Smith (eds) *Bold plans for school restructuring,* (pp. 25–51), Mahwah, NJ: Lawrence Erlbaum.

Cohen, D. K. (1995) "What is the system in systemic reform?", *Educational Researcher* 24, 9: 11–17, 31.

Cohen, D. K. and Spillane, J. P. (1993) "Policy and practice: The relationship between governance and instruction", in S. H. Fuhrman (ed.) *Designing coherent educational policy*, San Francisco: Jossey Bass.

Cole, M. (1996) *Cultural psychology: A once and future discipline*, Cambridge, MA: Harvard Belknap.

Comer, J. P., Haynes, N. M., Joyner, E. T., and BenAvie, M. (1996) *Rallying the whole village: The Comer process for reforming education*, New York: Teachers College Press.

Core Knowledge Foundation (1998) *Core knowledge sequence: Content guidelines for grades K–8*, Charlottesville, VA: Core Knowledge Foundation.

Consortium for Policy Research in Education (1998) "States and districts and comprehensive school reform. CPRE Policy Brief", Philadelphia, PA: University of Pennsylvania Graduate School of Education.

Corson, D. (1995) "Discursive power in educational organizations: An introduction", in Corson, D. (ed.) *Discourse and power in educational organizations*, Cresskill, NJ: Hampton Press.

Crandall, D. P., Loucks-Horsley, S., Baucher, J. E., Schmidt, W. B., Eiseman, J. W., Cox, P. L., Miles, M. B., Huberman, A. M., Taylor, B. L., Goldberg, J. A., Shive, G., Thompson, C. L. and Taylor, J. A. (1982) *Peoples, policies, and practices: Examining the chain of school improvement*, (vols. 1–10), Andover, MA: The NETWORK.

Cuban, L. (1986) *Teachers and machines: The classroom use of technology since 1920*, New York: Teachers College Press.

—— (1992) "What happens to reforms that last? The case of the junior high school", *American Educational Research Journal* 29, 2: 227–251.

—— (1998) "How schools change reforms: Redefining reform success and failure", *Teachers College Record* 99, 3: 153–177.

Clune, W. (1993) "The best path to systemic educational policy: Standard/centralized or differentiated/decentralized?", *Educational Evaluation and Policy Analysis* 15, 3: 233–254.

D'Agostino, J., Borman, G. D., Hedges, L.V. and Wong, K. K. (1998) "Longitudinal achievement and Chapter 1 coordination in high poverty schools: A multilevel analysis of the Prospects Data", *Journal of Education for Students Placed At Risk* 3, 4: 363–401.

D'Andrade, R. P. (1997) *Cognitive anthropology,* Cambridge: Cambridge University Press.

Darling-Hammond, L. (1988) "Policy and professionalism", in A. Lieberman (ed.) *Building a professional culture in schools*, New York: Teachers College Press.

Datnow, A. (1998) *The gender politics of educational change*, London: Falmer Press.

—— (1999) "How schools choose externally developed reform designs", Report No. 35. Baltimore, MD: Center for Research on the Education of Students Placed at Risk, Johns Hopkins University.

—— (2000) "Power and politics in the adoption of school reform models", *Educational Evaluation and Policy Analysis* 22, 4: 357–374.

Datnow, A., Borman, G. and Stringfield, S. (2000) "School reform through a highly specified curriculum: A study of the implementation and effects of the Core Knowledge Sequence", *The Elementary School Journal* 101, 2: 167–191.

Datnow, A. and Castellano, M. (2000a) "An 'Inside Look' at Success for All: A qualitative study of implementation and teaching and learning", Report No. 45.

Baltimore, MD: Center for Research on the Education of Students Placed at Risk, Johns Hopkins University.

Datnow, A. and Castellano, M. (2000b) "Teachers' responses to Success for All: How beliefs, experiences, and adaptations shape implementation", *American Educational Research Journal* 37, 3: 775–799.

Datnow, A. and Castellano, M. (2001) "Managing and guiding school reform: Leadership in Success for All schools", *Educational Administration Quarterly* 37, 2: 219–249.

Datnow, A. and Stringfield, S. (eds) (1997) "The Memphis Restructuring Initiative: Development and first-year evaluation from a large-scale reform effort", Special issue of *School Effectiveness and School Improvement* 8, 1: 1–162.

Datnow, A. and Stringfield, S. (2000) "Working together for reliable school reform", *Journal of Education for Students Placed At Risk* 5, 1: 183–204.

Datnow, A., Stringfield, S., Borman, G., Rachuba, L. and Castellano, M. (2001) "Comprehensive school reform in culturally and linguistically diverse contexts: Implementation and outcomes from a 4-year study", Santa Cruz, CA: Center for Research on Education, Diversity, and Excellence.

Datnow, A., Stringfield, S., McHugh, B. and Hacker, D. (1998) "Scaling up the Core Knowledge Sequence", *Education and Urban Society,* 30, 3: 409–432.

Datnow, A. and Yonezawa, S. (in press) "Observing school restructuring in multilingual, multiethnic classrooms: Balancing ethnographic and evaluative approaches", in H. Waxman, R. Tharp and R. Hilberg (eds) *Observational research in culturally and linguistically diverse classrooms,* Cambridge: Cambridge University Press.

Desimone, L. (2000) *Making comprehensive school reform work,* New York: ERIC Clearinghouse on Urban Education.

Dimaggio, P. and Powell, W. (1991) "Introduction", in W. Powell and P. Dimaggio (eds) *The new institutionalism in organizational analysis,* (pp. 1–38), Chicago: University of Chicago Press.

Durkheim, E. (1938) *The rules for sociological method,* Glencoe, IL: The Free Press.

Education Commission of the States (1999) *Comprehensive school reform: Five lessons from the field,* Denver, CO: Author.

Elmore, R. E. (1996) "Getting to scale with good educational practice", *Harvard Educational Review* 66, 1: 1–26.

Elmore, R. E. (2000) *Building a new structure for school leadership?,* New York: The Albert Shanker Institute.

Elmore, R. E. and Sykes, G. (1992) "Curriculum policy", in P. Jackson (ed.), *Handbook of Research on Curriculum,* (pp. 185–215), New York: Macmillan.

Elmore, R. E. and Burney, D. (1997a) *Investing in teacher learning: Staff development and instructional improvement in Community School District #2, New York City,* National Commission on Teaching and America's Future and the Consortium for Policy Research in Education.

Elmore, R. E. and Burney, D. (1997b). *School variation and systemic instructional improvement in Community School District #2, New York City,* Pittsburgh, PA: Learning Research and Development Center, High Performance Learning Communities Project.

Engestrom, Y. (1993) "Developmental studies on work as a testbench of activity theory", in S. Chaiklin and J. Lave (eds) *Understanding practice,* (pp. 64–103), Cambridge: Cambridge University Press.

Erickson, F. and Shultz, J. (1982) *The counselor as gatekeeper*, New York: Academic Press.

Evans, R. (1996) *The human side of school change: Reform, resistance, and the real-life problems of innovations*, San Francisco: Jossey Bass.

Firestone, W. A. and Donner, W. W. (1981) "Knowledge use in educational development: Tales from a two-way street", ERIC document 241583.

Foster, M. (1993) "Resisting racism: Personal testimonies of African-American teachers", in L. Weiss and M. Fine (eds) *Beyond silenced voices: Class, race, and gender in United States schools*, (pp. 273–288), Albany: State University of New York Press.

Foster, M. (1994) "The role of community and culture in school reform efforts: Examining the views of African-American teachers", *Educational Foundations* 8, 2: 5–26.

Frederick, J. (1992) "Ongoing principal development: The route to restructuring urban schools", *Education and Urban Society* 25, 1: 57–70.

Fullan, M. G. (1991) *The new meaning of educational change*, 2nd edn, New York: Teachers College Press.

—— (1993) *Change forces: Probing the depths of educational reform*, London: Falmer Press.

—— (1999) *Change forces: The sequel*, London: Falmer Press.

—— (2000) "The return of large-scale reform", *Journal of Educational Change* 1, 1: 5–17.

—— (2001) *The new meaning of educational change*, 3rd edn, New York: Teachers College Press.

Fullan, M. G. and Hargreaves, A. ([1992] 1996) *What's worth fighting for in your school?*, New York: Teachers College Press.

Fullan, M. G. and Miles, M. (1992) "Getting reform right: What works and what doesn't", *Phi Delta Kappan* 73, 10: 744–752.

Fuhrman, S. H. and Elmore, R. (1995) "Ruling out the rules: The evolution of deregulation in state education policy", *Teachers College Record* 97, 2: 279–309.

Fuhrman, S. H. and Fry, P. (1989) *Diversity amidst standardization: State differential treatment of districts*, New Brunswick, NJ; Center for Policy Research in Education.

Gamoran, A. (1996) "Goals 2000 in organizational context: Will it make a difference for states, districts, and schools?", in K. Borman, A. Sadovnik, P. Cookson and J. Spade (eds) *Implementing Educational Reform: Sociological Perspectives on Education Policy,* Norwood, NJ: Ablex Publishing.

Garfinkel, H. (1967) *Studies in ethnomethodology*, Englewood Cliffs, NJ: Prentice Hall.

Gee, J. P. (1996) "On mobots and classrooms: The converging languages of the new capitalism and schooling", *Organization* 3, 3: 386–407.

Gee, J. S., Michaels, S. and O'Conner, K. (1992) "Discourse analysis", in W. Millroy, J. Preissle and M. D. LeCompte (eds) *Handbook of qualitative research in education* (pp. 227–291), San Diego, CA: Academic Press.

Giddens, A. (1979) *Central problems in social theory*, Berkeley, CA: University of California Press.

—— (1984) *The constitution of society*, Berkeley, CA: University of California Press.

—— (1993) *New rules of sociological method*, Cambridge: Polity Press.

Goldring, E. and Rallis, S. F. (1993) *Principals of dynamic schools: Taking charge of change*, Corwin Press: Newbury Park, CA.

Goodson, I. (2001) *The personality of change*. Paper presented at the conference on Social Geographies of Educational Change, Barcelona, Spain.

Grant, R. (1989) "Women teachers' career pathways: Towards an alternative model of career", in S. Acker (ed.) *Teachers, gender, and careers*, London: Falmer Press.

Gross, N., Gaicquinta, J. and Bernstein, M. (1971) *Implementing organizational innovations: A sociological analysis of planned educational change*, New York: Basic books.

Guthrie, L. F. and Guthrie, P. G. (1998) "The 1997 evaluation of statewide AVID expansion, Final Report", Burlingame, CA: Center for Research, Evaluation And Training in Education.

Hall, G. and Loucks, S. (1976). *A developmental model for determining whether or not the treatment really is implemented*, Austin, TX: Research and Development Center for Teacher Education, University of Texas.

Hall, P. M. (1997) "Meta-power, social organization, and the shaping of social action", *Symbolic Interaction* 20, 4: 397–418.

Hall, P. M. and McGinty, P. J. W. (1997) "Policy as the transformation of intentions: Producing program from statutes", *The Sociological Quarterly* 38: 439–467.

—— (in press). "Social organization across space and time: The policy process, mesodomain analysis, and the breadth of perspective", in S. C. Chew and D. Knottnerus (eds) *Structure, culture, and history: Recent issues in social theory*, New York: Rowman & Littlefield.

Hallinger, P. and Hausman, C. (1994) "From Attila the Hun to Mary had a Little Lamb: Principal role ambiguity in restructured schools", in J. Murphy and K. S. Louis (eds) *Reshaping the principalship: Insights from transformational reform efforts,* (pp.154–176), Thousand Oaks, CA: Corwin Press.

Hallinger, P., Murphy, J. and Hausman, C. (1992) "Restructuring schools: Principals' perceptions of fundamental educational reform", *Educational Administration Quarterly* 28, 3: 330–349.

Hannah, M. T. (1979) "Mutual adaptation: Using outside information in educational practice", ERIC document 229469.

Hannan, M.T. and Freeman, J. (1989) *Organizational ecology*, Cambridge, MA: Harvard University Press.

Hannaway, J. and Carnoy, M. (eds) (1993) *Decentralization and school improvement,* San Francisco: Jossey-Bass.

Hargreaves, A. (1985) "The micro-macro problem in the sociology of education", in R. Burgess (ed.) *Issues in educational research*, London: Falmer Press.

—— (1994) *Changing teachers, changing times,* New York: Teachers College Press.

—— (1996) "Transforming knowledge: Blurring the boundaries between research, policy, and practice", *Educational Evaluation and Policy Analysis* 18, 2: 105–122.

—— (1998) "The emotions of educational change", in A. Hargreaves, A. Lieberman, M. Fullan and D. Hopkins (eds) *International handbook of educational change,* (pp. 558–570), Norwell, MA: Kluwer Academic Publishers.

Hargreaves, A., Earl, L. and Ryan, J. (1996) *Schooling for change: Reinventing education for early adolescents*, London: Falmer Press.

Hargreaves, A., and Fink, D. (2000) "The three dimensions of educational reform", *Educational Leadership* 57, 7: 30–34.

Hargreaves, A. and Fullan. M. (1998) *What's worth fighting for out there?* New York: Teachers College Press.

Hart, A. W. (1995) "Reconceiving school leadership: Emerging views", *Elementary School Journal* 96, 1: 9–28.

Hatch, T. (1998a) "The differences in theory that matter in the practice of school improvement", *American Educational Research Journal* 35, 1: 3–32.

—— (1998b) "How comprehensive can comprehensive reform be?" *Phi Delta Kappan* 79, 7: 518–523.

—— (2000) "What does it take to 'go to scale'? Reflections on the promise and the perils of comprehensive school reform", *Journal of Education for Students Placed At Risk* 5, 4: 339–354.

Hatch, T. and White, N. (1997) "The raw materials of educational reform: Rethinking the knowledge of school improvement", Unpublished paper, ATLAS Seminar, Cambridge, MA.

Havelock, R. G. (1969) *Planning for dissemination through dissemination and utilization of knowledge*, Ann Arbor, MI: Center for Research on Utilization of Scientific Knowledge.

Haycock, K. (1997) *Achievement in America*, Washington, DC: The Education Trust.

—— (1999) *Achievement in America*, Washington, DC: The Education Trust.

Haynes, N. (ed.) (1998) Special issue: Changing schools for changing times: The Comer Development Program, *Journal of Education for Students Placed At Risk* 3(1).

Heady, R. and Kilgore, S. (1996) "The Modern Red schoolhouse", in S. Stringfield, S. M. Ross and L. Smith (eds) *Bold plans for school restructuring: The new American schools designs*, (pp. 139–178), Mahwah, NJ: Erlbaum.

Healey, F. and De Stefano, J. (1997) *Education reform support: A framework for scaling up school reform*, Washington, DC: Abel 2 Clearinghouse for Basic Education.

Heck, R. H. and Hallinger, P. (1999) "Next generation methods for the study of leadership and school improvement", *Handbook of educational administration*, 2nd edn, (pp. 141–162), San Francisco: Jossey Bass.

Helsby, G. (1999) *Changing teachers' work*, Buckingham: Open University Press.

Herman, R., Aladjem, D., McMahon, P., Masem, E., Mulligan, I., O'Malley, A., Quinones, S., Reeve, A. and Woodruff, D. (1999) *An educators' guide to school-wide reform*, Washington, DC: American Institutes for Research.

Herman, R. and Stringfield, S. (1997) *Ten promising programs for educating disadvantaged students: Review of research on implementation and potential effect*, Arlington, VA: Educational Research Service.

Hess, F. (1999) *Spinning wheels: The politics of urban school reform*, Washington, DC: The Brookings Institute.

Hirsch, E. D., Jr. (1987) *Cultural literacy: What every American needs to know*, Boston, MA: Houghton Mifflin.

—— (ed.) (1993) *What your first grader needs to know: Fundamentals of a good first grade education*, New York: Delta.

—— (1996) *The schools we need and why we don't have them*, New York: Doubleday.

—— (1998) "Why general knowledge should be a goal of education in a democracy", *Common Knowledge* 11, 1/2.

Hopkins, D. and Wideen, M. F. (1984) *New perspectives on school improvement*, London: Falmer Press.

Houle, C. (1980) *Continuing learning in the professions*, San Francisco: Jossey Bass.

Hubbard, L. and Datnow, A. (2000) "A gendered look at educational reform", *Gender and Education* 12, 1: 115–130.

Hubbard, L. and Mehan, H. (1999a) "Scaling up an untracking program: A co-constructed process", *Journal of Education for Students Placed At Risk* 4, 1: 83–100.

—— (1999b) "Educational niche picking in a hostile environment", *Journal of Negro Education* 68, 2: 213–226.

Hubbard, L. and Ottoson, J. (1997) "When a bottom-up innovation meets itself as a top-down policy: The AVID Untracking Program", *Science Communications* 19, 1 September: 43.

Huberman, M. (1989) "The professional life cycle of teachers", *Teachers College Record* 91, 2: 30–57.

Iannacone, L. (1991) "Micropolitics of education: What and Why", *Education and Urban Society* 23, 4: 465–471.

Johnson, S. M. (1999) Response to Murphy's "Reconnecting teaching and school administration: A call for a united profession." Comments delivered at the annual meeting of the American Educational Research Association, Montreal, Canada.

Joyce, B. (1999) "The greatest literacy problem and Success for All", *Phi Delta Kappan* 81 (1): 129–31.

Kearns, D.T. and Anderson, J.L. (1996) "Sharing the vision: Creating new American schools", in S. Stringfield, S. M. Ross and L. Smith (eds) *Bold plans for school restructuring: The New American Schools designs*, (pp. 9–23), Mahwah, NJ: Erlbaum.

Kirst, M. and Meister, G. (1985) "Turbulence in American secondary schools. What reforms last?", *Curriculum Inquiry* 15, 169–186.

Klein, L. H., McCaffrey, D. and Stecher, B. (2000) *What do test scores in Texas tell us?* Santa Monica, CA: RAND.

Kohlberg, L. and Mayer, R. (1972) "Development as the Aim of Education", *Harvard Educational Review* 42 (4): 449–496.

Lave, J. (1993) "The practice of learning", in S. Chaiklin and J. Lave (eds) *Understanding practice: Perspectives on activity and context*, (pp. 3–34), Cambridge: Cambridge University Press.

Leadership (1993) *American School Board Journal*. 180 (Suppl.) A–15–A17.

Leithwood, K. and Jantzi, D. (1990) "Transformational leadership: How principals can help reform school cultures", *School Effectiveness and School Improvement* 1: 249–280.

Levin, H. (1987) "New schools for the disadvantaged", *Teacher Education Quarterly* 14, 4: 60–83.

Lieberman, A. (1990) *Schools as collaborative cultures*, London: Falmer Press.

—— (1999) Response to Murphy's "Reconnecting teaching and school administration: A call for a united profession." Comments delivered at the annual meeting of the American Educational Research Association, Montreal, Canada.

Lighthall, F. (1973) "Review of Smith and Keith, 1971", *Anatomy of An Educational Innovation, School Review* 3: 255–293.

Lipsky, M. (1980) *Street-level bureaucracy: Dilemmas of the individual in public services*, New York: Russell Sage Foundation.

Lipsky, M. (1982) *Street level bureaucracy*, New York: Russell Sage.

Little, J. W. (1990) "Contradictions of professional development in secondary schools", in M. W. McLaughlin, J. E. Talbert and N. Bascia (eds) *The contexts of teaching in secondary schools: Teachers' realities*, New York: Teachers College Press.

Lotan, R. and Navarette, C. (1986) "The process of mutual adaptation: A study of an innovative program", ERIC document 273580, Paper presented at the annual meeting of the American Educational Research Association, San Francisco.

Louis, K. S. (1990) "Social and community values and the quality of teachers' work life", in M. W. McLaughlin, J. E. Talbert and N. Bascia (eds) *The contexts of teaching in secondary schools: Teachers' realities*, New York: Teachers College Press.

—— (1994) "Improving urban and disadvantaged schools: Dissemination and utilization perspectives", *Knowledge and Policy* 4: 34–54.

Lusi, S. (1997) *The role of state departments of education in complex school reform*, New York and London: Teachers College Press.

Madden, N., Livingston, M. and Cummings, N. (1998) *Success for all, roots and wings: Principal's and facilitator's manual*, Baltimore, MD: Johns Hopkins University.

Malen, B. (1995) "The micropolitics of education: mapping multiple dimensions of power relations in school polities", in J. D. Scribner and D. H. Layton (eds) *The study of educational politics* (pp. 147–168), London: Falmer Press.

Marble, K. and Stephens, J. (1999) "Scale-up strategy of a national school reform and its evaluation design: Satellite centers of the Accelerated Schools Project", Paper presented at the annual meeting of the American Educational Research Association, April 19–23, Montreal, Canada.

Marshall, C. and Scribner, J. (1991) "It's all political: Inquiry into the micropolitics of education", *Education and Urban Society* 2, 34: 347–355.

Matthews, C. (1978) *Successful project: Examining the research. Keys to community Involvement series 8* Arlington, VA: National School Public Relations Association.

Mazzoni, T. L. (1995) "State policymaking and school reform: Influences and influentials", in J. D. Scribner and D. H. Layton (eds) *The study of educational politics*, (pp. 53–74), London: Falmer Press.

McDermott, R. P. (1980) "Profile: Ray Birdwhistell", *Kinesis Reports* 2: 1–4, 14–16.

—— (1993) "The acquisition of a child by a learning disability", in S. Chaiklin and J. Lave (eds) *Understanding practice* (pp. 269–305), Cambridge: Cambridge University Press.

McDonald, J. P., Hatch, T., Kirby, E., Ames, N., Haynes, N. and Joyner, E. (1999) *School reform behind the scenes*, New York: Teachers College Press.

McLaughlin, M. W. and Talbert, J. E. (1993a) *Contexts that matter for teaching and learning*, Stanford, CA: Stanford University Center for Research on the Context of Secondary School Teaching.

—— (1993b) "How the world of students and teachers challenges policy coherence", in S. H. Fuhrman (ed.) *Designing coherent educational policy*, San Francisco: Jossey Bass.

McLaughlin, M. W. (1994) "Strategic sites for teachers' professional development", in P. Grimmett and J. Neufeld (eds) *Teacher development and the struggle for authenticity*, New York: Teachers College Press.

McLaughlin, M. W., Talbert, J. E. and Bascia, N. (eds) (1990) *The contexts of teaching in secondary schools: Teachers' realities*, New York: Teachers College Press.

McNeil, L. M. (1988) *Contradictions of control: School structure and school knowledge*, New York: Routledge.

Mehan, H. (1993) "Beneath the skin and between the ears: A case study in the politics of representation", in S. Chaiklin and J. Lave (eds) *Understanding practice: Perspectives on activity and context*, (pp. 241–268), Cambridge: Cambridge University Press.

Mehan, H. A., Hertweck, A. and Meihls, J. L. (1986) *Handicapping the handicapped: Decision making in students' educational careers*, Stanford: Stanford University Press.

Mehan, H., Villanueva, I., Hubbard, L. and Lintz, A. (1996) *Constructing school success: The consequences of untracking low-achieving students*, Cambridge: Cambridge University Press.

Mehan, H. and Wood, H. (1975) *The reality of ethnomethodology*, New York: Wiley Interscience.

Miller, L. (1998) "Redefining teachers, reculturing schools: Connections, commitments, and challenges", in A. Hargreaves, A. Lieberman, M. Fullan and D. Hopkins (eds) *International handbook of educational change*, (pp. 529–543), The Netherlands: Kluwer Academic Publishers.

Mitchell, D. (1990) "Past issues and future directions", in D. Mitchell and M. Goertz (eds) *Education politics for the new century*, (pp. 153–167), London: Falmer Press.

Modern Red Schoolhouse Institute (no date) The Modern Red Schoolhouse Institute, Nashville, TN: Author. http://www.mrsh.org.

Muncey, D. and McQuillan, P. (1996) *Reform and resistance in schools and classrooms*, New Haven: Yale University Press.

Murphy, J. (1994) "Transformational change and the evolving role of the principal: Early empirical evidence", in J. Murphy and K. S. Louis (eds) *Reshaping the principalship: Insights from transformational reform efforts*, (pp. 20–53), Thousand Oaks, CA: Corwin Press.

Murphy, J. (1999a) "Reconnecting teaching and school administration: A call for a united profession", Paper presented at the annual meeting of the American Educational Research Association, Montreal, Canada.

Murphy, J. (1999b) *The quest for a center: Notes on the state of the profession of educational leadership*, Columbia, MO: University Council for Educational Administration.

Murphy, J. and Louis, K. S. (1999) "Introduction: Framing the project", *Handbook of educational administration,* 2nd edn, (pp. xxi–xvii), San Francisco: Jossey Bass.

Murray, C. (1984) *Losing ground: American social policy, 1950–1980*, New York: Basic Books.

National Center for Education Statistics (1992) *Schools and staffing in the United States*, Washington, DC: Author.

National Council on Education and the Economy (1983) *A nation at risk*, Washington DC: Author.

Natriello, G. (1996) "National standards for assessments and performance: Reactions, knowledge base, and recommendations for research", in K. Borman, A. Sadovnik, P. Cookson, and J. Spade (eds) *Implementing educational reform: Sociological perspectives on education policy,* (pp. 65–80), Norwood, NJ: Ablex Publishing.

New American Schools (1997) *Bringing success to scale: Sharing the vision of New American Schools,* Arlington, VA: Author.

Neufeld, B. (1995) "Learning in the context of SDP: What are the opportunities?

What is the context?" Paper presented at the annual meeting of the American Educational Research Association, San Francisco, CA.

Nias, J. (1998) "Why teachers need their colleagues: A developmental perspective", in A. Hargreaves, A. Lieberman, M. Fullan and D. Hopkins (eds) *International handbook of educational change*, Hingman, MA: Kluwer.

Noblit, G., Berry, B. and Demsey, V. (1991) "Political responses to reform: A comparative case study", *Education and Urban Society*, 23, 4: 379–395.

Nunnery, J. A. (1998) "Reform ideology and the locus of the development problem in educational restructuring", *Education and Urban Society* 30, 3: 277–295.

Nunnery, J., Slavin, R. E., Madden, N. A., Ross, S. M., Smith, L. J., Hunter, P. and Stubbs, J. (1997) "Effects of full and partial implementation of Success for All on student reading achievement in English and Spanish", Paper presented at the annual meeting of the American Educational Research Association, Chicago, IL.

Oakes, J. and Guiton, G. (1995) "Matchmaking: The dynamics of high school tracking decisions", *American Educational Research Journal* 32, 1: 3–33.

Oakes, J. and Lipton, M. (1992) "Detracking schools: Early lessons from the field", *Phi Delta Kappan* 73, 6: 448–454.

Oakes, J., Quartz, K. H., Ryan, S. and Lipton, M. (1999) *Becoming good American schools: The struggle for civic virtue in educational reform*, San Francisco: Jossey Bass.

Oakes, J. and Wells, A. S. (1996) *Beyond the technicalities of school reform: Policy lessons from detracking schools*, Los Angeles: UCLA.

Oakes, J., Wells, A. S., Jones, M. and Datnow, A. (1997) "Detracking: The social construction of ability, cultural politics, and resistance to reform", *Teachers College Record* 98, 3: 482–510.

O'Day, J. and Smith, M. (1993) "Systemic reform and educational opportunity", in S. H. Fuhrman (ed.) *Designing coherent education policy*, San Francisco: Jossey Bass.

Olsen, L. (2000) "NAS launches loan fund to support adoption of school designs", *Education Week* 19, 26 (March 8): 8.

Pogrow, S. (1998) "What is an exemplary program, and why should anyone care? A reaction to Slavin and Klein", *Educational Researcher*, 22–29.

Popkewitz, T. S., Tabachnick, B. R. and Wehlage, G. (1981) *The myth of educational reform: A study of school responses to a program of change*, Madison, WI: University of Wisconsin Press.

Pressman, J. L. and Wildavsky, A. (1973) *Implementation*, Berkeley, CA: University of California Press.

Prestine, N. (1993) "Shared decision making in restructuring essential schools: The role of the principal", *Planning and Changing* 22, 3–4: 160–177.

Purkey, S. and Smith, M. (1983) "Effective schools: A review", *Elementary School Journal* 83, 4: 428–452.

Regan, H. B. and Brooks, G. H. (1995) *Out of women's experience: Creating relational leadership*, Thousand Oaks, CA: Corwin Press.

Restine, N. (1993) *Women in administration: Facilitators for change*, Newbury Park, CA: Corwin Press.

Richardson, M. D., Flanigan, J. L. and Blackbourn, R. L. (1991, March) "An analysis of KERA: Kentucky's answer to educational equity", Paper presented at the annual meeting of the American Educational Finance Association, Williamsburg, VA.

Riseborough, G. (1981). "Teacher careers and comprehensive schooling: An empirical study", *Sociology* 15, 3: 352–381.

Rogoff, B. (1995) "Observing sociocultural activity on three planes: Participatory appropriation, guided participation, and apprenticeship", in J. V. Wertsch, P. Del Rio and A. Alvarez (eds) *Sociocultural studies of mind*, (pp. 139–164), Cambridge: Cambridge University Press.

—— (1998) "Cognition as a collaborative process", in D. Kuhn and R. S. Siegler (eds) *Cognition, perception and language [Vol. 2], Handbook of child psychology* (5th edn) (pp. 679–744), New York: Wiley.

Ross, S. M., Henry, D., Phillipsen, L., Evans, K., Smith, L. and Buggey, T. (1997) "Matching restructuring programs to schools: Selection, negotiation, and preparation", *School Effectiveness and School Improvement* 8, 1: 45–71.

Ross, S. M., Alberg, M. and Nunnery, J. (1999) "Selection and evaluation of locally developed versus externally developed schoolwide programs", in G. Orfield and E. H. Debray (eds) *Hard work for good schools: Facts not fads in Title I reform*, (pp. 147–158), Cambridge: Harvard University, The Civil Rights Project.

Rowan, B. (2001) "The ecology of school improvement: Notes on the school improvement industry in the U.S.", Paper presented at the conference on Social Geographies of Educational Change, Barcelona, Spain.

Sarason, S. (1982) *The culture of the school and the problem of change*, 2nd edn, Boston, MA: Allyn & Bacon.

Sarason, S. (1990) *The predictable failure of educational reform*, San Francisco: Jossey Bass.

Sarason, S. (1996) *Revisiting "the culture of the school and the problem of change"*, New York: Teachers College Press.

Sarason, S. (1997) "Revisiting the creation of settings", *Mind Culture and Activity*, 4, 3: 175–182.

School Development Program (no date) "School Development Program new district presentation", New Haven, CT: Yale Child Study Center.

Schorr, L. (1997) *Common purpose: strengthening families and neighborhoods to rebuild America*, New York: Doubleday, Anchor Books.

Scott, W. R. (1998) *Organizations: Rational, natural, and open systems*, Upper Saddle River, NJ: Prentice-Hall.

Schutz, A. (1962) *Collected papers I: The problem of social theory*, The Hague: Martinus Nijhoff.

Senge, P. (1990) *The fifth discipline: The art and practice of learning*, New York: Doubleday.

Sergiovanni, T. J., Burlingame, M., Coombs, F. and Thurston, P. W. (1992) *Educational governance and administration*, (3rd edn), Boston, MA. Allyn and Bacon.

Shapiro, M. (1987) *The politics of representation*, Madison, WI: University of Wisconsin Press.

Shweder, R. A. (1996) "The view from manywheres", *Anthropology Newsletter* 37, 9: 1, 4–5.

Sikes, P. J. (1992) "Imposed change and the experienced teacher", in M. Fullan and A. Hargreaves (eds) *Teacher development and educational change*, London: Falmer Press.

Sikes, P. J., Measor, L. and Woods, P. (1985) *Teacher careers: Crises and continuities*, London: Falmer Press.

Silberman, C. (1970) *Crisis in the classroom: The remaking of American education*, New York: Random House.

Simon, H. (1957) *Administrative behavior*, 2nd edn, New York: Macmillan.

Simon, K. and Gerstein, A. (no date) "The Coalition of Essential Schools: A principle-based approach to school reform", http://www.essentialschools.org/aboutus/ceschapter.html.

Simon, K. and Gerstein, A. (2000) "The Coalition of Essential Schools: A principle-based approach to school reform", http://www.essentialschools.org/aboutus/ceschapter.html.

Sirotnik, K. and Oakes, J. (1986) "Critical inquiry for school renewal: Liberating theory and practice", in K. Sirotnik and J. Oakes (eds) *Critical perspectives on the organization and improvement of schooling*, (pp. 3–93), Boston, MA: Kluwer-Nijhoff.

Siskin, L. S. (1994) *Realms of knowledge: Academic departments in secondary schools*, Bristol, PA: Falmer Press.

Sizer, T.R. (1984) *Horace's compromise*, Boston, MA: Houghton Mifflin.

Sjöström, S. (1997) *Party or patient? Discursive practices relating to coercion in psychiatric and legal settings*, Umeå: Boréa Bokförlag.

Slavin, R. (1996) *Education for all*, Lisse, Netherlands: Swets & Zeitlinger.

Slavin, R. (1998) "Far and wide: Developing and disseminating research-based programs", *American Educator* (Fall): 8–11, 45.

Slavin, R. (1999). "Rejoinder: Yes, control groups are essential in program evaluation: A response to Pogrow", *Educational Researcher*, 36–38.

Slavin, R. E. and Fashola, O. (1998) *Show me the evidence!* Thousand Oaks, CA: Corwin.

Slavin, R. E. and Madden, N. A. (1998) "Disseminating Success for All: Lessons for policy and practice, Revised technical report", Baltimore, MD: Center for Research on the Education of Students Placed At Risk, Johns Hopkins University Press.

Slavin, R. E, Madden, N., Dolan, L. and Wasik, B. (1996) *Every child, every school: Success for all*, Thousand Oaks, CA: Corwin Press.

Smith, L. and Keith, P. (1971) *Anatomy of an educational innovation*, New York: John Wiley & Sons.

Smith, L., Ross, S., McNelis, M., Squires, M., Wasson, R., Maxwell, S., Weddle, W., Nath, L., Grehan, A. and Buggey, T. (1998) "The Memphis restructuring initiative: Analysis of activities and outcomes that impact implementation success", *Education and Urban Society* 30, 3: 296–325.

Smith, M. S. and O'Day, J. (1991) "Systemic school reform", in S. Fuhrman and B. Malen (eds) *The politics of curriculum and testing*, London: Falmer Press.

Smylie, M. A. (1997) "Research on teacher leadership: Assessing the state of the art", in B. Biddle, T. Good, and I. Goodson (eds) *International handbook of teachers and teaching I*, (pp. 521–592), Boston, MA: Kluwer.

Smylie, M. A. and Brownlee-Conyers, J. (1992) "Teacher leaders and their principals: Exploring the development of new working relationships", *Educational Administration Quarterly* 28, 2: 150–184.

Smylie, M. A. and Denny, J. W. (1990) "Teacher leadership: Tensions and ambiguities in organizational perspective", *Educational Administration Quarterly* 26, 3: 235–259.

Snyder, J., Bolin, F. and Zumwalt, K. (1992) "Curriculum implementation", in P. Jackson (ed.) *Handbook of research on curriculum*, (pp. 402–435), New York: Macmillan.

Squires, D. (1998) "Towards a balanced curriculum: Aligning standards, curriculum, and assessments", *ERS Spectrum* 16, 3: 17–24.

References

Stallings, J. and Kaskowitz, D. (1974) *Follow through classroom observation evaluation. 1972–1973* (SRI Project (URU–7370), Menlo Park, CA: Stanford Research Institute.

Star, S. L. and Bowker, G. C. (1997) "Of Lungs and lungers: The classified story of tuberculosis", *Mind Culture and Activity* 4, 1: 3–23.

Steele, C. (1997) "A threat in the air: how stereotypes shape intellectual identity and performance", *American Psychologist* June: 613–629.

Stigler, J. and Hiebert, J. (1999) *The teaching gap: Best ideas from the world's teachers for improving education in the classroom*, New York: The Free Press.

Stoll, L. and Myers, K. (1998) *No quick fixes*, London: Falmer Press.

Stringfield, S. (1998) "Science, cynicism, and Diogenes' double-edged lamp", *Education Week* 17 (43), 45, 48.

Stringfield, S. and Datnow, A. (1998) "Introduction: Scaling up school restructuring designs in urban schools", *Education and Urban Society* 30, 3: 269–276.

Stringfield, S., Datnow, A., Borman, G. and Rachuba, L. (1999) "National evaluation of Core Knowledge Sequence Implementation: Final report", Baltimore, MD: Center for Social Organization of Schools, Johns Hopkins University.

Stringfield, S., Datnow, A., Ross, S. and Snively, F. (1998) "Scaling up school restructuring in multicultural, multilingual contexts", *Education and Urban Society* 30, 3: 326–357.

Stringfield, S. and McHugh, B. (1998) "Implementation and effects of the Maryland Core Knowledge project", Baltimore: Johns Hopkins University, Center for Social Organization of Schools.

Stringfield, S., Millsap, M., Herman, R., Yoder, N., Brigham, N., Nesselrodt, P., Schaffer, E., Karweit, N., Levin, M. and Stevens, R. (1997) "Special strategies studies, final report", Washington, DC: U.S. Department of Education.

Stringfield, S. and Ross, S. M. (1997) "A reflection at mile three of a marathon: The Memphis Restructuring Initiative in mid-stride", *School Effectiveness and School Improvement* 8,1: 151–161.

Stringfield, S., Ross, S. and Smith, L. (eds) (1996) *Bold plans for school restructuring: The new American schools development corporation models*, Mahwah, NJ: Lawrence Erlbaum.

Sunderman, G. and Nardini, G. (1998) *Constraints on institutionalizing school reform: Lessons from Chicago*, Oak Brook, IL: North Central Regional Educational Laboratory.

Swanson, M. C. (1997) Personal Interview in San Diego, California.

Tharp, R. (2000) "Under the microscope", *CREDE Talking Leaves*, 4, 2: 1, 6.

Tharp, R. and Gallimore, R. (1995) *Rousing minds to life*, Cambridge: Cambridge University Press.

Tharp, R. G. (1997) "From at risk to excellence: Research, theory, and principles for practice, research report #1", Santa Cruz, CA: Center for Research on Education, Diversity and Excellence.

Thomas, W. I. and Thomas, D. S. (1928) *The child in America: Behavior problems and programs*, New York: Knopf.

Tucker, A. (1999) *A response to An Educators' Guide to Schoolwide Reform*, Oakland CA: Coalition of Essential Schools National Office.

Tyack, D. (1990) "Restructuring in historical perspective: Tinkering toward utopia", *Teachers College Record* 92 (2): 169–191.

Tyack, D. and Cuban, L. (1995) *Tinkering toward utopia,* Cambridge, MA: Harvard University Press.

Tyack, D. and Tobin, W. (1994) "The 'grammar' of schooling: Why has it been so hard to change?", *American Educational Research Journal* 31: 453–479.

U.S. Department of Education (1994) *Goals 2000 Educate America Act: Making American education great again*, Washington, DC: Author.

U.S. Department of Education (1999) *CSRD in the field: Fall 1999 update*, Washington, DC: Author.

Vinovskis, M. A. (1996) "An analysis of the concept and uses of systemic educational reform", *American Educational Research Journal* 33, 1: 53–85.

Wasley, P. (1989) "Lead teachers and teachers who lead: Reform rhetoric and real practice", Paper presented at the annual meeting of the American Educational Research Association, San Francisco, CA. ERIC document no. 311018.

Wason, P. C. and Johnson-Laird, P. N. (1972) *Psychology of reasoning: Structure and content*, Cambridge, MA: Harvard University Press.

Weick, K. E. (1995) *Sensemaking in organizations*, Thousand Oaks, CA: Sage.

Weiss, C. (1995) "The four 'I's' of school reform: How interests, ideology, information, and institution affect teachers and principals", *Harvard Educational Review* 65, 4: 571–592.

Wells, A. S., Hirshberg, D. H., Lipton, M. and Oakes, J. (1995) "Bounding the case within its context: A constructivist approach to studying detracking reform", *Educational Researcher* 24, 5: 18–24.

Wells, A. S. and Oakes, J. (1996) "Potential pitfalls of systemic reform: Early lessons from detracking research", *Sociology of Education,* Special Issue: 135–143.

Wieder, D. L. (1973) *Language and social reality*, The Hague: Mouton.

Wilcox, K. (1982) "Differential socialization in the classroom: Implications for educational opportunity", in G. Spindler, and L. Spindler (eds) *Doing the ethnography of schooling*, (pp. 268–309), New York: Harcourt, Brace, World.

Witte, J. F. (2000) *The market approach to education*, Princeton, NJ: Princeton University Press.

Wise, A. (1977) "Why educational policies often fail: The hyperationalization hypothesis", *Curriculum Studies* 9, 1: 43–57.

Wittgenstein, L. (1952) *Philosophical investigations*, London: Basil Blackwell.

Wodak, R. (1995) "Power, discourse, and styles of female leadership in school committee meetings", in D. Corson (ed.) *Discourse and power in educational organizations,* (pp. 31–54), Cresskill, NJ: Hampton Press.

Woolard, K. (1989) "Sentences in the language prison: the rhetorical structure of an American language debate", *American Ethnologist* 16, 2: 268–278

Yonezawa, S. (1998) Bay Elementary School Case Report, Baltimore, MD: Center for Social Organization of Schools, Johns Hopkins University.

Yonezawa, S. and Datnow, A. (1999) "Supporting multiple reform designs in a culturally and linguistically diverse school district", *Journal of Education of Students Placed At Risk 4*, 1: 101–125.

Yonezawa, S. and Stringfield, S. (2000) *Special strategies for educating disadvantaged students follow-up study: Examining the sustainability of research based school reforms*, Baltimore, MD: Johns Hopkins University CRESPAR.

Index

Some names and pseudonyms which do not refer to real places or persons have been included in this index to allow cross-referencing.

abandonment of reform *see* expiration
absorption of reform 124
abstract theories 121
academic standards 110
Accelerated Schools reform 1, 91
accountability 19, 23, 35–7, 62, 133–4, 137–9; *see also* test scores
Achievement Via Individual Determination (AVID) program 1, 3–4, 6, 9–10, 22–5, 31–5, 45–8, 52–5, 58, 60, 65–6, 70–8, 81–6, 91–2, 97–9, 102, 118, 125–30, 136, 139, 146–7; in California and Kentucky 133; eligibility of students for 105–8; scale of program 130; scaling up of 94–5
affirmative action 106–8, 122
African-American students 18, 53–5, 105, 125, 129
agency: definition of 62; in school reform 63–6, 71–3, 118, 129, 141
Allen, George 52
Annenberg Principalship Program 70
ATLAS reform design team 91, 104
Audrey Cohen College System of Education 4–5, 25–6, 49–50, 55, 78, 82–5, 97–8, 111–12, 120, 147–9
AVID *see* Achievement Via Individual Determination

Baker, Linda 127
Bascia, N. 43
Bay Area Coalition 101
Bayside Elementary School 25, 125
Beacon (company) 97
belief systems 43, 53, 56, 129–31
beneficiaries of reform 60
Berends, M. 71
Berman, P. 42
Bernstein, M. 41
bilingual education 49–50

Black, I. 27
Blackmore, J. 71
Bowker, G. C. 12
Boysen, Thomas 23, 126
breadth of educational reform 117, 130
Brofenbrenner, U. 13
Brown, A. 129
Brown University 95–6
Bushweller, K. 106
business practices and terminology 3, 115, 141

California 34; AVID in 132–3; Civil Rights Initiative *see* Proposition 209; English-only teaching policy 121–2; *see also* University of California
Callaway Elementary School 32–3, 49
Campione, J. 129
care-giving by teachers 73, 87
Carnegie Foundation 19
Castellano, Marisa 10
change: local nature of 39–61; overall process of 36, 141; pressure for 18
change agents 62, 79, 83
chaos theory 11
Coalition of Essential Schools (CES) 1, 3–4, 7, 43, 45, 48–51, 67, 70, 74, 78, 91, 97, 101–2, 110, 113–14, 127, 132, 149–51; scaling up of reform 95–6
co-construction perspective 10–12, 16, 40–4, 59, 138–9
Cole, M. 12–13
collaboration among teachers 73–6
collective beliefs about education 56
"College Partnership" program 48, 125
Comer, James 103
Comer School Development Program 1, 3–4, 7, 29–30, 47–51, 56, 67, 70, 73–8 *passim*, 91–2, 97, 100–4, 109–11, 134, 151–3

competition between schools 143
complexity theory 11
compliance, culture of 71
Comprehensive School Reform
    Demonstration (CSRD) program 1, 21,
    37, 92, 137, 143
"concept dissemination" approach 4
conferences 70, 77–8
consensus on reform 14
constraints on reform 27–8, 45–7, 52, 54,
    124
context, definition of 13, 44
"contrived collegiality" 73
Core Knowledge Sequence and Core
    Knowledge Foundation 1, 3–4, 6–7,
    30–3, 49, 51, 70, 72, 76–8, 82–3, 97, 100,
    102, 108–10, 132, 134, 153–4
creativity in teaching 57, 71
"critical friends" 45
Cuban, L. 58–9, 117, 143
culture 16–17, 52–8, 60, 131; of schools
    62–3, 67, 75, 118, 121–4, 128–30; on
    societal level 63
curriculum development 77, 121

Dana Foundation 98
decentralization of administration 19, 101
democratic processes 96, 113
depth of educational reform 117, 130
design teams 3, 41, 58–9; business
    orientation of 115, 141; change in
    90–116, 140–1; guidelines for 60–1
Desimone, L. 60, 134
Developmental Studies Center 110
Dimaggio, P. 116
disadvantaged children 20–1, 54
Disseminating Efforts Supporting School
    Improvement (DESSI) project 41
district-level policies and standards 50–1,
    100, 131–2
district superintendents 23–5
Durkheim, E. 15

Edison Project 3, 143
Education Commission of the States 19
Education Development Center 91
Education Partners (company) 99
Education Week 145
Educational Research 145
Elmore, R. E. 142
embedded conception of context 13
employability of students 127
"Essentials for Literacy" program 110–11
ethnomethodology 15–16, 144
Evans, Samuel 23–4, 31–2

expiration of reform 120, 125, 135–6, 141

facilitators, role of 80–9
factionalism among teachers 75
fairs and exhibitions of reform design 27,
    126
Fashola, O. 20, 144
federal special education mandates 43
Fink, D. 117, 126, 130
flagship schools 32–3, 134
Florida 20
Forest Elementary School 29–30, 47–8, 70
"franchise" approach to school reform 5,
    112–13
Freeport, Virginia 32, 48
Fullan, M. G. 11, 13, 59, 62, 121, 123, 141–2

Gee, J. P. 128–9
Gee, J. S. 14
generalists, teachers as 48
Gerstein, A. 95–6, 113
Giaquinta, J. 41
Giddens, A. 15–16
goals of education 127, 142
grading systems for schools 133–4
Graham, Susan 81
Gross, N. 14
Guthrie, L. F. and P. G. 106

Haitian students 49
Hall, G. 41
Hall, P. M. 12, 59, 63, 139
Hargreaves, A. 43, 59, 63, 117, 126, 128,
    130
Hatch, T. 92, 104
Haynes, N. 47
Helsby, G. 11
Herman, R. 20, 144
Hess, F. 141
Hirsch, E. D. 97
Holly Elementary School 56, 67
Houle, C. 92
Hudson Institute 97
hyperrationalization 121

ideologies and response to change 31,
    53–8, 61, 128–9
implementation of reform: as inter-related
    conditions and consequences 11–12;
    meaning of 3–4; variations in 40
Improving America's Schools Act (IASA)
    21
Individually Guided Education 43
inequality, educational 18
insensitivity, failures due to 121–3

instructional leadership 88
intelligence, attitudes to 56, 60

Jetty Elementary School 30, 82–3
John Hopkins University 94
Johnson, L.B. 21
Jonesville 32
junior high schools 124

Kamahameha Early Education Program 37
Keith, P. 43, 119
Kensington School 43
Kentucky 22, 52, 132–3
Kentucky Education Reform Act 20, 22–3, 52
Keys Elementary School 55, 120
Kilgore, Sally 97

Latino students 18, 105
Lave, J. 12–13
"layering" of reforms 47–8, 79
leadership 64–70, 76, 85–8; styles of 67–8; training in 114; *see also* teacher leaders
"learning communities" 129
lesson plans 4, 69, 72
Lighthall, F. 119
Limestone School 74
Limited English Proficient (LEP) students 49–50
linguistic diversity 49–50
Loucks, S. 41

McDermott, R. P. 12–13
McDonald, J. P. 91, 114–15
McGinty, P. J. W. 12, 59
machine technologies 124–5
McLaughlin, M. W. 11, 13, 42
McQuillan, P. 43, 144
Madden, N. A. 91–2, 94, 99–100, 112
Madison High School 65–6, 84–5
Malen, B. 21–2
management theory 41
Mangrove Elementary School 46
Marble, K. 91
marketization of school reform 143
Maryland School Performance Accountability Program 20
master teachers 80
Mazzoni, T. L. 25
Memphis University 99
"meso" level of analysis 63
micropolitics in education 25–8, 64, 84
Miller, L. 80
Mitchell, D. 143

Modern Red Schoolhouse 3–5, 29, 45, 51, 67–9, 78–9, 98, 104, 110, 114, 122–5, 154–6; scaling up of reform 96–8
modification of reform designs 39, 45–50, 56–61, 112–16, 123–4, 140
monitoring: of design teams 96; of teachers 69, 84–5, 88
motivations for school reform 18–22
multidirectional reform 33–4, 44, 112
"multiple processes" perspective 117
Muncey, D. 43, 144
Murray, C. 122
mutual adaptation 40–4

A Nation at Risk 19
National Rifle Association 122
National Writing Project 110
Native American students 105
networks, professional 69–70
New American Schools reform design 1–3, 27, 94
New Mexico Elementary Network Center 101
New York District 2 37
news media 18
Newton Elementary School 50
"niche" programmes 131, 137
non-profit status 94–7
North Carolina 31–2, 45, 53–4, 108
Nunnery, J. 41

Oakes, J. 37, 43, 54, 60, 128, 130, 141
Oakwood school district 54
O'Neill, Tip 39
Orchid Elementary School 46
organizational theory 11, 26
"ownership" of reforms 71, 136, 145

Palm Valley High School 53, 58, 108, 129
perspective on school reform process 14, 16, 29, 33–6, 58, 140; *see also* co-construction perspective; technical-relational perspective
Peterson Elementary School 28–9
Phi Delta Kappan 145
"policy churn" 141
political processes 15–16, 21–2, 140, 144; see also micropolitics
Popkewitz, T. S. 43
Porter-Obey amendments (1998) 92
Powell, W. 116
power relations 14, 17, 22–8, 35–6, 80, 83–4, 89, 126, 140
power-sharing 67
Pressman, J. L. 11, 41, 43

principals of schools: engagement in
teaching and learning 69; expansion of
professional networks 69–70; influence
of 30–1; role of 64–9, 87–8, 125–6
privatization of school reform 143
professional lives of teachers 73
professional opportunities outside school
77–8
Project Zero 91
Proposition 209 106, 108, 122
prospects for reform 141–3
Prudential Insurance 97
Purpose Centered System of Education 55
"push-pull" of reform 34

racism 55
Rand Change Agent Study 42–3, 144–5
reading periods 46
reading programs 46, 111–13, 131–2, 134
Redwood High School 81
reform co-ordinators 80–1, 85–9
regional organizations of design teams
98–102
relational sense of context 12–14
replication of reform 123
representation, politics of 28–9
"research-based" reform models 28, 92, 144
resistance to reform by teachers 72, 79, 88;
see also "subversion"
"resource specialists" 82
resources needed for reform 136–7
Rogoff, B. 11
Ross, Steve 8

San Diego 23, 94–5, 130
Sarason, S. 59, 121
Sawgrass Elementary School 25–6, 29
scaling up 1, 92–3; definition of 2; method-
ology for 8–10; problems with 10;
staff for 102–4
school change theories 63
Schorr, L. 123
self-belief of students 53, 129–30
Shweder, R. A. 15
Silberman, C. 121
Simon, K. 113
Sirotnik, K. 37
site teams 74–5
Sizer, Ted 95–6
Slavin, R. E. 20, 91–4, 99–100, 112, 144
Smith, L. 43, 119
social construction of students' ability 53–6
social structures 15, 118, 139
Socratic approach 45
Special Strategies studies 20, 117

Star, S. L. 12
state-level policies and standards 51–2,
105–7, 111–12, 132–5, 139
Stephens, J. 91
stereotypical views of students 54–5
stress 78, 81, 86–7
Stringfield, Sam 8, 20, 117
structural determinism 13
structuration theory 15–16
"subversion" of reform 118–21
Success for All (SFA) 1, 3, 5–6, 10, 25, 28–9,
46–50, 57, 66–72, 78, 81–6 *passim*, 91,
97–104 *passim*, 109–13, 120, 131, 133,
145, 156–7; scaling up of 93–4
success, differing criteria of 58, 135, 137
Summer Institutes 70, 77–8
Sunland County 25–33 *passim*, 46–51, 55–6,
66, 74, 79, 82–3, 93, 102, 104, 112, 118,
122, 126–7, 131–3, 136
sustainability of reform 117–36, 141
Swanson, Mary Catherine 34, 91
systemic reform 19–20, 100–2

Tabachnick, B. R. 43
Talbert, J. E. 11, 13
Tanner Bill (California, 1980) 132
teacher autonomy 19, 57
teacher empowerment 67, 76–7, 87–8
teacher involvement in reform 35–8, 71–9,
87
teacher leaders 79–89
teachers' relationships with one another
73–5
technical-relational perspective 40–2, 60
Tennessee Comprehensive Assessment
Program 20
test scores 112, 133–7, 145
Texas 20, 144–5
Tharp, R. 11, 90
Thomas, W. I. and D. S. 14
Title I program 20–1, 92
Tobin, W. 128
top-down implementation of policies 19,
36, 122
tracking 9, 54, 130–1
Tupelo Elementary School 29, 122–3
turnover of staff 126–8
tutoring 45–6
Tyack, D. 128, 143

unions 85
University of California 106

Virginia 23–4, 32, 52, 107
vocational education 127

voting by teachers on reform 35

Walnut Grove 32
web sites 109–10
Wehlage, G. 43
Weiss, C. 38
WestEd (educational laboratory) 99–100
White Wake school district 24, 98
whole-school reform 2, 20, 67, 137

Wilcox, K. 13
Wildavsky, A. 11–12, 41, 43
Wodak, R. 28
women teachers 72–3, 86–7
Woolard, K. 122

Yale University 97, 100
Yonezawa, S. 117